PHILOSOPHY OF HISTORY AND ACTION

PHILOSOPHY OF
HISTORY AND ACTION

Papers Presented at the
First Jerusalem Philosophical Encounter
December 1974

Edited by

YIRMIAHU YOVEL

The Hebrew University of Jerusalem, Israel

D. REIDEL PUBLISHING COMPANY

DORDRECHT : HOLLAND / BOSTON : U.S.A.
LONDON : ENGLAND

THE MAGNES PRESS, THE HEBREW UNIVERSITY
JERUSALEM

Library of Congress Cataloging in Publication Data

Jerusalem Philosophical Encounter, 1st, 1974.
    Philosophy of history and action.

    (Philosophical studies series in philosophy ; v.11)
    1. History — Philosophy — Congresses. I. Yovel, Yirmiahu. II. Title.
D16.8.J43   1974   901   78-14886
ISBN 90-277-0890-8

Published by D. Reidel Publishing Company,
P. O. Box 17, Dordrecht, Holland

Sold and distributed in the U.S.A., Canada, and Mexico
by D. Reidel Publishing Company, Inc.
Lincoln Building, 160 Old Derby Street, Hingham,
Mass. 02043, U.S.A.

Sold and distributed in Israel
by The Magnes Press, The Hebrew University, Jerusalem

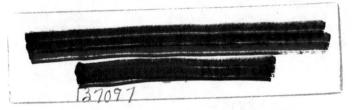

37097

Printed in Israel
for The Magnes Press, The Hebrew University, Jerusalem
by Sivan Press Ltd. Jerusalem

To Nathan Rotenstreich at Sixty

TABLE OF CONTENTS

PREFACE   ix

ACKNOWLEDGMENTS   xi

PART ONE: HISTORY, INTERPRETATION AND ACTION

PAUL RICOEUR / History and Hermeneutics   3
Comments by Charles Taylor   21

ABRAHAM KAPLAN / Historical Interpretation   27
Comments by Isaiah Berlin   38

DONALD DAVIDSON / Intending   41
Comments by Stuart Hampshire   61

NATHAN ROTENSTREICH / Historical Actions or Historical Events   69

EDDY M. ZEMACH / Events   85

ELAZAR WEINRYB / Descriptions of Actions and their Place in
   History   **97**

PART TWO: THE PHILOSOPHY OF HISTORY FROM KANT TO SARTRE

YIRMIAHU YOVEL / Kant and the History of Reason   115

CHARLES TAYLOR / Hegel's *Sittlichkeit* and the Crisis of
   Representative Institutions   133
Comments by Shlomo Avineri   155

JACQUES D'HONDT / Marx et les leçons de l'histoire   159

WERNER BECKER / Demokratie und die dialektische Theorie der
   Geschichte   177

TABLE OF CONTENTS

MENACHEM BRINKER / Transhistoricity and the Impossibility of
Aufhebung: Remarks on J.-P. Sartre's Philosophy of History   191

PART THREE: FAREWELL TO THE PHILOSOPHY OF HISTORY?

RAYMOND POLIN / Farewell to the Philosophy of History   201

PANEL DISCUSSION / Is a Philosophy of History Possible?   219

INDEX   241

PREFACE

This volume contains the proceedings of the First Jerusalem Philosophical Encounter — started by the Hebrew University Institute of Philosophy (now the S.H. Bergman Centre for Philosophical Studies), which took place on December 28-31, 1974.

In recent years the culture-gap that separates philosophers seems slowly — indeed much too slowly — to be narrowing. Although short-circuits in communication still do happen and mutual disrespect has not vanished, it is becoming unfashionable to demonstrate ignorance of another philosophical tradition or to shrug it off with a supercilious smile. Perhaps dialectically, the insufficiency of any self-centred view that tries to immunize itself to challenges from without starts to disturb it from within. Moreover, as the culture- (and language-) bound nature of many philosophical divergencies is sinking more deeply into consciousness, the irony of an attitude of intolerance to them becomes more apparent.

Our aim was to make a modest contribution to this development. We did not, however, mean to confuse genuine differences and problems in communication. Consequently, the more realistic term "encounter" was preferred to the idealizing "dialogue." The Israeli hosts, themselves trained in a variety of philosophical traditions, felt that there is something in-between real dialogue on the one hand and mutual estrangement on the other, and wished to provide a meeting place for it. As this volume appears two more Jerusalem Philosophical Encounters have taken place: one in 1976 on the philosophy of language (*Meaning and Use*, also published by D. Reidel Publishing Company and the Magnes Press, the Hebrew University) and the other in 1977 on Spinoza (in collaboration with the Institut International de Philosophie, to be published in their *Entretiens* by Martinus Nijhoff).

This volume is divided into three parts. Part One discusses systematic issues in the philosophy of history and action, representing a number of contemporary viewpoints, such as the hermeneutical, the analytical, and the

ix

phenomenological. Part Two represents the subject in historical perspective from Kant to Hegel, Marx, contemporary Marxism and Sartre. Part Three discusses what is living and what is dead in the philosophy of history, starting with Raymond Polin's challenging address and continuing with a panel discussion. I wish to thank all the distinguished colleagues and guests who have delivered papers and participated in the discussion.

It gives me particular pleasure to dedicate this volume to Professor Nathan Rotenstreich — teacher, friend, and colleague. Professor Rotenstreich's impressive work — writing, teaching, and translating philosophy — has made him the foremost figure in Israeli philosophical life. His range, depth, and variety can hardly be matched. He is also a socially involved scholar, taking stands on public issues and providing leadership to higher education in Israel. The philosophy of history is one of Rotenstreich's direct concerns; he has written on it numerous articles and a systematic book (*Between Past and Present*) and has also dealt specifically with problems in Jewish history. It was, therefore, only natural to insist that his own contribution be included in the meeting.

As always, I am deeply indebted to Ms. Eva Shorr (of the S.H. Bergman Centre for Philosophical Studies, the Hebrew University) for her meticulous work and invaluable help in all stages of preparing this work for publication.

Thanks are also due to the Israel Academy of Sciences and Humanities and the Van Leer Jerusalem Foundation that helped make the Encounter possible.

The Hebrew University of Jerusalem   Yirmiahu Yovel

ACKNOWLEDGMENTS

Acknowledgment is gratefully made to the following publishers who have granted permission to use selections from their publications:

Glencoe Press for: Abraham Kaplan, *In Pursuit of Wisdom*, Los Angeles 1977, § 68, which is a former version of his "Historical Interpretation."

Cambridge University Press for: Charles Taylor, *Hegel*, Cambridge 1976, pp. 380-386, reprinted here.

PART ONE

HISTORY, INTERPRETATION, AND ACTION

PAUL RICOEUR

HISTORY AND HERMENEUTICS

In this paper, I shall attempt to promote a *reciprocity* of arguments between philosophical hermeneutics and the method of historical inquiry. In the case of philosophical hermeneutics — on which I am focusing the discussion here — this concern for hearing arguments presented by the other side is not a frequent occurrence. Hermeneutics is better prepared to take the "way upward," the path of the *Rückfrage* which carries it from the historical inquiry of historians towards the consideration of the historicity of human experience in general. The "way downward" towards historical inquiry is a path less known to it. Yet it is on this path that we encounter the most significant questions for hermeneutics itself. The dialectic of the "way upward," Plato has taught us, is arduous. But how much more so is this "second navigation!"

I. FROM HISTORICAL METHODOLOGY TO HERMENEUTICS

Following the path outlined above, the contribution of philosophical hermeneutics is not intended to improve the methodology of history, still less to elaborate an alternative methodology. Indeed, it is not a methodology at all. Its purpose is quite different. It is to expose the dependence of historical inquiry (*Historie*) on the historical condition (*Geschichte*) of human existence. If this consideration has any bearing on methodology, this will appear only later, by a sort of rebound effect, when hermeneutics has shed light on some paradoxes nurtured within the historical methodology. But before this, hermeneutics must come to terms with (in the sense of the *Ausseinandersetzung*) history at a level more profound than that of its method, at the level of the *interest* which could be termed its soul. I am using the word "interest" as Kant uses it when he considers the interest of reason in this or that undertaking, whether theoretical or practical. It is by reflecting directly on the interest that animates historical knowledge that hermeneutics indirectly designates its object and its method.

3

Yirmiahu Yovel (ed.), Philosophy of History and Action, 3–20 . All Rights Reserved.
Copyright © 1978 by D. Reidel Publishing Company, Dordrecht, Holland.

1. The Interest for "Knowledge" in Historical Inquiry

The interest of reason in historical inquiry is to constitute a truly *scientific* and *objective* body of knowledge, i.e., a body of knowledge which satisfies Kant's criteria of objectivity in the *Second Analogy of Experience*. In essence, the analytical argument in the analogies runs as follows: it must be possible to distinguish between an "objective" succession in the phenomenon and a merely "subjective" succession in my representation. That is, it must be possible to oppose two kinds of temporal relation, one subjected to order, the other indifferent to order. The recourse to the criterion of objectivity established in the *Analogies* has a direct bearing on our discussion. This criterion applies directly to the temporality of human experience. It distinguishes and delineates two modes of temporality, unordered succession on the one hand and ordered succession on the other. Objectivity consists in the ability to apply this distinction to every sort of experience. It is of little importance to know whether the three Kantian analogies — permanence, causality, and reciprocal action — do indeed identify a truly permanent trait in the conceptual structure of experience. It is not in fact certain that in elaborating these we designate a condition to which we are unavoidably committed if we wish to employ the notions of experience and object in a manner intelligible to ourselves and to others. In regard to what it states, however, the theory of the *Principles* — as extracted from the complicated argument of the *Analogies* — does seem to be able to serve as the ground for any analysis of the conceptual schema of our experience, as P.F. Strawson suggests in *The Bounds of Sense*.

This, however, is not all there is to the argument. Our notion of experience and of objectivity, in the strict sense of the word, does not only presuppose a series, an order, a connectedness (causal or not); this connectedness must also be such that experience is *one* in order therefore to be *mine*. This is the meaning of the *Transcendental Deduction*: there is no connectedness without unity, no unity without self-consciousness. In other words: an ordered experience is an experience which can be ascribed to a consciousness which is *one* in such a way as to allow each person to call that experience *his*. Here again, it is of slight importance that Kant was led to a risky hypostasis — or rather, encouraged this hypostasis — by calling upon a subsisting and permanent *I* accompanying all our representations. What is central to the argument is that the connectedness of experience requires a principle higher than the concepual network governing this connectedness, that this connectedness is subordinate to the condition of the self-ascription of experience, the ascription not merely of an ordered but of a unified experience.

How, we might ask, does this ground of the notion of experience and of objects concern the interest of the historian? The historian is concerned insofar as he is motivated as a man of science by the desire for his object and his science to meet the requirements of an experience which is not only ordered but unified as well. By the same token, his interest lies in reducing the gap between the social sciences and the natural sciences as much as possible. This requirement is inaccurately described when it is presented as a prejudice supported by the domination of natural science, namely as an improper extension of the methodology of natural science to the field of social sciences. Of course, at the level of the history of ideas, one can observe the fascination exerted by the experimental method on social scientists. They find in it a ready-made model serving to link together facts, hypotheses, laws and theories. But when reflection addresses itself to the roots of the interests at stake, this sort of transfer from one field to the other stems from a profound need which can be expressed as follows: if it is true that experience, in the strict sense of the word, must be at once connected and unified, then the difference between natural science and social science is inessential. For if it were essential, the idea of the connectedness of experience would be threatened and along with it, the singular character of the conceptual network underlying this connectedness. The same argument which excludes a plurality of worlds excludes an ultimate pluralism of methods and of objective domains.

Of course, the analytical argument drawn from an explanation of the notions of experience and object does not prevent us from retaining something of the Aristotelian thesis that "one must not expect the same rigorousness in every sort of discussion, any more than one requires it in works of art..., for a cultured man is one who seeks rigorousness in each kind of thing only to the extent to which the nature of the subject permits" (*Nichomachean Ethics*, 1094 b 11). This thesis cannot, however, be placed on the same level as the requirement of connectedness and unity. At best it forms a secondary rule, appropriate for regional differences but subordinate to the idea of ordered and unified experience.

2. Hermeneutical Reflection

I should like to introduce hermeneutical reflection here, not at the level of the "quarrel of methods" — of the *Methodenstreit* between *Natur-* and *Geisteswissenschaft* — but at that of the conflict of interests.

If the interest which demands that the difference between natural science and social science be made entirely relative is based upon the requirement of constituting an ordered and unified experience, and if this requirement is ultimately based upon the possibility that "the *I think* accompanies all my representations," then it is this very possibility that must be examined. This can, in fact, signify nothing other than the condition that I can, potentially, ascribe experience to myself as ordered and as unified. Henceforth, the entire project to construct a foundation is focused on the possibility of the self-ascription of experience.

It is here that the conflict of interest arises. Are we to hold along with Kant that the conflict opposes some "ethical" principle to the "theoretical" interest for objective knowledge? It seems to me that the hermeneutical perspective can initially be described — in a negative fashion — as an attempt to dig deeper than the opposition between "theoretical" and "practical." This opposition can, in fact, only lead to subtracting "belief" from "knowledge" without thereby increasing knowledge and so without transgressing the principle of meaning which governs our use of the notions of experience and object. Hermeneutics claims instead to generate a crisis within the very concept of the *theoretical* as expressed by the principle of the connectedness and unity of experience. This crisis results from a reflection upon the conditions of self-ascription. It is only after a long journey backwards, following prolonged questioning of the Kantian *I think*, master of the unity and the connectedness of experience, that the interest governing this very question can be identified.

Let us attempt to follow this questioning, as it moves from *Historie* back to *Geschichte*, from historical inquiry back to the historical *condition*. The first step back consists in recognizing that the self-ascription of experience is not a primary, sovereign, self-constitutive act. Instead it has always been preceded by the experience of *belonging-to*...what knowledge attempts to posit in front of the subject as its object.

This *belonging-to* can be ignored with no apparent harm to the constitution of physical objects. Galilean and Newtonian science, in fact, arose from the decisive split between the physical world and the world of perception, which had determined the constitution of Ancient and Medieval cosmologies. In thus breaking the ties between the physical object and the perceptive field, the new mathematical science of nature actually constituted the physical object as such. The object then became what I can oppose to myself, what I can distinguish and place in front of the subjective flow of my experience. And yet, even at the level of natural science, it should not be forgotten that it is because I first find myself thrown into situations I have not chosen, because I am affected by things I receive but have not created, that I can assign myself the task of orienting myself, of projecting my own possibilities into these situations. The most primordial sort of understanding is nothing other than this project of determining what affects me as *this* or as *that*, namely the project of *thinking* what I *receive*. Underlying the conceptual network developed by an analytical argument, there is thus a much more primordial relation between receiving and determining which is properly the domain of an ontology of finitude. The analytical argument is situated at the level of the principle of meaning without which we could make no intelligible use of the notions of experience and object. Hermeneutical reflection digs under this principle and exposes it as merely the rule to which the users of ordinary language are committed. Behind this rule, hermeneutics aims at the finite and transcendent condition of a being who is *affected* in his receptive capacity before he is able to *determine* his situation conceptually. It is this primordial belonging-to, that cannot be destroyed by the opposition between subjective and objective succession, which constitutes experience.

This antecedence of the experience of belonging-to, which cannot be cancelled by physical experience, is even less in danger of being contradicted by historical experience. The historical object can never really be placed before me as the *other* of my temporal representations. It presents a temporality which is not foreign to my own. My temporality is primordially related, by means of what Husserl terms *Paarung* — a sort of pairing — to the temporality of others whom I apprehend as other subjects, other selves, subjects analogous to myself. According to this pairing, one temporal flux accompanies another temporal flux; yet this accompanying does not correspond to the way in which the *I think* accompanies all *my* representations, even when this is understood as an "I can ascribe to myself" all my representations. Instead, an *I can* accompanies another *I can*, analogous in its capacity to ascribe its experiences to itself. But this is not all. The foreignness of historical reality cannot even be included in the otherness of intersubjectivity. The temporality belonging to historical reality consists in the following: the pairing of one temporal flux to another appears as a relation of simultaneity which, in turn, is only a cross-section of an all-encompassing flux which, in addition to coexistence, also includes succession. What is encompassed by historical temporality is a threefold relation; my personal history relates at once to contemporaries, predecessors, and successors (to use the language of Alfred Schutz in his phenomenology of the social world).

My temporality *belongs to* this higher-order temporality. And this belonging-to no longer seems capable of objectification in the sense required by the Kantian analytical argument, i.e., an opposition between objective and subjective succession. If the physical object can still be constituted by this distinction and by this opposition between the subjective modality of unordered succession and the objective modality of ordered succession, the historical object calls for a different sort of constitution which includes a multitude of temporal fields themselves related as contemporaneous, anterior and posterior within an all-encompassing temporal field that is history itself. As a result of this enigma, history eludes the limiting conceptual framework by which we make intelligible to ourselves what we call experience and the objects of experience. This enigma does not involve severing ethics from physics but rather removing the historical from the sway of the natural.

This belonging-to, however, is not unintelligible. It is the condition for what we understand, even in ordinary language, when we speak of the past as what is *transmitted* to us through traditions. It is within the framework of this transmission that we can speak — as we have just done above — of our predecessors and our successors. The intelligibility belonging to the historical field cannot be reduced to the course of things, to the governing order which in Kant's example in *The Second Analogy* limits us to seeing the boat floating down the river. There is no doubt that human events are interwoven with the course of things. The boat sails down the river and we along with it. Nevertheless, even if we have a perfect right to speak of the ordered and objective sequence, which is properly referred to as the course of things, in terms of the law of causality alone, understood as ordered succession — we are also justified in seeking to express the transmission of tradition, which binds us to our predecessors and to our contemporaries, in absolutely specific categories. In this regard, we speak of human agents who initiate events of which they are the authors; who interpret their actions in terms of motives; who take into account the actions, motives and goals of other agents; who submit their goals to norms and their norms to institutions; who may consider these institutions as mutable or as immutable, and so on. In short, historical transmission demands to be *thought* otherwise than as ordered succession. The basic reason is that the higher-order temporality of history is made up of temporal fields, of temporal fluxes similar to my own. If *analogy* is invoked here as the transcendental principle of the relation of one temporal flux to another, this is not done in order to introduce a kind of reasoning by analogy — in a falsely empirical sense — by which we could infer the existence of our contemporaries, our predecessors and our successors. Reasoning by analogy is an illusion and has no verifiable status in the empirical acquisition of human experience. The analogy at issue here is a transcendental *principle* and not empirical *reasoning*. This principle signifies that others, all others before, with and after me, exert the ego function, that each of us is able to ascribe to himself his own experience *like* others. The function of analogy as a transcendental principle is to preserve the equality of the signification *I* — equality in the sense that others are equally egos — throughout all dimensions forming the domain of this higher-order temporality. My predecessors, my contemporaries and my successors were able, are able and will be able to designate themselves as *I* and to ascribe their experience to themselves. This is why the transmission of tradition can — under certain conditions which we shall put forth later — simulate the ordered succession of things. Under these conditions, it can lend itself to a kind of causal explanation. However, the conditions for this simulation are themselves to be understood as resulting from the reification through which historical reality has lost its original status. If, in fact, human relations throughout history have for the most part been reified to the point where the course of history is no longer distinguished from the course of things, this represents history's misfortune not its primordial constitution. *Utopia* bears witness to this by untiringly directing the *imagination* toward an historical situation freed from reification. The imagination would have a mere de-reifying function did it not point to possibilities really implied by the primordial constitution of the historical bond, to the possibilities that the actual course of history has in some sense frozen or petrified.

This remark on utopia permits us to glimpse the answer to a question raised earlier. We asked what interest carries us back from history as science to our belonging to a lived history which precedes any relation to an objective history. This interest, it seems to me, can be termed the interest for communication. The term "communication" must, however, be taken here in a broad enough sense to enable us, at least for the moment, not to take sides with Gadamer or Habermas in the disagreement between them on this subject. The interest for communication is not an interest for simply renewing traditions received from the past, which would call for the counterweight of another interest, turned toward the future — the interest for liberation. The interest for communication is not backward-looking nor does it call for a futurist complement. On the one hand, it is hard to see from where the interest for liberation would draw its force if the voice of human freedom did not echo from the furthest reaches of our most ancient traditions — Hebrew and Greek — if this voice were not both that of the Exodus and that of the Greek city and of the Stoics. On the other hand, it is difficult to see what end the recapitulation of our heritage would serve if the resistance to reification did not lie at the very heart of our memory. Utopia and recollection cannot be separated; each would perish without the other. I shall therefore not return to the quarrel mentioned earlier. It is not to the ethical and political questions of communication that I wish to address myself here, but to the properly epistemological issues involved in communication. That is, I should like to consider communication as a transcendental principle apt to conflict with the principle of meaning which directs us to unify our experience and to hold the regional difference between history and nature to be of secondary importance.

The interest for communication can be termed *practical*, in contrast to the interest for knowledge, that is, for the connectedness and unity of experience. Practical, however, is not the same as ethical. We must be careful not to fall back into the old neo-Kantian dichotomy between value judgments and judgments of fact. What we have here is a practical interest, an interest for a "competence" — in the sense in which Chomsky distinguishes between competence and performance. This competence is precisely what can be reified, what simulates the simple objective connectedness which we call the course of things under the conditions of reification. The sense of this competence can be expressed in terms that are less negative in the two following ways. First, in terms of the notion of a higher-order temporality — the all-encompassing historical temporality mentioned above — we can say that this competence consists in preserving our "openness" to our contemporaries, to our predecessors and even to our successors, in spite of the reification of our projects, norms and institutions. Preserving our openness in this way means allowing ourselves to be affected by the effects of history, keeping ourselves open to history's efficacity. This is, in fact, Gadamer's concept of *wirkungsgeschichtliches Bewusstsein* reinterpreted in terms of competence. A consciousness open to history is at once the consciousness of being affected, the project of allowing oneself to be affected, and the competence to remain affected. A second way of expressing the sense of this competence is suggested here: if the analogy of the ego is the transcendental principle by which we distinguish historical connectedness from the connectedness of things, the *competence* which concerns us historically is the unfailing ability to discern the difference between the two kinds of connectedness. It allows us to identify, despite all evidence to the contrary, the analogy of the ego not only in the short term relationships of friendship and love but in long term relationships with contemporaries, predecessors and successors.

By the same token, this discriminatory competence — meaning this competence to discern history as such — places the interest for communication in conflict with the interest for knowledge. The latter appears in contrast to the former as a competence not to discern history as such, not to take into account the difference between the historical and the natural, by virtue of the principle of meaning which forbids our conceiving a plurality of experiences as well as a plurality of worlds.

II. FROM HISTORICITY TO HISTORY

The way back from philosophical hermeneutics towards the methodology of the historical sciences is the most arduous. Yet, it is along here that hermeneutics has to test its ability to contribute to an authentic critique of the historical method. Its task does not end with the "return to the essential"; it ends only when hermeneutics enters into a renewed dialogue with the historical sciences. Now, the return to the essential can itself constitute an obstacle to the second part of the hermeneutic task. Indeed, there is a danger that hermeneutics will cast itself in the role of simply opposing methodology. This occurs when the objectification implied by this methodology is held to be identical with the alienation which represents the perversion of our belonging-to history. The way back towards science is possible only if hermeneutics can account for a principle of the externalization of experience which is not as such already a form of alienation but which is later perverted and, consequently, presupposed by alienation. This principle of externalization must be implied in the very mediation which constitutes the bond of our belonging-to history and must be the basis of the movement towards objectification in general. In other words, this must be a feature of the mediation described above as the transmission of a tradition, a mediation which appeared to us to be the very first characteristic of historical reality.

1. Temporal Distance and "Methodological" Distantiation

We become concretely aware of this principle of externalization in the case of temporal distance. The consequence of the separation in time between us and our predecessors is that we have access to the past only through traces, marks, inscriptions, documents, archives, monuments of all kinds which are the "facts" of history. To the extent that these "facts" may be said to be "observable," history may participate in observation and explanation along the lines of a model of intelligibility resembling that of natural science. Marc Bloch's plea in behalf of history attests strongly to this relation between observation and explanation in the science of history.

But temporal distance is not in itself a principle. For the objection remains that the perversion of the historical bond begins with the reference to exterior marks. The first misfortune is held to be the externalization of memory in physical marks. Plato's celebrated argument against writing in the *Phaedrus* applies equally well to historical objectification insofar as this argument opposes two sorts of memory, one "interior" — that of true reminiscence — the other "exterior," compelled to rely upon marks and imprints. Besides, the argument drawn from the distinction between interior reminiscence and exterior means of recollection concerns both history and writing to the extent that history is a particularly explicit case of recollection by means of marks and traces. Plato's sharp attack on externalization in marks and his impassioned plea for reminiscence free of external mediation prevent us from simply hiding behind the fact of temporal distance. This is why I am introducing a principle of distantiation which involves *setting at a distance* rather than distance alone.

Distantiation is invoked as a principle in an effort to show that the experience of belonging-to, on which historicity is based, itself stands in need of something like externalization in order to be apprehended, articulated and understood.

For different reasons, François Dagognet attempted to demonstrate this in his work, *Ecriture et iconographie*. Taking his argument from Plato's comparison between "letters" and "icons," he has developed a general theory of inscription under the concept of iconicity which is in direct opposition to the Platonic theory of images as mere shadows, diminished reality. Dagognet shows that the effect of icons — in writing as well as in painting and in all the graphic forms by means of which thought represents and describes the universe — is to *augment* reality and not to diminish it. This is accomplished in various ways which are linked by the common feature of summing up experience, encompassing it by means of a small number of clearly distinct signs, and thereby amplifying it by means of the combinatory power of a concise system of signs. Dagognet opposes this augmentary effect to the erosion of differences and dissimilarities to which ordinary vision is prone due to the effacement and weakening of contrasts. Graphic images thus work to combat the entropy that affects ordinary perception. Now, externalization into marks is the sole cause of this intensification of our experience. Similarly, it would appear to me that our perception of history is likewise intensified and augmented by this process of externalization which consists in the deposit of traces and inscriptions. Temporal distance, then, which is simply given, is of little importance beside the distantiation resulting from inscription. Once again, the objectification of historical experience and that of writing share the same fate, both are hopes for rehabilitation as they were objects of reprobation. It is as writing that historical experience is set at a distance. If the science of history is a science that proceeds by means of traces, if it begins with an "external" critique which employs documents from archives, this is because historical experience is itself a continual process of externalization, which permits of inscription and perpetuation in archives.

This conjunction of historical objectification and externalization through writing is of tremendous importance for hermeneutics. Even if we say with Dilthey that historical understanding ultimately relies on our power to transport ourselves into a foreign psychic life, understanding becomes a hermeneutical task only when it is mediated by written signs and, in general, by an inscription. Understanding can then justly be called interpretation, that is, textual exegesis. History is given as a *text* offered not only to our understanding but to our interpretation. Understanding between our contemporaries and ourselves is mediated by something like a text. This mediation confers upon temporal distance its full meaning. The issue here is not the measurable distance which separates us from the past. This distance can be thought of as the place and the instance of a textual or quasi-textual mediation. The size of this gap is of little importance since the same sort of mediation can arise between our contemporaries and ourselves, as witnessed by the role played in human communication by written messages from living authors in letters, newspapers and in all the mass media.

It is therefore necessary to move back from the simple fact of distance to the distance formed by the externalization in inscription in an effort to grasp and to circumscribe the principle of distantiation.

But we must move beyond inscription in order to discover the extent to which distantiation is implied by the relation of belonging-to. Before any actual inscription, experience contains a fundamental capacity for inscription which makes writing possible. Inquiring into the conditions for understanding, before any interpretation of written signs, Dilthey noted that externalization in signs is the first condition for understanding others. Moreover, it is because these signs and the experience they express have a certain inner connection – a *Zusammenhang* – an inner form, that they can be present to the understanding. Thus objectification is absolutely primitive and radical. It begins when life is not simply lived but understands itself and offers itself for understanding by others through its inner connection. It is because of this characteristic that life can be said and described.

Dilthey's analysis is confirmed by a similar reflection on the conditions of the possibility of writing in the form of discourse, that is, in a structure which precedes the split into spoken and written discourse. If writing is possible, it is because discourse already possesses its own form of externalization which can be inscribed on a material base, in an external medium, in marks and in archives. *Saying* is an act externalized in a proposition, which – to use Frege's expression – can be written on the wall. *Saying* moves beyond itself in the "*said.*" The "said" is what signifies and what will continue to signify when *saying* disappears. Hegel described this in his chapter on the dialectic of experience and language in the *Phenomenology of Mind.* I say: day is dawning. But when the day is no longer dawning, what was aimed at, spoken of, meant in my saying remains as what was said. This is why it can be written. The expressible character of experience, therefore, comes before the power of inscription. This verbal articulation is the element of language which forms the ground for what, following Dilthey, we have termed the inner connection of experience. Experience is expressible insofar as it is discursive, and its discursiveness is also what makes it capable of being inscribed.

Historical science takes up this spontaneous distancing in a deliberate and methodical act of distantiation.

This is a *methodological* act in the same sense as the Cartesian doubt. Returning to our earlier reflection on the transmission of traditions, we can say that a tradition is capable of transmission when we do not confine ourselves to living in it but begin to set it at a distance like an object. This is the case even if this distantiation should one day disappear into mere repetition which, itself, would in any case constitute something different from the initial naïve state. This methodical doubt at times prolongs a sceptical, non deliberate doubt which may be experienced as a violent discord within consciousness. Hegel calls this crisis of tradition "alienation" in the celebrated chapter of the *Phenomenology* entitled *"Geist."* Culture — *Bildung* — proceeds, to a large extent, from the pain of becoming a stranger to one's own past as fashioned by tradition at the level of mere custom. This is the price paid in order that the "ethical substance" — *die Sittlichkeit* — may become "subject."

Methodical doubt is the same sort of doubt but it is deliberate. In fact, history as a distinct discipline was born of such negative activity of this pain of alienation. Then the relation to the past becomes a question: Why war? asks the Greek historian. In particular, why this war between Hellenes, destroying the panhellenic dream? It is not difficult to see that the will to know which takes hold of the person who raises the question cannot help but place the entire inquiry within the perspective of the physical explanation of nature. To look for the *aition* of war is to question as one questions in physics where what is sought is the "cause" — or causes — of motion.

A bridge is thus built between the truth of our belonging-to history and the method of historical science. The former requires the latter insofar as sceptical doubt is taken up in methodical doubt and insofar as objective answers are sought to a question conceived in anguish.

The methodical mind can thus take possession of everything in our historical bond which can lend itself to objectification and inscription. History then truly becomes the text of human action.

2. The Moment of "Critical" Distantiation

A further step brings us closer not only to the *method* but also to the *interest* which rules the historical method. We said above that this interest requires that the objectivity of historical science be joined to that of the natural sciences in such a way that the network of experience becomes a single network and that experience as a whole can in every instance be ascribed to an individual consciousness. Does the interest for communication, which makes us seek a distinct epistemological status for history, require as its dialectical counterpart the interest for objectivity?

My thesis is that this implication of one interest by another can be demonstrated if the "methodical" moment of distantiation is reduced to a "critical" moment and if we find what is required by this critical moment in the human experience of belonging-to.

The critical reduction no longer concerns the method of history but more precisely the reflective consciousness of the method and, consequently, the consciousness of the historian himself. As the term "critical" already suggests, this consciousness judges, raises the *quaestio juris*, evaluates claims and sets a limit on them. It is, to borrow the expression Eric Weil employs in his interpretation of Kant, the "judiciary." This consciousness of method is itself, at least implicitly, philosophical consciousness. It proclaims the primacy of judgment in our comportment in the world. Accordingly, it rules out the prejudices considered as the primary evil which have crept into historical judgment through the weight of tradition. Today this critical consciousness is more directly involved in the critical social sciences such as the critique of ideologies and psychoanalysis. The critical consciousness rebounds onto history itself, giving it an explicit awareness of its method through the multiple and varied contacts between historical science and the social sciences.

The social sciences are critical in the sense that they do not take their starting point in historical consciousness itself in order to broaden and elucidate this consciousness. Instead, they treat it from the outset as "false consciousness" and apply to it the various techniques of *suspicion*. The level of reference is thus displaced to unconscious structures and deep-rooted conflicts linked either to individual repression or to collective repression. In both cases, the systematic distortion of communication requires an indirect explanation which is no longer in line with the direct understanding of the historical condition. This explanation by unconscious structures and conflicts may not be self-sufficient. An explanation in terms of the unconscious or in terms of social structures not recognized by consciousness when it acts intentionally loses its meaning if no way is offered of reintegrating the contents thus revealed in the process of self-understanding. What good would it do an agent acting intentionally to know that all his intentions are slanted by forces unknown to him, if this discovery cannot finally be transposed into increased lucidity? It would thus appear that, ultimately, explanation in terms of unconscious structures is only a phase in the process of understanding, for otherwise understanding itself would have no meaning. Reconverting explanation into understanding in this way is not, however, what is at issue here. What we are interested in is why this detour by the most extreme sort of objectification is necessary; we want to know the meaning of this indirect phase for historical understanding.

History as science cannot remain untouched by this development of the critical sciences, even though these sciences, as we said earlier, are not themselves historical and even though history, for its part, cannot be absorbed by these sciences without losing its status as a science of past events based on traces, marks, and inscriptions. This concerns history less, it seems to me, at the level of its method than at that of its own reflective consciousness. This is not to say that historical explanation is in no way affected as to its method by the lessons of psychoanalysis and ideology-critique, for as a result of its contact with them it does arrive at a more precise sense of the structures constituting its object. Nevertheless, complex as a historical method enriched by psychoanalysis and ideology-critique may become, history does not lose its identity and simply allow itself to be absorbed by the critical sciences. The historical as such resists this dissolution. It is the historian who, in the reflective consciousness of his method, is profoundly affected and changed. The suspicion of the critical sciences causes his methodical doubt to become ever more radical. In spite of the influence of the critical sciences this doubt has always been part of his field of study for it directly constitutes the methodology of this pursuit. It is in this sense that the critical moment is incorporated into the historian's interest for his object at the level of the reflective consciousness of his method.

What kind of connection can be found between our experience of belonging-to history and this critical moment of distantiation?

As we stated above, the final step hermeneutics takes in the direction of historical science involves the interests in which their respective attitudes are grounded. It seems to me that this step is required by the very structure of understanding, its structure of anticipation. This structure contains the seeds both of a certain rehabilitation of prejudice as pre-judgment and of a critical requirement in regard to prejudices insofar as they create an obstacle for an authentic relationship with the thing itself. In other words, the critical moment is required by the work of partitioning into authentic and inauthentic experience; this work takes place at the level of the structure of anticipation, at the level of pre-understanding.

Let us then take this as our starting point.

The very term "fore-structure of understanding" (*Vor-struktur des Verstehens*) comes, as we know, from Heidegger. Paragraph 32 of *Sein und Zeit* lists a series of expressions possessing the prefix *vor-* (*Vor-habe, Vor-sicht, Vor-griff*). All these expressions point to a fundamental characteristic of understanding, namely that no one — not the historian, the literary critic, the art critic, or the exegete — can approach his object without some previous notion of that object. What is called the hermeneutic circle on the purely philological level is only a "derived form" of this originary fore-structure of understanding. H.G. Gadamer is not mistaken in taking the argument even further and in seeking in the history of jurisprudence a level of *prae-judicium* which would no longer include the pejorative connotation of the pre-judged but which would still carry the traces of its relation to the fore-structure of understanding. This relative rehabilitation of pre-judgment leads to the recognition (*Anerkennung*) of authority, insofar as authority offers us a cultural heritage. Tradition is therefore what precedes historical investigation in that it assures the "preservation" (*Bewahrung*) of the heritage of the past in a manner which cannot be reduced to the mere "perseverance" of natural forces.

This concept of fore-structure, and the manner in which it is developed by Heidegger and by Gadamer, does not consider the return path of this fore-structure which constitutes our historical being. It is, however, on this way back that hermeneutics confronts the critical moment in its most distinctive form, namely in ideology-critique. And yet this confrontation is implied by the very notion of fore-structure:

[In] this circle of understanding... is hidden a positive possibility of the most primitive kind of knowing. To be sure, we genuinely take hold of this possibility only when, in our interpretation [*Auslegung*], we have understood that our first, last, and constant task is never to allow our fore-having, fore-sight, and fore-conception to be presented to us by fancies and popular conceptions, but rather to make the scientific theme secure by working out these fore-structures in terms of the things themselves (*Being and Time*, Oxford, 1967, p. 195).

A critical partitioning into pre-understanding and pre-judice is therefore required by the hermeneutics of understanding itself. This partitioning, in turn, requires that the critical moment be included in the movement directed from the ontology of understanding towards the methodology of interpretation. But for structural reasons, the former cannot return to the region of dialogue with the social sciences.

H.G Gadamer indicates the direction to be taken here. If tradition "preserves" the heritage of the past, and if we reply to this voice of the past with an anticipation of its meaning, this reciprocal relation must undergo the rigors of criticism if the past is to keep some "signification" for us. Indeed, only the test of criticism can enable us to discern what is worth questioning. It alone can enable us to decide between what in pre-understanding is mere "fancy" and "popular conceptions" and what is authentically a "fore-structure in terms of the things themselves." In this respect, historical experience does not escape Socrates' warning: a life which is not "examined" is not worthy of the name.

CONCLUSION

Has the argument of the "way downward" from hermeneutics to historical science abolished the argument of the "way upward" from the methodology of history to the ontology of historicity?

Not at all.

The first argument states that historical transmission requires categories different from those which rule physical succession. The second concerns the relation between historical and social sciences. Both paradoxes are set against the paradox of history's two-fold foundation in a two-fold interest.

The difference between historical science and natural science is unessential to the extent that history also relies on "facts" and proceeds from "observation" to "explanation" and "theory." But this same difference is essential to the extent that history cannot rid itself of the categories of meaningful action, such as project, motive, evaluation, norm, institution, and ultimately the category of the historical agent acting intentionally. The objectivity of history therefore remains merely analogous to that of natural science, and history can never be a sub-section of natural science.

In the same way, history tends to become one of the critical social sciences to the extent that it takes into account not only the motives of which historical agents are aware, but also concealed motives. History would thus appear to enjoy the status of strict objectivity accorded to these sciences. Yet history remains tied, in spite of all its efforts to the contrary, to the nature of *events* which characterize men's action on the course of things, and to the nature of *succession* between generations, founded on the primordial relation between contemporaries and predecessors.

Finally, the ambiguous nature of the historical method betrays the allegiance of history to two different systems of interest: an interest for objective knowledge and an interest for communication. We have shown that these interests neither altogether exclude nor altogether include one another; they act instead as the two foci of an ellipse. The dialectical relation between these two interests is what ultimately justifies the paradoxes of methodology. The objectivity of history moves tangentially towards the objectivity of the natural sciences and towards that of the social sciences, but it cannot be completely absorbed by either. The parallelism between their methods cannot erase the difference in their foundations.

The two arguments presented in this essay come together and form a single argument which I should like to call a "deduction" (in the Kantian sense of the word) of the process of history.

Université de Paris
and the University of Chicago

CHARLES TAYLOR

COMMENTS

There is a great deal in Professor Ricoeur's paper. Perhaps we can regard it, however, as composed of a base and a superstructure, in the sense that it relies upon there being a fundamental distinction between the situation in which we find ourselves in relation to historical inquiry on the one hand, and that in relation to the natural sciences on the other. The entire development of the argument, and the formulation of our current dilemmas in the latter part of the paper, are based on this distinction. Let me therefore focus on the distinction itself, because it is an extremely difficult one to get clear. Once it has become clear, one can go on to what depends on it. But I shall confine my own remarks to this distinction alone.

The distinction comes out in a number of ways in the paper, but above all in what Ricoeur says about ourselves as subjects engaged in historical inquiry — that we have to take account of the way in which we, as subjects, belong to a certain historical epoch, or a historical belt of transmissions, of tradition. In order to bring out what this means, let me introduce a term of art: self-understanding, in a specific sense of self-understanding which need not outlive the present discussion (as I do not think it is widely usable, but it will help today). By this I shall mean the understanding we have of ourselves through our classification of different kinds of human motivation, or different kinds of human possibilities, as we see them, ones which are essential to our achieving certain fundamental modes of human life as we understand it.

For instance, in a given civilization like ours, there is a conception of what it is to be an individual, that is, an autonomous human being, a fully-realized individual as against one who is, in some way, not autonomous. Or there is a conception of what it is to be a rational human being, or a productive human being. These are cases of what I mean by concepts which characterize a certain type of human motivation, or a certain type of human possibility.

Now, all of these concepts are only comprehensible contrastively. That is,

21

Yirmiahu Yovel (ed.), Philosophy of History and Action, 21–25. All Rights Reserved.
Copyright © 1978 by D. Reidel Publishing Company, Dordrecht, Holland.

we understand what rationality is by means of a certain set of notions of what can breach it, ones constituting irrationality; we understand autonomy as contrasted with heteronomy. And because of the necessity of contrast here, our understanding of what the life forms are — what it is to be an autonomous or a rational man — goes along with, and is intimately related to, an understanding of the life form of a heteronomous or an irrational human being, and so on.

This means that we understand ourselves only by understanding certain other kinds of human beings, other kinds of life possibilities. Sometimes, of course, these are realized, as far as we are concerned, by other people in our close milieu. In other cases one of the alternatives may seem to characterize our civilization virtually as a whole. In particular, ours is a historical civilization, in the sense that we have defined ourselves by certain notions of progress, or development, or maturation relative to earlier civilizations. It is a central feature of our civilization that an important part of the contrasts in terms of which we define ourselves is historical. That is, we consider ourselves to be *moderns* who are rational, who have a certain ideal of autonomy, and we define this partly by the contrast with *earlier* civilizations, which we believe to have lacked those notions in important ways. And we won through to those notions of autonomy and rationality and so on—notably, for instance, in the seventeenth century revolution—by a negation of certain earlier life ideals or notions of human possibility.

This aspect of our self-understanding is still very much alive today. If you ask someone today who believes in those ideals to tell you what they mean, he will sooner or later be forced into talking about the seventeenth century revolution, Galileo, Newton and so on. And he will talk about it as an act of historical negation of what went on before. The same goes for other traditions; to Marxists, for instance, it is even more relevant.

In our civilization, consequently, the universal human necessity of defining one set of possibilities by contrast with others, is to an important degree a matter of historical understanding, because an important category of the "others" with whom we contrast ourselves are those from whom we sprang.

This does not mean, of course, that we never employ purely contemporary contrasts as part of our self-definition. It may be, for instance, that many people in the Western world, to a considerable degree, define their notion of autonomy also by how they see the Soviet world. Or it may be that in twenty years time, we shall all be defining ourselves in considerable measure by contrast with contemporary Chinese civilization. But even if ours is not an exclusively historical consciousness, it involves attitudes to history in a very important way.

We can sum up what I have been saying so far in the statement that, in our civilization, there can be no self-understanding without historical understanding, without some understanding of what the people who preceded us were like. The important point that Ricoeur makes will come out if it is *also* possible to convert that proposition as I think it is. That is, I want to claim that there is also no historical understanding without, in the sense I explained, self-understanding. Let me try to outline, in the brief time available, my justification for this claim.

I think this claim follows if we accept one basic assumption: that we cannot have something describable as historical understanding, without having a set of notions of history which fulfil the criteria of what Weber called "meaning adequacy" as opposed to mere "causal adequacy." That is, we would be dissatisfied with a historical account of what brought about the French Revolution, or of what went on in the Roman Empire, if it did not give us an idea of how people acted, thereby being "meaning adequate" in Weber's sense.

The only way you could deny this bold assumption I am making, is if you could imagine a historical account which gave us an explanation in terms of generalizations about or correlations of human behaviour, one which was purely, in Weber's sense, "causally adequate." That is, founded purely on the fact that we discover these generalizations to hold by counting over instances. And although many people have issued promissory notes about the possibility of doing this, I defy anyone to give me one historical account of any event, any time, which anyone will take as adequate, but which is based purely on this foundation.

So in default of an argument in principle for making that assumption, I shall simply issue this challenge and take it as granted that we make it a condition of adequacy of historical explanations that such explanations be "meaning adequate." If this is so, then I think one could show that the background of *any* conception of "meaning adequacy" in Weber's sense is precisely one or more of those classifications of different kinds of human possibility that I mentioned before. If this is so in turn, then the particular human possibilities we see ourselves as realizing are always there as a perhaps unspoken part of the contrast. Thus, there is always some element of contrasting "them" with "us" which is involved in our understanding of another epoch. If that is so, then one can indeed convert the proposition I advanced earlier — that there is no self-understanding without historical understanding — and claim also that there is no historical understanding without self-understanding. From which it follows that there is quite a different predicament here in historical inquiry than in inquiry in natural science. And this is precisely the distinction underlying Ricoeur's paper.

That is, natural scientists attempt to abstract totally from the predicament of the subject who is doing the inquiry, and to discover a language such as the language of mathematics, or the language of mathematics plus reference to certain physical events, and so on, which should be ideally understandable in a way which involves no reference at all to the historical or life situation of any of those engaging in the inquiry. Ideally, if we met some intelligent beings with a completely different physical base than ourselves — say intelligent gaseous clouds in Alpha Centauri in the year 2025 — we should be able to communicate with them about particle physics, to exchange equations in some way. So in this sense there is an ideal of those sciences which involves complete abstraction. But if what Ricoeur is saying, and what I am trying to say, about history is true, this is completely impossible in historical inquiry.

It follows from this that an important element of self-criticism is required in any historical inquiry. In other words, the inquiry is always going awry, because we are always distorting it, because we have this other very important interest which we do not have in the inquiry into nature. Since the way we understand ourselves, and therefore our entire practice, is bound up with a certain projective interpretation of others.

If you start interpreting the Middle Ages differently than as being dark ages in which all human learning and light disappeared, you threaten the whole life project of a Macaulay, of the Whig historians and their successors in modern civilization. And they naturally have an interest in defending this interpretation, which is, one might say, our life interest. Therefore, the only way the discussion can proceed is by uncovering these distortions that we project in virtue of the fact that the whole way we put our own lives together is bound up with them.

Another example: we are engaged now in trying to discover how to understand the process of political development in the world, particularly in connection with those countries which now call themselves "developing countries," in the modern jargon. As a matter of fact, there are a number of theories put forward in contemporary American political science, called theories of development, which I think are all guilty of the most horrendous distortion in this process.

The way in which this distortion comes about is intimately bound up with, or dependent on, the way Americans, and Westerners in general, see themselves, understand themselves, as occupying one among the many human possibilities. And one does not get to the real discussion of how this is distorting our understanding of what development is in Kenya or Uganda or India, without bringing into the discussion the whole set of conceptions of what man is which underlie it, and underlie the presupposed conception of Western civilization, autonomy and so on. One really does not begin to raise the issues without doing that.

Thus in historical inquiry, there is a necessity — particularly by using the routes that Ricoeur mentioned at the end, such as the critical sciences or psychoanalysis — to try to get to an understanding of how one is projecting wrongly onto the historical epoch. One does not begin to get a revision of historical understanding without this. In this sense there is no historical understanding without self-understanding. We cannot detach it from our predicament as an agent, from where we are, from the historical period we belong to, as we rightly try to do in physics.

All Souls College
Oxford

ABRAHAM KAPLAN

HISTORICAL INTERPRETATION

The philosophy of history differs from many other fields of philosophy in this respect, that while its general questions are relatively easy to deal with, specific problems are much more difficult. By contrast, in the philosophy of science, for instance, general questions like the nature and basis of scientific knowledge are still unsettling, while specific problems like the logic of measurement or the relation between physical and mathematical geometry have been dealt with rather well.

Here I present some of the specific problems in the philosophy of history, especially the problems of historical interpretation. I distinguish various types of history, and corresponding types of historical interpretation. In a particular body of historical writing several types can be simultaneously present and intertwined, as they are in the work of such writers as James Bryce and Alexis de Tocqueville. The types must be distinguished nevertheless, because each poses distinct methodological problems.

There is need in the philosophy of history for more than an understanding of what is true "in principle" about the writing of history. We need to understand what in fact historians do. In principle, the description, interpretation and explanation of what happened in history may be no different from what applies to any other sort of happenings; in practice, there are many special problems. It is absurd to proclaim conclusions about what is true "in the last analysis," while we are still floundering in the first analysis.

What historians actually do confronts us at once with the problem of what is to be identified as a *historical fact*. The materials of the historian do not themselves constitute his subject-matter. The *materials* are traces or remains of certain processes and events: documents, inscriptions, coins, ruins, perhaps memories. The *subject-matter* is not these remains but the events themselves, "what actually happened," as von Ranke has it.

The problem is that we cannot, as he supposed, "let history speak for itself." It is historians who speak, not history, and what they say is not

27

Yirmiahu Yovel (ed.), Philosophy of History and Action, 27-37, Dordrecht, Reidel, 1978.
Revised from In Pursuit of Wisdom, Los Angeles, Glencoe, 1977, §68.

determined solely by what actually happened — as is amply illustrated, for example, by the periodic Soviet rewriting of history. If history is more than a fable agreed upon (Voltaire), a shallow village tale (Emerson), a distillation of rumor (Carlyle), or simply a huge Mississippi of falsehood (Matthew Arnold), this can only be if it rests on an objective basis of historical fact. Though the historian may aspire to let the facts speak for themselves, he has still the task of determining what the facts are.

Historians constantly face such questions as whether Kennedy's assassin had co-conspirators, where in America Norsemen landed before Columbus, when the Dead Sea scrolls were inscribed, or who authored a certain one of the Federalist Papers. A comprehensive answer to such questions about a particular domain of events is a *historical chronicle*. Examples are the facts about church history recorded by Eusebius in the fourth century, or the facts about land-ownership recorded in the Domesday Book in the eleventh century. A historical chronicle is the outcome of a set of decisions by which the materials of history are interpreted as providing the historian with a certain subject-matter.

That the statements of chronicle are specific rather than general is not in itself problematic, as used to be thought by those who attached great importance to the difference between ideographic and nomothetic disciplines. Establishing facts may be quite as difficult, and have quite as much scientific significance, as formulating valid generalizations. For the practising historian there is little to recommend the Baconian notion that science begins with an assemblage of facts, from which it then extracts universal laws. Such a "beginning" is in practice a point at which the historian would quite often be content to leave off. A historical chronicle has the same logical structure and function as an ephemeris, an almanac or an atlas, and may occupy the historian just as these others occupy the geographer or astronomer.

The sameness of the logic is a matter of principle; in practice the historian faces a distinctive difficulty. It is that his materials lie in the present while his subject-matter is the past. (This is a difficulty for the astronomer as well, who interprets the image on his photographic plate as the trace of a light-ray emitted long ago.) In the most fundamental terms the problem here is the relation between meaning and verification. The evidence is present, but what it is evidence *for* is something past. What the statements of chronicle mean is something quite other than what verifies them.

The question is how we move from evidence to meaning, from present to past. That there is an intimate connection between meaning and verification is by now a truism, but just what the connection is remains obscure, especially in the case of history. As time goes on we not only uncover new historical evidence but also new meanings in the evidence we already have. Both processes affect what we accept as historical fact. But it is not our acceptance which makes it factual.

The possibility of construing reference to the past as a logical construction out of present evidence was explored by G.H. Mead in his *Philosophy of the Present.* While sharing the underlying pragmatism of his theory of meaning, I am not persuaded that it is literally the past, rather than our view of the past, which changes with the changing present. It is true not only that the past illuminates the present, but also that the present throws new light on the past. The question is whether we then see the past differently or whether there is something different to be seen. If the realist insists that we only see it differently, the pragmatist asks how the reality can be distinguished from what we see as real, without an outright begging of the question. Yet how otherwise are we to distinguish between an objective history and a fable agreed upon? Perhaps Orwell's slogan in *1984,* "Who controls the past controls the future" is not the whole story; are we to add, "Who controls the present controls the past"?

The first sense of historical interpretation, then, is that historical remains are taken to be traces of certain happenings; a subject-matter is inferred or construed from materials. Interpretation is involved in the sheer determination of historical fact.

The historian not only determines what happened; he reconstructs what happened, presenting it as the effect of certain causes and as the cause of certain effects. In such a reconstruction, discrete historical *facts* are interpreted to constitute inter-connected historical *events.* The task is to establish linkages, as particular in themselves as are the facts being linked. What part was played by Trotsky in the Bolshevik Revolution, or by the Munich Pact in the outbreak of World War II? Whether Caesar crossed the Rubicon is a question of historical fact; an answer to the question what difference it made presents it as a historical event.

The outcome of this second type of historical interpretation is not a chronicle but a *narrative,* the presentation of a sequence of events bound together in a causal network, as in the histories written by Herodotus and

Gibbon. The difference between chronicle and narrative is like that between an anamnesis, the background data about a patient, and a case history, which details the onset and course of a disease. When the astronomer asks whether quasars are relatively near or very distant he is, as it were, on the level of chronicle; when he asks about the source of their astonishingly great energies, he is preparing a narrative. If the quasars are very distant they have much higher energies, which are presumably produced by quite different processes, than those to be expected if the quasars are nearby. We cannot think fruitfully about causal relations in ignorance of their relata; narrative depends on chronicle, events on facts. Yet we can decide what are the facts only on the basis of the causal connections between what happened and their traces. One chronicle may be better than another just because it allows for a better narrative.

The basic problem here was prefigured by Kant, in his insistence that an objective world can be conceptualized only as existing in a causal order — or rather, in a unified causal system, not in isolated causal streaks, as Reichenbach called them. Every event enters into an unlimited network of causal relations with all other events. The difficulty is that the causal relations by which we come to know it as an objective event are not necessarily those which make it significant. The knowledge of causes and effects which allows the historian to interpret his findings as traces of certain historical facts does not automatically provide a basis for interpreting the facts as the elements of a certain narrative.

To know not only that something happened, but just *what* it was that happened, requires consideration of a much larger network of causal relations, perhaps also one which is much more finely reticulated. What constituted the "fall" of Rome is a matter which hinges less on the determination of facts, like the capture of the city by Alaric, than on their interpretation as having certain causes and consequences. Which causes and consequences is as much a matter of the historian's choice as of objective necessities. He makes not only the inductive leap from traces to facts which produces a chronicle, but also the inductive leap from established facts to events having a certain significance which produces a narrative. Writing history is a risky business.

Yet it is not as demanding as doctrinaire philosophies of science sometimes make out. Narrative gives significance to events by presenting their connections with other events; it does not necessarily display events as governed by general laws. Such a display might very well endow the events with a more profound significance, but the generalizations are correspondingly harder to come by. We may have far better reason to assert a particular causal connection than to proclaim a general law governing connections of that kind. The historian may know what started a particular war without knowing how wars in general start. What he does know is knowledge for all that, and it may be quite significant. Geology is a science just as is geophysics. and the *Descent of Man* is as much a scientific treatise as is the *Origin of Species.*

Presenting particular events as instances of general laws is another type of historical interpretation, whose outcome may be called a *historical analysis*, notably illustrated in Marxist-Leninist historical writing. Such an analysis embodies or presupposes a narrative, and purports also to tell us why events had to happen as they did. Methodological problems of the discovery and formulation of general laws present themselves in historical research as they do everywhere in science. In history, the difficulties are multiplied by certain distinctive features of its subject-matter.

One of these is the central role played in history by *chance* — the problem of Cleopatra's nose (had it been shorter, said Pascal, the whole aspect of the world would have been altered). Lenin was fond of the expression, "It is no accident that...," but accidents do happen, and they may have profound consequences. The familiar reply is that, first, laws may formulate only statistical regularities, and second, a specific event may be accidental while the occurrence of some event of that kind may be necessary (the assassin's bullet at Sarajevo might have missed, but in any case World War I would soon have been triggered in one way or another).

The trouble is that in practice the statistical data are not forthcoming. Moreover, what would have happened, as recent analyses of counterfactual conditionals have made us aware, is impossible to say without appeal to general laws, and whether we *can* appeal to them is just the point at issue. The interpretations characteristic of sweeping philosophies of history often beg the question, invoking "laws" which owe their plausibility to their being tautologies. Pendulum theories of history, for example, are empty unless they specify how much reverse movement is to be expected and within what time interval, for there are random fluctuations in every process, and nothing lasts forever.

The existence of laws of history, presupposed by historical analyses, is sometimes mistakenly supposed to entail a doctrine of historical inevitability, which Isaiah Berlin has convincingly criticized. In the eighteenth century Vico aimed at formulating an "eternal, ideal history, invariably followed by all nations." By the time of Marx, historical inevitability took on a connotation of compulsion: we can only delay or ease the birth-pangs of the new society which will inevitably come to be. Here the problem of self-fulfilling predictions confronts us, as well as the methodological considerations which differentiate conditional predictions from flat forecasts. That there are laws of history does not mean that the future is fore-ordained, but only that real possibilities for the future are no more chaotic than are present actualities, and the past conditions by which they were produced.

Ideologues of the Right also purport to represent the wave of the future. Interpretation of events by reference to general features of the historical process may be associated with a doctrine of historicism, that the inexorable laws of history, in disclosing what *must* happen, show what *should* happen. The laws are taken to define a moral order as well as an order of nature. Karl Popper has focussed attention on the resulting espousal of a closed society, blueprinted in Plato's world of Ideas and in Hegel's dialectic of world Reason. So far as concerns the logic of the laws invoked, rather than their content, interpretation which produces historical analysis does not entail any specific ideological commitment, any more than do the interpretations which produce historical narratives or chronicles.

A fourth type of interpretation presents events in the light of the *purposes* of the actions constituting the events, or by which the events are produced. The result may be called a *historical account*, like those given by Thucydides and Macaulay. This is one of the familiar senses in which we speak of understanding an action, and derivatively, understanding a historical event or process. It is only *one* of the senses, however: we also speak of understanding an event when we know its causes, or the laws by which it is governed. Historical narrative (in terms of causes) and historical analyses (in terms of laws) also provide understanding.

Some philosophers of history, like Croce and Collingwood, seem to think that only historical accounts are acceptable, for they see historical events only as expressions of human purposes. But the fact that the historian himself has purposes in his writing of history may lead him to exaggerate the role of purposes in the events he is writing about. Such mechanisms of projection are well-known in other disciplines dealing with human subject-matter. The problem for a historical account is not only that accidental outcomes must be acknowledged. Purposiveness is also limited by nomological processes. There may be as much significance for the historian in the disappearance of herring from the Baltic Sea in a certain period as in the policies of the Hanseatic League at that time; the movement of the herring, even if not accidental, was certainly not purposive (in human terms, that is to say).

The exaggeration of the element of purposiveness in history is illustrated by the nineteenth century myth of the role of the hero. Hegel, Carlyle, Emerson, Nietzsche and others conceived of the hero as the embodiment of historically significant purposes — his own, or those of some social or metaphysical entity. Sidney Hook's distinction between an eventful man and an event-making man conveys the relevant criticism: individuals singled out as historically significant may only happen to have been at a certain place and time, and enter into history only because of that circumstance. They may be involved in important events, but their purposes may have contributed nothing to the significance of these events.

There are historically important events which undeniably do call for purposive interpretation. How is the ascription of particular purposes to be warranted? Comparatively direct knowledge of purposes, as from letters and diaries, is both rare and unreliable. In general, the indirect and hazardous inferences that must be made are validated by the *coherence* of the interpretation (how well it fits with all we already know of that kind of behaviour), and the *comprehensiveness* of the interpretation (its capacity to make sense of all the specific data we have).

A common pattern of inference by which we ascribe purposes might be called the *circle of interpretation*. We interpret given actions as manifesting certain purposes, then invoke these purposes to justify that understanding of the actions. The circle is not necessarily a vicious one; its usefulness depends on the diameter of the circle, as it were. Certain actions of a historical figure may lead the historian to perceive him as having been engaged in an unremitting struggle for power; that the perception is sustained when additional actions are examined is taken to validate the initial interpretation. If we can continue to understand things in a certain way we become more confident that we have understood them rightly all along.

A more serious difficulty arises from the circumstance that purposes need not be deliberate, conscious, and intended. Purposes with anticipation might be called *motivational*, distinguished from *functional* purposes which are embodied in goal-directed behaviour without implied awareness, as in cybernetic and other telic mechanisms. This distinction between functions and motivations corresponds to Dewey's distinction between ends and ends-in-view. Even when events can be interpreted as purposive, the historian might err in ascribing motives when outcomes are in fact unanticipated consequences of decisions made on the basis of quite other considerations. The conspiratorial view of history, for instance, sees everything that happens as having been deliberately brought about; the paranoid projects on to others the omnipotence which figures in his own delusions. A war might have definitely resulted from certain policies, which will form the substance of the historical account, yet it may be that nobody intended war.

The mistake of resorting to a motivational rather than a functional account is often defended — and compounded — by invoking fictitious entities to serve as the locus of the alleged intentions. These are usually personified abstract or collective agencies of action: social classes, society, the State, the People, universal Reason, or History itself. Invoking such entities in historical accounts is sometimes called historical *holism*. There is no objection to holistic concepts if their causal workings are sufficiently specified empirically to identify the telic pattern of the mechanisms involved — as is often done, say, in ecology. If social classes, for example, are said to act so as to satisfy class interests, what is asserted is no more a matter of motivations than when we state that the early amphibians evolved a kidney so as to provide a stable saline environment for body cells. Both are meaningful purposive interpretations when they are construed functionally rather than motivationally.

Historical accounts characteristically make use of *purposive units*. Corresponding to functions and motivations, respectively, are concepts of *historical policies* (the *Drang nach Osten*, the Cold War). (Periods may also play a part in historical narrative, being specified chiefly in terms of causes and effects, as with the concepts of the Bronze Age, or the Age of Discovery.) All concepts presuppose judgments of relevance; such judgments are especially hard to make in connection with purposive units. We can find almost any purpose we choose if we are free to decide which outcomes we will call "side-effects" or "by-products" and which we will identify as the "major" or "significant" consequences. Everything all together does not fit any empirically recognizable purpose; some selection must be made. There cannot be any such thing as universal history, and neither does history consist only of past politics. What history "really" is about is an inescapable choice of the historian, shaping his subsequent interpretations. History does not speak for itself even to announce its identity.

Historic purposes are often specified on some mythological basis, exmplified by the familiar religious philosophies of history. Events are then taken as symbols; the task of the historian is essentially to read and expound the symbolism. Thereby historical interpretation becomes a type of *hermeneutic.* The operative norms are not continuous with those governing inquiry, but have their own sources which, to my mind, lie somewhere between the subject-matters of metaphysics and of psychoanalysis.

Historical explanation comprises all the types of historical interpretation save the determination of fact, and so is provided by all types of history save chronicle. We explain events by uncovering their causes, by presenting them as instances of general laws, or by disclosing the purposes they serve. Prevailing philosophies of science take as paradigmatic nomological explanation, so that only historical analysis would qualify as a scientific approach to the writing of history. In these philosophies, historical narratives and accounts are construed as preparations for historical analyses to which they must lead or be reduced. What is invoked here is known as the *deductive model* of scientific explanation: explanation in terms of general laws from which, together with appropriate antecedents, the events to be explained are deducible. Whatever the merits of this model in principle, in practice it has little application to what most historians do. Our knowledge of general historical laws is sketchy at best.

Ironically, it is the most speculative historians who come closest to the logical form demanded by these stringent philosophies of science. Vico, Hegel, Marx, Spengler and Toynbee all formulated generalizations purportedly providing a basis for historical analyses. Many of the formulations are so vague, however, that it is hard to know what can be strictly deduced from them, and the circle of interpretation so all-embracing that the analyses must be swallowed whole or not at all. The weakness of these histories is that they claim such universality. It is all very well to aim at the widest possible generalization, but hardly reasonable to suppose that we can attain it without induction from intermediate generalizations of more limited scope. Historians who want to be Newtons would be well-advised to be sure they have identified their Galileos and Keplers.

Historical narratives and accounts exemplify what might be called the *pattern model* of explanation, as distinguished from the deductive model. Here events are explained by exhibiting their place in a pattern of either causes or purposes. (Fitting into the pattern might be construed in terms of appropriate deductions, but this would be at best an artificial *post-hoc* reconstruction, far from the historian's actual methodology.) The usefulness of such explanations depends on their capacity to provide both for the continuing flow of new historical data and the continuing growth in our understanding of human behaviour. For this reason the writing of history is intimately involved with all the other disciplines engaged in the study of man (as well as with the natural sciences basic to the interpretation of historical traces, as in the case of carbon-dating). In its own nature history is one of the social sciences, whatever place it be assigned in the academic division of labour.

Yet it belongs to the humanities as well. The historian may attempt to *recreate* the events he deals with, in an imaginative evocation which may have as much in common with art as with science. The interpretation of historical events, like the critic's interpretation of a work of art, may call for its own artistic skills. Aristotle held poetry to be more philosophical than history, but there is much to recommend Macaulay's description of history as a compound of both poetry and philosophy. The historian needs imagination as all scientists do, for it is imagination which is the source of the conceptual schemes with which we interpret experience. But the historian's need for imagination may be especially great, to offset the deadening effect of contemplating only what is already over and done with. The truth is, we never are done with the past; the historian's re-creation of the past helps convey this truth.

In our day, this may be the most important service that history can provide. Santayana's aphorism that the penalty for ignoring history is that we are condemned to repeat it is, if anything, too indulgent. We may stand condemned even if we know history, but know it only as something pale and bloodless, remote from the springs of our own action and passion. Historical interpretation at its best unites science and art so as to link the past to the emerging future. In Shaw's *Caesar and Cleopatra* Theodotus pleads with Caesar to put out the fire in the library of Alexandria: "What is burning there is the memory of mankind." To which Caesar rejoins, "A shameful memory, let it burn." The more shame if we do let the memory die; for how, then, can we hope for a less shameful world to come?

University of Haifa

ISAIAH BERLIN

COMMENTS

I want to address myself briefly to one of the points made by Prof. Kaplan, not by way of criticism but by way of elucidation; it also partly bears on the discussion this mornmg by Professor Ricoeur and Professor Taylor.

I wish to tell a story. If history is ever philosophy teaching by examples, this story about the beginnings of cultural history might perhaps be an illustration of this function. It began, as far as I know, some time in the fifteenth century, earlier than is usually supposed. As everyone knows, during the Renaissance there was a tremendous rise of interest in the classical world. So far as we can tell — and, of course, evidence for these impressions is seldom decisive and we do not always know exactly how to interpret it — the interest of the Renaissance in the classical world was not primarily historical. It was supposed that the Romans or the Greeks knew the answers to some of the perennial questions of men — about how life should be lived, or what made works of art beautiful, or how buildings and cities should be built, or what legal or political systems would ensure order and justice. It was believed that these great truths had been distorted in the Middle Ages by the Church, by monkish superstitions, by clerical interests and the like, with which they were all too familiar and which they deeply disliked and, indeed, despised. They therefore wished to rescue classical texts, and the truths they contained, from the corrupt versions which they thought came into being partly by accident, partly as a result of deliberate distortion by fanatical or unscrupulous editors.

To this end they began to restore and emend classical texts. They proceeded by the best scientific methods that were open to them, by comparing words and usages and structures, and so working out certain rules of grammar and style in the best Baconian manner. This led to an inductive discipline by which they established the etymology, syntax, use and meaning of certain key words and expressions, a method still in use. The lawyers were particularly concerned with this, since they thought that Justinian's seventy-five editors had turned the entire corpus of Roman law

Yirmiahu Yovel (ed.), Philosophy of History and Action, 38–40. All Rights Reserved.

into a vast chronological chaos: jurisprudence of different periods had been confused, jumbled together, and needed sorting out. They set to work to achieve this.

In the course of these labours they appear to have discovered that the classical world, so far from a world which all wise men could recognize as being the repository of timeless values, was a far stranger world than they expected, not at all like their own. This produced a sense of the possibility, indeed, the reality of alternative cultures, rather the sort of thing that Prof. Taylor talked about this morning, namely, that there existed a whole world, with social and personal relationships, moral, intellectual and political values, significantly different from their own, but which, nevertheless, formed a coherent whole: a world which needed interpretation, but could not be interpreted fully within the concepts or ideals of their own civilization.

This story has been told by others, particularly well by Prof. J.G.A. Pocock who has written an excellent chapter on it. The sense of sharp contrast between their own culture and that of the classical world emerges in the new tone to be found in the writings of prominent French jurists, especially the Reformers among them, in the late sixteenth century, who tend to say that they are not concerned with the rules of Roman law, that it is not authoritative for them; that Rome was Rome, while they were what they were; and what was Rome to them? This was a revolutionary thing to declare, since Rome hitherto had been close to being regarded as an almost ideal civilization; the best social structure yet established by men. If Rome were simply a different and alien order of being, not relevant to the lives of Frenchmen, Germans, Flemings, the appeals to Roman law, whether they were made by the champions of the Papacy or the Empire, no longer carried decisive weight.

Yet it all began with the wish merely to reconstruct the meanings of words. I am addressing this to Prof. Kaplan because this is the locus at which purely technical research to establish facts about, let us say, Norsemen in Minnesota, which he mentioned, or to restore a particular word in the fourth line of a particular chapter of an ancient text — which began as a pure piece of detective work, quite unconnected with large cultural considerations — can by degrees become part of a general attempt to interpret a complete culture: the line he drew between these enterprises does not always hold.

When Renaissance scholars began to reconstruct legal texts, and came to concepts like manumission, for example, they began to ask themselves what exactly manumission was, and therefore what slavery was, and therefore what ownership and property relations were, and therefore what kind of structure of society it was in which slaves occurred, for what reason and in what circumstances slaves were manumitted, and how and why, and what kind of social structure it was that emerged from the differences of status between various classes in Roman society.

Thus what appeared to be mere textual reconstruction, sheer work of grammatical emendation, ended by revealing vast new horizons. This is how, for example, the Donation of Constantine was shown to be a forgery. The Donation of Constantine was, of course, very important in the great Medieval conflict of authority, the struggle for supremacy between the Emperor and the Pope. But its exposure as a forgery by Valla or Dumoulin rests on mainly grammatical considerations, which in their turn rest upon the interpretation of the meanings of words, which in their turn rest upon the consideration of the meanings of these words within the specific context of what had begun to be a gradual reconstruction of the social history of Constantine's Rome, not indeed, by narrative historians, but by Renaissance lawyers and antiquaries in search of something quite different. That is why I do not think the two activities, *pace* Professor Kaplan, can be clearly distinguished from one another.

In a sense, of course, these lawyers were politically motivated. They wished to abolish the relics of the Middle Ages, to reform their own societies, to resist the centralizing ambitions of the Pope, or the Emperor, or even, at times, the King of France. But the actual work which they performed was the reconstruction of another civilization which, by the end of the sixteenth century, was conceived as somewhat alien to their own. The very notion that there was more than one human civilization, that there could exist cultures equally complete and developed yet different, that human nature was therefore not, in some sense, unchanging; that words did not mean the same at different times in different circumstances; that cultural conditions could be different, and could be understood only in terms of the contrast with, or differences from, one another, began in Renaissance scholarship. This is the true beginning of the revolution promoted by Herder and Hegel, of which Charles Taylor spoke so eloquently in his paper. Odd, but, I think, true.

All Souls College, Oxford

INTENDING

Someone may intend to build a squirrel house without having decided to do it, deliberated about it, formed an intention to do it, or reasoned about it. And despite his intention, he may never build a squirrel house, try to build one, or do anything whatever with the intention of getting a squirrel house built. Pure intending of this kind, intending that may occur without practical reasoning, action, or consequence, poses a problem if we want to give an account of the concept of intention that does not invoke unanalysed episodes or attitudes like willing, mysterious acts of the will, or kinds of causation foreign to science.

When action is added to intention, for example when someone nails two boards together with the intention of building a squirrel house, then it may at first seem that the same problem does not necessarily arise. We are able to explain what goes on in such a case without assuming or postulating any odd or special events, episodes, attitudes or acts. Here is how we may explain it. Someone who acts with a certain intention acts for a reason; he has something in mind that he wants to promote or accomplish. A man who nails boards together with the intention of building a squirrel house must want to build a squirrel house, or think that he ought to (no doubt for further reasons), and he must believe that by nailing the boards together he will advance his project. Reference to other attitudes besides wanting, or thinking he ought, may help specify the agent's reasons, but it seems that some positive, or pro-, attitude must be involved. When we talk of reasons in this way, we do not require that the reasons be good ones. We learn something about a man's reasons for starting a war when we learn that he did it with the intention of ending all wars, even if we know that his belief that starting a war would end all wars was false. Similarly, a desire to humiliate an acquaintance may be someone's reason for cutting him at a party though an observer might, in a more normative vein, think that that was no reason. The falsity of a belief, or the patent wrongness of a value or desire, does not disqualify the belief or desire from providing an explanatory

41

Yirmiahu Yovel (ed.), Philosophy of History and Action, 41-60. Dordrecht, D. Reidel, 1978.

reason. On the other hand, beliefs and desires tell us an agent's reasons for acting only if those attitudes are appropriately related to the action as viewed by the actor. To serve as reasons for an action, beliefs and desires need not be reasonable, but a normative element nevertheless enters, since the action   must be reasonable in the light of the beliefs and desires (naturally it may not be reasonable in the light of further considerations).

What does it mean to say that an action, as viewed by the agent, is reasonable in the light of his beliefs and desires? Suppose that a man boards an airplane marked "London" with the intention of boarding an airplane headed for London, England. His reasons for boarding the plane marked "London" are given by his desire to board a plane headed for London, England, and his belief that the plane marked "London" is headed for London, England. His reasons explain why he intentionally boarded the plane marked "London." As it happens, the plane marked "London" was headed for London, Ontario, not London, England, and so his reasons cannot explain why he boarded a plane headed for London, England. They can explain why he boarded a plane headed for London, Ontario, but only when the reasons are conjoined to the fact that the plane marked "London" was headed for London, Ontario; and of course his reasons cannot explain why he intentionally boarded a plane headed for London, Ontario, since he had no such intention.[1]

The relation between reasons and intentions may be appreciated by comparing these statements:

(1)   His reason for boarding the plane marked "London" was that he wanted to board a plane headed for London, England, and he believed the plane marked "London" was headed for London, England.

(2)   His intention in boarding the plane marked "London" was to board a plane headed for London, England.

The first of these sentences entails the second, but not conversely. The failure of the converse is due to two differences between (1) and (2). First, from (2) it is not possible to reconstruct the specific pro-attitude mentioned in (1). Given (2), there must be some appropriate pro-attitude, but it does not have to be wanting. And second, the description of the action ("boarding the plane marked 'London'") occupies an opaque context in (1), but a transparent context in (2). Thus "boarding the plane headed for

London, Ontario" describes the same action as "boarding the plane marked 'London,'" since the plane marked "London" *was* the plane headed for London, Ontario. But substitution of "boarding the plane headed for London, Ontario" for "boarding the plane marked 'London'" will turn (1) false, while leaving (2) true. Of course the description of the intention in (2), like the description of the contents of the belief and pro-attitude in (1), occupies an opaque context.

Finally, there is this relation between statements with the forms of (1) and (2): although (2) does not entail (1), if (2) is true, *some* statement with the form of (1) is true (with perhaps another description of the action, and with an appropriate pro-attitude and belief filled in). Statement (1), unlike (2), must describe the agent's action in a way that makes clear a sense in which the action was reasonable in the light of the agent's reasons. So we can say, if an agent does A with the intention of doing B, there is some description of A which reveals the action as reasonable in the light of reasons the agent had in performing it.

When is an action (described in a particular way) reasonable in the light of specific beliefs and pro-attitudes? One way to approach the matter is through a rather abstract account of practical reasoning. We cannot suppose that whenever an agent acts intentionally he goes through a process of deliberation or reasoning, marshalls evidence and principles, and draws conclusions. Nevertheless, if someone acts with an intention, he must have attitudes and beliefs from which, had he been aware of them and had the time, he *could* have reasoned that his action was desirable (or had some other positive attribute). If we can characterize the reasoning that would serve, we will in effect have described the logical relations between descriptions of beliefs and desires, and the description of an action when the former give the reasons with which the latter was performed. We are to imagine, then, that the agent's beliefs and desires provide him with the premises of an argument. In the case of belief, it is clear at once what the premise is. Take an example: someone adds sage to the stew with the intention of improving the taste. We may describe his belief: He believes that adding sage to the stew will improve its taste. So his corresponding premise is: Adding sage to the stew will improve its taste.

The agent's pro-attitude is perhaps a desire or want; let us suppose he wants to improve the taste of the stew. But what is the corresponding premise? If we were to look for the proposition toward which his desire is directed, the proposition he wants true, it would be something like: He does something that improves the taste of the stew (more briefly: He improves the taste of the stew). This cannot be his premise, however, for nothing interesting follows from the two premises: Adding sage to the stew will improve its taste, and the agent improves the taste of the stew. The trouble is that the attitude of *approval* which the agent has toward the second proposition has been left out. It cannot be put back in by making the premise "The agent wants to improve the taste of the stew": we do not want a *description* of his desire, but an *expression* of it in a form in which he might use it to arrive at an action. The natural expression of his desire is, it seems to me, evaluative in form; for example, "It is desirable to improve the taste of the stew," or "I ought to improve the taste of the stew." We may suppose different pro-attitudes are expressed with other evaluative words in place of "desirable."

There is no short proof that evaluative sentences express desires and other pro-attitudes in the same way that the sentence "Snow is white" expresses the belief that snow is white. But the following consideration will perhaps help show what is involved. If someone who knows English says honestly "Snow is white," then he believes snow is white. If my thesis is correct, someone who says honestly "It is desirable that I stop smoking" has some pro-attitude towards his stopping smoking. He feels some inclination to do it: in fact he will do it if nothing stands in the way, he knows how, and he has no contrary values or desires. Given this assumption, it is reasonable to generalize: if explicit value judgments represent pro-attitudes, all pro-attitudes may be expressed by value judgments that are at least implicit.

This last stipulation allows us to give a uniform account of acting with an intention. If someone performs an action of type A with the intention of performing an action of type B, then he must have a pro-attitude toward actions of type B (which may be expressed in the form: an action of type B is good (or has some other positive attribute)) and a belief that in performing an action of type A he will be (or probably will be) performing an action of type B (the belief may be expressed in the obvious way). The expressions of the belief and desire entail that actions of type A are, or probably will be, good (or desirable, just, dutiful, etc.). The description of the action provided by the phrase substituted for "A" gives the description under which the desire and the belief rationalize the action. So to bring things back to our example, the desire to improve the taste of the stew and the belief that adding sage to the stew will improve its taste serve to rationalize an action described as "adding sage to the stew". (This more or less standard account of practical reasoning will be radically modified presently.)

There must be such rationalizing beliefs and desires if an action is done for a reason, but of course the presence of such beliefs and desires when the action is done does not suffice to insure that what is done is done with the appropriate intention, or even with any intention at all. Someone might want tasty stew and believe sage would do the trick and put in sage thinking it was parsley; or put in sage because his hand was joggled. So we must add that the agent put in the sage because of his reasons. This "because" is a source of trouble; it implies, so I believe, and have argued at length, the notion of cause. But not any causal relation will do, since an agent might have attitudes and beliefs that would rationalize an action, and they might cause him to perform it, and yet because of some anomaly in the causal chain, the action would not be intentional in the expected sense, or perhaps in any sense.[2]

We end up, then, with this incomplete and unsatisfactory account of acting with an intention: an action is performed with a certain intention if it is caused in the right way by attitudes and beliefs that rationalize it.[3]

If this account is correct, then acting with an intention does not require that there be any mysterious act of the will or special attitude or episode of willing. For the account needs only desires (or other pro-attitudes), beliefs, and the actions themselves. There is indeed the relation between these, causal or otherwise, to be analysed, but that is not an embarrassing entity that has to be added to the world's furniture. We would not, it is true, have shown how to *define* the concept of acting with an intention; the reduction is not definitional but ontological. But the ontological reduction, if it succeeds, is enough to answer many puzzles about the relation between the mind and the body, and to explain the possibility of autoromous action in a world of causality.

This brings me back to the problem I mentioned at the start, for the strategy that appears to work for acting with an intention has no obvious application to pure intending, that is, intending that is not necessarily accompanied by action. If someone digs a pit with the intention of trapping a tiger, it is perhaps plausible that no entity at all, act, event or disposition, corresponds to the noun phrase "the intention of trapping a tiger" — this is what our survey has led us to hope. But it is not likely that if a man has the intention of trapping a tiger, his intention is not a state, disposition or attitude of some sort. Yet if this is so, it is quite incredible that this state or attitude (and the connected event or act of *forming an intention*) should play no role in acting with an intention. Our inability to give a satisfactory account of pure intending on the basis of our account of intentional action thus reflects back on the account of intentional action itself. And I believe the account I have outlined will be seen to be incomplete when we have an adequate analysis of pure intending.

Of course, we perform many intentional actions without forming an intention to perform them, and often intentional action is not preceded by an intention. So it would not be surprising if something were present in pure intending that is not always present in intentional action. But it would be astonishing if that extra element were foreign to our understanding of intentional action. For consider some simple action, like writing the word "action." Some temporal segments of this action are themselves actions: for example, first I write the letter "a." This I do with the intention of initiating an action that will not be complete until I have written the rest of the word. It is hard to see how the attitude towards the complete act which I have as I write the letter "a" differs from the pure intention I may have had a moment before. To be sure, my intention has now begun to be realized, but why should that necessarily change my attitude? It seems that in any intentional action that takes much time, or involves preparatory steps, something like pure intending must be present.

We began with pure intending — intending without conscious deliberation or overt consequence — because it left no room for doubt that intending is a state or event separate from the intended action or the reasons that prompted the action. Once the existence of pure intending is recognized, there is no reason not to allow that intention of exactly the same kind is also present when the intended action eventuates. So though I may, in what follows, seem sometimes to concentrate on the rather special case of unfulfilled intentions, the subject in fact is all intending — intending abstracted from a context which may include any degree of deliberation, and any degree of success in execution. Pure intending merely shows that there is something there to be abstracted.

What success we had in coping with the concept of intentional action came from treating talk of the intention with which an action is done as talk of beliefs, desires, and actions. This suggests that we try treating pure intentions — intendings abstracted from normal outcomes — as actions, beliefs or pro-attitudes of some sort. The rest of this paper is concerned with these possibilities.

Is pure intending an action? It may be objected that intending to do something is not a change or event of any kind, and so cannot be something the agent does. But this objection is met by an adjustment in the thesis; we should say that the action is forming an intention, while pure intending is the state of an agent who has formed an intention (and has not changed his mind). Thus all the weight is put on the idea of forming an intention. It will be said that most intentions are not formed, at least if forming an intention requires conscious deliberation or decision. What we need then is the broader and more neutral concept of coming to have an intention — a change that may take place so slowly or unnoticed that the agent cannot say when it happens. Still, it is an event, and we could decide to call it an action, or at least something the agent does.

I see no reason to reject this proposal; the worst that can be said of it is that it provides so little illumination. The state of intention just is what results from coming to have an intention — but what sort of a state is it? The coming to have an intention we might try connecting with desires and beliefs as we did other intentional actions (again with a causal chain that works "in the right way"). But the story does not have the substantial quality of the account of intentional action because the purported action is not familiar or observable, even to the agent himself.

Another approach focuses on overt speech acts. *Saying* that one intends to do something, or that one will do it, is undeniably an action, and it has some of the characteristics of forming an intention. Saying, under appropriate circumstances, that one intends to do something, or that one will do it, can commit one to doing it; if the deed does not follow, it is appropriate to ask for an explanation. Actually to identify saying one intends to do something with forming an intention would be to endorse a sort of performative theory of intention; just as saying one promises to do something may be promising to do it, so saying one intends to do it may be intending (or forming the intention) to do it. Of course one may form an intention without saying anything aloud, but this gap may be filled with the notion of speaking to oneself, "saying in one's heart."[4] A variant theory would make forming an intention like (or identical with) addressing a command to oneself.

I think it is easy to see that forming an intention is quite different from saying something, even to oneself, and that intending to do something is quite different from having said something. For one thing, the performative character of commands and promises which makes certain speech acts surprisingly momentous depends on highly specific conventions, and there are no such conventions governing the formation of intentions. Promising involves assuming an obligation, but even if there are obligations to oneself, intending does not normally create one. If an agent does not do what he intended to do, he does not normally owe himself an explanation or apology, especially if he simply changed his mind; yet this is just the case that calls for explanation or apology when a promise has been made to another and broken. A command may be disobeyed, but only while it is in force. But if an agent does not do what he intended because he has changed his mind, the original intention is no longer in force. Perhaps it is enough to discredit these theories to point out that promising and commanding, as we usually understand them, are necessarily public performances, while forming an intention is not. Forming an intention may be an action, but it is not a performance, and having an intention is not generally the aftermath of one.

None of this is to deny that saying "I intend to do it" or "I will do it" is much like, or on occasion identical with, promising to do it. If I say any of these things in the right context, I entitle a hearer to believe I will do it, and since I know I entitle him to believe it, I entitle him to believe I believe I will do it. Perhaps a simpler way to put it is this: if I say "I intend to do it" or "I will do it" or "I promise to do it" under certain conditions, then I *represent myself* as believing that I will. I may not believe I will, I may not intend that my hearer believe I will, but I have given him ground for complaint if I do not. These facts suggest that if I not only say "I intend" or "I will" in such a way as to represent myself as believing I will, but I am sincere as well, then my sincerity guarantees both that I intend to do it and that I believe I will. Some such line of argument has led many philosophers to hold that intending to do something entails believing one will, and has led a few philosophers to the more extreme view that to intend to do something is identical with a sort of belief that one will.

Is intending to act a belief that one will? The argument just sketched does not even show that intending implies belief. The argument proves that a man who sincerely says "I intend to do it" or "I will do it" under certain conditions must believe he will do it. But it may be the saying, not the intention, that implies the belief. And I think we can see this is the case. The trouble is that we have asked the notion of sincerity to do two different pieces of work. We began by considering cases where, by saying "I intend to" or "I will," I entitle a hearer to believe I will. And here it is obvious that if I am sincere, if things are as I represent them, then I must believe I will. But it is an assumption unsupported by the argument that any time I sincerely say I intend to do something I must believe I will do it, for sincerity in this case merely requires that I know I intend to do it. We are agreed that there are cases where sincerity in the utterer of "I intend to" requires him to believe he will, but the argument requires that these cases include all those in which the speaker knows or believes he intends to do it.

Once we have distinguished the question how belief is involved in avowals of intention from the question how belief is involved in intention, we ought to be struck with how dubious the latter connection is.

It is a mistake to suppose that if an agent is doing something intentionally, he must know that he is doing it. For suppose a man is writing his will with the intention of providing for the welfare of his children. He may be in doubt about his success, and remain so to his death; yet in writing his will he may in fact be providing for the welfare of his children, and if so, he is certainly doing it intentionally. Some sceptics may think this example fails because they refuse to allow that a man may *now* be providing for the welfare of his children if that welfare includes events yet to happen. So here is another example: in writing heavily on this page I may be intending to produce ten legible carbon copies. I do not know, or believe with any confidence, that I am succeeding. But if I am producing ten legible carbon copies, I am certainly doing it intentionally. These examples do not prove that pure intending may not imply belief, for the examples involve acting with an intention. Nevertheless, it is hard to imagine that the point does not carry over to pure intending. As he writes his will, the man not only is acting with the intention of securing the welfare of his children, he also intends to secure the welfare of his children. If he can be in doubt whether he is now doing what he intends, surely he can be in doubt whether he will do what he intends.

The thesis that intending implies believing is sometimes defended by claiming that expressions of intention are generally incomplete or elliptical. Thus the man writing his will should be described as intending to try to secure the welfare of his children, not as intending to secure it, and the man with the carbon paper is merely intending to try to produce his copies. The phrases sound wrong: we should be much more apt to say he *is* trying, and intends to do it. But where the action˙is entirely in the future, we do sometimes allow that we intend to try, and we see this as more accurate than the bald statement of intention when the outcome is sufficiently in doubt. Nevertheless, I do not think the claim of ellipsis can be used to defend the general thesis.

Without doubt many intentions are conditional in form — one intends to do something only if certain conditions are satisfied — and without doubt we often suppress mention of the conditions for one reason or another. So elliptical statements of intention are common. Grice gives us this exchange:

> X. I intend to go to that concert on Tuesday.
> Y. You will enjoy that.
> X. I may not be there.
> Y. I am afraid I don't understand.
> X. The police are going to ask me some awkward questions on Tuesday afternoon, and I may be in prison by Tuesday evening.
> Y. Then you should have said to begin with, "I intend to go to the concert if I am not in prison," or, if you wished to be more reticent, something like, "I should probably be going," or "I hope to go," or, "I aim to go," or, "I intend to go if I can." [5]

Grice does not speak of ellipsis here, but he does think that this example, and others like it, make a strong case for the view that "X intends to do A" is true, when "intends" is used in the *strict* sense, only if X is sure that he will do A. The man in the example must intend *something*, and so if we knew what it was, we could say that his remark "I intend to go to the concert" was elliptical for what he would have said if he had used "intend" in the strict sense. What would he have said? "I hope to go" is not more accurate about the intention, since it declares no intention at all; similarly for "I aim to go" and "I should probably be going." "I intend to go if I can" is vague and general given the particularity of X's doubts, but there seems something worse wrong with it. For if an agent cannot intend what he believes to be impossible, then he asserts neither more nor less by saying "I intend to do it if I can" than he would by saying "I intend to do it." How about "I intend to go to the concert if I am not in prison"? Intuitively, this comes closest to conveying the truth about the situation as X sees it. But is it *literally* more accurate? It is hard to see how. On the view Grice is arguing for, if X said in the strict sense, and honestly, "I intend to be at the concert," he would imply that he believed he would be there. If X said in the strict sense, and honestly, "I intend to be at the concert if I am not in jail," he would imply that he believed he would be at the concert if he were not in jail. Now obviously the first belief implies the second, but is not implied by it, and so an expression of the second belief makes a lesser claim, and may be thought to be more accurate. Of course, the stronger claim cannot, by its contents, lead Y into error about what X will do, for whether X says he will be at the concert, or only that he will be there if he is not in jail, both X and Y know X will not be at the concert if he is in jail. Where Y might be misled is with respect to what X believes he will do, and hence intends, if the thesis we are examining is true. For on the thesis, "I intend to be at the concert if I am not in jail" implies a weaker belief than "I intend to be at the concert." If this is right, then greater accuracy still would result from further provisos, since X also does not believe he will be at the concert if he changes his mind, or if something besides imprisonment prevents him. We are thus led further and further toward the nearly empty "I intend to do it if nothing prevents me, if I don't change my mind, if nothing untoward happens." This tells us almost nothing about what the agent believes about the future, or what he will in fact do.

I think X spoke correctly and accurately, but misleadingly, when he said "I intend to go to the concert." He could have corrected the impression while still being accurate by saying "I now intend to go to the concert, but since I may be put in jail, I may not be there." A man who says "I intend to be there, but I may not be" does not contradict himself, he is at worst inscrutable until he says more. We should realize there is something wrong with the idea that most statements of intention are elliptical until tempered by our doubts about what we shall in fact do when it is noticed that there is no satisfactory *general* method for supplying the more accurate statement for which the original statement went proxy. And the reason is clear: there can be no finite list of things we think might prevent us from doing what we intend, or of circumstances that might cause us to stay our hand. If we are reasonably sure something will prevent us from acting, this does, perhaps, baffle intention, but if we are simply uncertain, as is often the case, intention is not necessarily dulled. We can be clear what it is we intend to do while being in the dark as to the details, and therefore the pitfalls. If this is so, being more accurate about what we intend cannot be a matter of being more accurate about what we believe we will bring off.

There are genuine conditional intentions, but I do not think they come in the form "I intend to do it if I can" or "if I don't change my mind." Genuine conditional intentions are appropriate when we explicitly consider what to do in various contingencies; for example, someone may intend to go home early from a party if the music is too loud. If we ask for the difference between conditions that really do make the statement of an intention more accurate, and bogus conditions like "if I can" or "if nothing comes up" or "if I don't change my mind," it seems to me clear that the difference is this: bona fide conditions are ones that are reasons for acting that are contemporary with the intention. Someone may not like loud music now, and that may be why he now intends to go home early from the party if the music is too loud. His not being able to go home early is not a reason for or against his going home early, and so it is not a relevant condition for an intention, though if he believes he cannot do it, that may prevent his having the intention. Changing his mind is a tricky case, but in general someone is not apt to view a possible future change of intention as a reason to modify his present intention unless he thinks the future change will itself be brought about by something he would now consider a reason.

The contrast that has emerged between the circumstances we do sometimes allow to condition our intentions and the circumstances we would allow if intentions implied the belief that we will do what we intend seems to me to indicate pretty conclusively that we do not necessarily believe we will do what we intend to do, and that we do not state our intentions more accurately by making them conditional on all the circumstances in whose presence we think we would act.

These last considerations point to the strongest argument against identifying pure intending with the belief one will do what one intends. This is that reasons for intending to do something are in general quite different from reasons for believing one will do it. Here is why I intend to reef the main: I see a squall coming, I want to prevent the boat from capsizing, and I believe that reefing the main will prevent the boat from capsizing. I would put my reasons for intending to reef the main this way: a squall is coming, it would be a shame to capsize the boat, and reefing the main will prevent the boat from capsizing. But these reasons for intending to reef the main in themselves give me no reason to believe I will reef the main. Given a lot more assumptions, that a squall is coming may be a reason to believe I believe a squall is coming, and given some even more fancy assumptions, that it would be a shame to capsize the boat may be a reason to believe I want to prevent the boat from capsizing. And given that I have these beliefs and desires, it may be reasonable to suppose I intend to reef the main, and will in fact do so. So there may be a loose connection between reasons of the two kinds, but they are not at all identical (individual reasons may be the same, but a smallest natural set of reasons that supports the intention to act cannot be a set that supports the belief that the act will take place).

It is often maintained that an intention is a belief not arrived at by reasoning from evidence, or that an intention is a belief about one's future action that differs in some other way in its origin from an ordinary prediction. But such claims do not help the thesis. How someone arrived at a belief, what reasons he would give in support of it, what sustains his faith, these are matters that are simply irrelevant to the question what constitute reasons for the belief; the former events are accidents that befall a belief, and cannot change its logical status without making it a new belief.

Is intending to do something the same as wanting to do it? Clearly reasons for intending to do something are very much like reasons for action, indeed one might hold that they are exactly the same except for time. As John Donne says, "To will implies delay," but we may reduce the delay to a moment. I am writing the letter "a" of "action," and I intend to write the letter "c" as soon as I finish the "a." The reason I intend to write the letter "c" as soon as I finish the "a" is that I want to write the word "action," and I know that to do this I must, after writing the letter "a," write the letter "c." Now I have finished the "a" and have begun "c"! What is my reason for writing the "c"? It is that I want to write the word "action," and I know that to do this I must... So far the reasons sound identical, but if we look closer a tiny difference will emerge. When I am writing the "a" I intend to write the "c" in just a moment, and part of my reason is that I believe this moment looms in the immediate future; when I am writing the "c," my reasons include the belief that *now* is the time to write the "c" if I am to write "action," as I wish to. Aristotle sometimes neglects this difference and as a result says things that sound fatuous. He is apt to give as an example of practical reasoning something of this sort: I want to be warm, I believe a house will keep me warm, straightway I build a house. It is an important doctrine that the conclusion of a piece of practical reasoning may be an action; it is also important that the conclusion may be the formation of an intention to do something in the future.

Now I would like to draw attention to an aspect of this picture of what it is like to form an intention that seems to make for a difficulty. Consider again a case of intentional action. I want to eat something sweet, that is, I hold that my eating something sweet is desirable. I believe this candy is sweet, and so my eating this candy will be a case of my eating something sweet, and I conclude that my eating this candy is desirable. Since nothing stands in the way, I eat the candy — the conclusion is the action. But this also means I could express the conclusion by using a demonstrative reference to the action: "This action of mine, this eating by me of this candy now, is desirable." What seems so important about the possibility of a demonstrative reference to the action is that it is a case where it makes sense to couple a value judgment directly to action. My evaluative reason for acting was, "My eating something sweet is desirable." But of course this cannot mean that any action of mine whatsoever that is an eating of something sweet is something it makes sense to do — my judgment merely deals with actions in so far as they are sweet-consuming. Some such actions, even all of them, may have plenty else wrong with them. It is only when I come to an actual action that it makes sense to judge it as a whole as desirable or not; up until that moment there was no object with which I was acquainted to judge. Of course I can still say of the completed action that it is desirable in so far as it is this or that, but in choosing to perform it I went beyond this; my choice represented, or perhaps was, a judgment that the action itself was desirable.

And now the trouble about pure intending is that there is no action to judge simply good or desirable. All we can judge at the stage of pure intending is the desirability of actions of a sort, and actions of a sort are generally judged on the basis of the aspect that defines the sort. Such judgments, however, do not always lead to reasonable action, or we would be eating everything sweet we could lay our hands on (as Anscombe pointed out in *Intention*).[6]

The major step in clearing up these matters is to make a firm distinction between the kind of judgment that corresponds to a desire like wanting to eat something sweet and the kind of judgment that can be the conclusion of a piece of practical reasoning — that can correspond to an intentional action.[7] The first sort of judgment is often thought to have the form of a law: any action that is an eating of something sweet is desirable. If practical reasoning is deductive, this is what we should expect (and it seems to be how Aristotle and Hume, for example, thought of practical reasoning). But there is a fundamental objection to this idea, as can be seen when we consider an action that has both a desirable and an undesirable aspect. For suppose the propositional expression of a desire to eat something sweet were a universally quantified conditional. While holding it desirable to eat something sweet, we may also hold that it is undesirable to eat something poisonous. But one and the same object may be sweet and poisonous, and so one and the same action may be the eating of something sweet and something poisonous. Our evaluative principles, which seem consistent, can then lead us to conclude that the same action is both desirable and undesirable. If undesirable actions are not desirable, we have derived a contradiction from premises all of which are plausible. The cure is to recognize that we have assigned the wrong form to evaluative principles. If they are judgments to the effect that *in so far as* an action has a certain characteristic it is good (or desirable, etc.), then they must not be construed in such a way that detachment works, or we will find ourselves concluding directly that the action is simply desirable when all that is warranted is the conclusion that it is desirable in a certain respect. Let us call judgments that actions are desirable in so far as they have a certain attribute *prima facie* judgments.

Prima facie judgments cannot be directly associated with actions, for it is not reasonable to perform an action merely because it has a desirable characteristic. It is a reason for acting that the action is believed to have some desirable characteristic, but the fact that the action is performed represents a further judgment that the desirable characteristic was enough to act on — that other considerations did not outweigh it. The judgment that corresponds to, or perhaps is identical with, the action cannot, therefore, be a *prima facie* judgment; it must be an all-out or unconditional judgment which, if we were to express it in words, would have a form like "This action is desirable."

It can now be seen that our earlier account of acting with an intention was misleading or at least incomplete in an important respect. The reasons that determine the description under which an action is intended do not allow us to *deduce* that the action is simply worth performing; all we can deduce is that the action has a feature that argues in its favour. This is enough, however, to allow us to give the intention with which the action was performed. What is misleading is that the reasons that enter this account do not generally constitute all the reasons the agent considered in acting, and so knowing the intention with which someone acted does not allow us to reconstruct his actual reasoning. For we may not know how the agent got from his desires and other attitudes — his *prima facie* reasons — to the conclusion that a certain action was desirable.[8]

In the case of intentional action, at least when the action is of brief duration, nothing seems to stand in the way of an Aristotelian identification of the action with a judgment of a certain kind — an all-out, unconditional judgment that the action is desirable (or has some other positive characteristic). The identification of the action with the conclusion of a piece of practical reasoning is not essential to the view I am endorsing, but the fact that it can be made explains why, in our original account of intentional action, what was needed to relate it to pure intending remained hidden.

In the case of pure intending, I now suggest that the intention simply is an all-out judgment. Forming an intention, deciding, choosing and deliberating are various modes of arriving at the judgment, but it is possible to come to have such a judgment or attitude without any of these modes applying.

Let me elaborate on this suggestion and try to defend it against some objections. A few pages ago I remarked that an all-out judgment makes sense only when there is an action present (or past) that is known by acquaintance. Otherwise (I argued) the judgment must be general, that is, cover all actions of a certain sort, and among these there are bound to be actions some of which are desirable and some not. Yet an intention cannot single out a particular action in an intelligible sense, since it is directed to the future. The puzzle arises, I think, because we have overlooked an important distinction. It would be mad to hold that any action of mine in the immediate future that is the eating of something sweet would be desirable. But there is nothing absurd in my judging that any action of mine in the immediate future that is the eating of something sweet would be desirable *given the rest of what I believe about the immediate future.* I do not believe I will eat a poisonous candy, and so that is not one of the actions of eating something sweet that my all-out judgment includes. It would be a mistake to try to improve the statement of my intention by saying "I intend to eat something sweet, provided it isn't poisonous." As we saw, this is a mistake because if this is the road I must travel, I will never get my intentions right. There are *endless* circumstances under which I would not eat something sweet, and I cannot begin to foresee them all. The point is, I do not believe anything will come up to make my eating undesirable or impossible. That belief is not part of what I intend, but an assumption without which I would not have the intention. The intention is not conditional in form; rather, the existence of the intention is conditioned by my beliefs.

I intend to eat a hearty breakfast tomorrow. You know, and I know, that I will not eat a hearty breakfast tomorrow if I am not hungry. And I am not certain I will be hungry, I just think I will be. Under these conditions it is not only not more accurate to say "I intend to eat a hearty breakfast if I'm hungry," it is *less* accurate. I have the second intention as well as the first, but the first implies the second, and not vice versa, and so the first is a more complete account of my intentions. If you knew only that I intended to eat a hearty breakfast if I was hungry, you would not know that I believe I will be hungry, which is actually the case. But you might figure this out if you knew I intend to eat a hearty breakfast tomorrow.

I think this view of the matter explains the trouble we had about the relation between intending to do something and believing one will — why, on the one hand, it is so strange to say "I intend to do it but perhaps I won't," and yet is so impossible to increase the accuracy of statements of intention by making the content of the intention conditional on how things turn out. The explanation is that the intention assumes, but does not contain a reference to, a certain view of the future. A present intention with respect to the future is in itself like an interim report: given what I now know and believe, here is my judgment of what kind of action is desirable. Since the intention is based on one's best estimate of the situation, it merely distorts matters to say the agent intends to act in the way he does only if his estimate turns out to be right. A present intention does not need to be anything like a resolve or a commitment (though *saying* one intends to do something may sometimes have this character). My intention is based on my present view of the situation; there is no reason in general why I should act as I now intend if my present view turns out to be wrong.

We can now see why adding "if I can" never makes the statement of an intention more accurate, although it may serve to cancel an unwanted natural suggestion of the act of saying one intends to do something. To intend to perform an action is, on my account, to hold that it is desirable to perform an action of a certain sort in the light of what one believes is and will be the case. But if one believes no such action is possible, then there can be no judgment that such an action consistent with one's beliefs is desirable. There can be no such intention.

If an intention is just a judgment that an action of a certain sort is desirable, what is there to distinguish an intention from a mere wish? We may put aside wishes for things that are not consistent with what one believes, for these are ruled out by our conception of an intention. And we may put aside wishes that do not correspond to all-out judgments. ("I wish I could go to London next week": my going to London next week may be consistent with all I believe, but not with all I want. This wish is idle because it is based on some only of my *prima facie* reasons.) But once we put these cases aside, there is no need to distinguish intentions from wishes. For a judgment that something I think I can do — that I think I see my way clear to doing — a judgment that such an action is desirable not only for one or another reason, but in the light of all my reasons, a judgment like this is not a mere wish. It *is* an intention. (This is not to deny that there are borderline cases.)

How well have we coped with the problem with which we began? That problem was, in effect, to give an account of intending (and of forming an intention) that would mesh in a satisfactory way with our account of acting with an intention, and would not sacrifice the merits of that account. With respect to the first point, finding an account of intending that would mesh with our account of intentional action, we devised a satisfactory way of relating the two concepts, but only by introducing a new element, an all-out judgment, into the analysis of intentional action. Given this sort of judgment and the idea of such a judgment made in the light of what is believed about the future course of affairs, we were able, I think, to arrive at a plausible view of intending.

There remains the question whether the sort of judgment to which I have appealed, an all-out judgment, can be understood without appeal to the notions of intention or will. I asked at the beginning of this last section of my paper whether intending to do something is wanting to do it; if it were, we might consider that our aim had been achieved. What we intend to do we want, in some very broad sense of want, to do. But this does not mean that intending is a form of wanting. For consider the actions that I want to perform and that are consistent with what I believe. Among them are the actions I intend to perform, and many more. I want to go to London next week, but I do not intend to, not because I think I cannot, but because it would interfere with other things I want more. This suggests strongly that wanting and desiring are best viewed as corresponding to, or constituting, *prima facie* judgments.

If this is correct, we cannot claim that we have made out a case for viewing intentions as something familiar, a kind of wanting, where we can distinguish the kind without having to use the concept of intention or will. What we can say, however, is that intending and wanting belong to the same genus of pro-attitudes expressed by value judgments. Wants, desires, principles, prejudices, felt duties and obligations provide reasons for actions and intentions, and are expressed by *prima facie* judgments; intentions and the judgments that go with intentional actions are distinguished by their all-out or unconditional form. Pure intendings constitute a subclass of the all-out judgments, those directed to future actions of the agent, and made in the light of his beliefs.

The University of Chicago

NOTES

Note. I have tried to profit from the generous advice of Max Black, Michael Bratman, Paul Grice, Stuart Hampshire, Gilbert Harman, David Sachs, and Irving Thalberg.

[1] I take the "intentionally" to govern the entire phrase "boarded a plane headed for London, Ontario." On an alternative reading, only the boarding would be intentional. Similarly, in (1) below his reason extends to the marking on the plane.

[2] See my "Freedom to Act," in *Essays on Freedom of Action*, ed. T. Honderich, London, 1973.

[3] This is where my "Actions, Reasons and Causes," *The Journal of Philosophy* 60 (1963): pp. 685-700, left things. At that time I believed it would be possible to characterize "the right way" in non-circular terms.

[4] See P.T. Geach, *Mental Acts*, London, 1957.

[5] H.P. Grice, "Intention and Uncertainty," British Academy Lecture, Oxford, 1971, pp. 4, 5.

[6] G.E.M. Anscombe, *Intention*, Oxford, 1957, p. 59.

[7] No weight should be given the word "judgment." I am considering here the *form* of propositions that express desires and other attitudes. I do not suppose that someone who wants to eat something sweet necessarily *judges* that it would be good to eat something sweet; perhaps we can just say he *holds* that his eating something sweet has some positive characteristic. By distinguishing among the propositional expressions of attitudes I hope to mark differences among the attitudes.

[8] I have said more about the form of *prima facie* evaluative judgments, and the importance of distinguishing them from unconditional judgments, in "How is Weakness of the Will Possible?" in *Moral Concepts*, ed. J. Feinberg, Oxford, 1969.

STUART HAMPSHIRE

COMMENTS

This particular topic seems to me to be certainly at the centre of the philosophy of history. One of the problems that we spoke of in the very first session here was what was called the categories of meaningful action, and the concept of intention just is the concept that marks the relation between thought and meaning and action, and it is by far the most substantial of these concepts, whether for the historian or for the lawyer. So I think we are at the centre of our proper concern.

Davidson's paper points to the fact that intentions are concerned, characteristically, though not exclusively, with the future – that is one feature of them – and often with a comparatively distant future. For human beings, unlike (as we believe) other creatures, can form intentions to do things – which they describe to themselves in certain specific terms – at a remote future, dated or undated, open or fixed.

Secondly, it is characteristic of intentions that they issue in what he called declarations of intention. Moreover, the part that they play, particularly in social life and communication, distinguishes intentions – not only declarations of intention but intentions themselves – from things closely related to them, such as purposes and, as I would say, desires – though Davidson would not say desires.

Thirdly, and arising from that, it is essential to, or necessary to, the having of intentions, that we should possess the linguistic equipment to express them. This is sometimes expressed aphoristically by saying that an animal can pursue a cat with, in a sense, the intention of destroying it, but it cannot have the intention of destroying it tomorrow.

So these are features that make intentions distinct from some other psychological verbs which take objects closely related to them, and which are also associated with the explanation of action. I think I would be ready to argue, following what Davidson says, that an explanation of an action in terms of intention – what the action was to the agent at the time, how he thought of it, what description he was acting under – is different from an explanation either in terms of purpose or in terms of function. That

61

Yirmiahu Yovel (ed.), Philosophy of History and Action, 61–68. All Rights Reserved.
Copyright © 1978 by D. Reidel Publishing Company, Dordrecht, Holland.

difference is a matter of the utmost importance to historians, because if they were to confuse these things, they would confuse their history.

All these points emerge quite clearly from Davidson's paper. I bring them out now simply in order to relate what he said more directly to some other things that have been said here.

Lastly, he makes the point that statements of intention may be either categorical or conditional. So also may be intentions themselves. That is, I may intend to go away if somebody does not arrive at a certain time, or I may simply intend to go away. That distinction has some importance.

Let us now examine Davidson's account of intention itself. He is concerned with pure intentions, i.e., intentions distilled, as it were, from the ordinary mixtures in which they are found, namely, with prior deliberations about later actions. He is concerned with, as it were, the pure gold of intention when all the dross of features surrounding intention have been removed.

I myself have no doubt whatever that there are pure intentions. There are many philosophers who would say that if you aim, as Davidson has aimed, at isolating an intention from either its manifestation in action, or its genesis in a prior deliberation, you are left with a nonentity. This seems to me to be false. I am inclined to argue on Davidson's side, that hopes, intentions, wants, may be episodes that occur in isolation from their natural expression which is in behaviour, and in isolation from the kind of preceding deliberation which ordinarily goes, or often goes, with that propositional attitude.

On the other hand, I have a doubt about Davidson's starting point. That is, he asks what is an intention. He asks this with a kind of reductionist interest in mind, and he speaks of intending as a mysterious act. I think we should distinguish between two things that might be meant here: a mysterious act of the will and a mysterious entity. What he seems to find mysterious about pure intentions is that if I *intend* to do something tomorrow but later change my mind — or the circumstances fail to arise — so the intention does not issue in an action, then there is a mystery about there being this particular kind of thought, in the sense that if I *want* to do something tomorrow, there is not a mystery, or in the sense that if I *hope* to do something tomorrow, there is not a mystery.

I think there is a very good historical reason why he should find a mystery here, and he hints that this is the reason why he does in fact find the mystery. It is that the notion of intention is associated with something called an "act of will." Now, there is a history of suspicion of acts of will, a very long history of suspicion that there are no such things. Indeed, it is a central issue in ethics, as everybody knows, whether or not you think you can give an account of rational action without mentioning acts of will. For instance, Aristotle, like Davidson, does not mention acts of will. And, of course, it would be very instructive in any case if you showed that intention is reducible to belief plus desire, and that therefore we understand its nature, in the clear sense of understanding what constitutes it or makes it up — if you showed that it is a something plus something else, and we did not know that before.

What seems to me challengeable, at least, is that there is something intrinsically unintelligible about the notion of intending placed alongside its close conjugates — I mean the verbs that are just like it, such as hoping, or wanting, or being determined to, and others. There could be a whole string of such psychological verbs. I admit that Davidson has, I think, a special reason. The special reason comes from ethics. It does for many people, perhaps. So that is a question — why?

Let me add one other thing, that the notion of pure hoping, pure intending, raises all sorts of epistemological problems, familiar to philosophers in any case. Namely, how do we, as the subjects intending to give up cigarettes, discriminate between this and wanting or vaguely wishing to give up cigarettes? Certainly, it might be quite difficult for ourselves to distinguish between those things, and even more difficult for our friends to distinguish whether we seriously, as we say, intend to give them up, or whether we have rather a vague velleity to do so.

So there are epistemological problems in pure intention just because you isolate it from the natural evidence for an intention which is provided by its manifestation in behaviour.

That, then, is one question. I should like now to concentrate on one more question — for in this very rich paper I can only choose from what I take to be the main points — which comes out especially towards the end of the paper. Here it is said that to intend to perform an action is to judge that it is desirable to perform an action of a certain sort in the light of what one believes is, and will be, the case. That is, Davidson is saying in the Aristotelian tradition, though with a certain qualification, that an intention, in the setting which he has given, is a judgement.

He proposes, in essence, a reduction of intention to judgement — not to belief, but to judgement — and this does have striking parallels, of course, with the Nicomachean Ethics. Indeed, he comes close to identifying intention with what Aristotle calls *proairesis*, a word which is often translated as "choice," but some people translate it as "intention." Such a choice, as people will recall, is defined by Aristotle in just this way — as being made up of two bits. One is *orexis*, or desire, and the other is deliberation. Well, about deliberation there are problems. But *orexis* of those things that are within our power comes very near to what Davidson says about things which might prevent us from doing what we intend.

It is notorious, and very much in Davidson's mind — since he has written on the subject — that anyone who says that an intention is a kind of judgement, has to be ready to deal with the problem of *akrasia*, that is, the so-called weakness of the will. For it is a somewhat notorious fact that people often do not set themselves to do, or do not intend or choose to do — even in the cases of intentions for the future — what they believe they should do. It would be very strange not to acknowledge this fact of human psychology, that we often fail to do what we think ought to be done, or is to be done. There arises a gap because of temptation, or because of impetuosity, even the kind of impetuosity that does not make the action unintentional.

So *akrasia*, or weakness of the will, can occur. Davidson has a perfectly clear answer to the problem, within his setting, which is again very similar to Aristotle's — namely, that we must distinguish between "*prima facie*" judgements of what is desirable and "all things considered" or "all-in" judgements of what is desirable. I suppose he would argue — though he does not here argue in detail, as he has elsewhere, I believe — that there is an account to be given of weakness of the will in terms of a gap between these two.

We come to the really difficult question, to which I do not know the answer, but which I think is of the utmost importance for any narrative writing about persons, i.e., for history. Namely, if you accept this kind of account you have the problem — which was a problem already for Aristotle — that if you are thinking of the future, then you are thinking of an action identified under certain descriptions, that is, you are not thinking of an action which you can point to in the sense in which you do point to actions.

For example, if I said, "I am going to do this, do this after me," I would have pointed to an action, to what Aristotle calls a *tode ti*, a "some particular thing." That is, I can do something and then say "Do the same thing" without saying *what* that same thing is. Of course, I can only do that in a certain setting which suggests the criterion of identity ("the something") for imitation.

But if I were thinking of, say, crowning the King tomorrow — or whatever action it is in the remoter future — I have to pick out this action by a set of descriptions. It is a necessary truth that for any given action alluded to by Davidson, there are an indefinite range of descriptions that could be given of that action, though which would be appropriate would be chosen relative to the purposes for which you were writing the story or giving the account. Therefore, there is a sense — a puzzling sense — in which intentions are always concerned with actions identified under a certain description, and therefore they have — to express it in traditional Aristotelian terminology — a certain generality attached to them. This puzzled Aristotle, because it was clear to him that one of the most important things about action, first of all, is that it depends upon a practical skill in execution, upon a *dynamis*, which is a capacity for doing things well. Secondly, it depends upon perception of the particular circumstances in which you are.

Thus, if you act on a certain maxim, then the maxim will never exactly fit the circumstances — or generally will not exactly fit the circumstances in which you act, because the circumstances indefinitely ramify in descriptions that could be given of them. Consequently, future occasions are picked out by descriptions, and if you ask yourself the question "Is the action that I actually perform when tomorrow comes the *same* as the action that I intended to perform?" you get a very difficult question of identity. That is a question which puzzled Aristotle. As far as I know, no very clear answer has been given to it, and it is particularly difficult for Aristotle and Davidson.

The particular action, therefore, is envisaged as being an action of a certain kind. For Davidson a present intention with respect to the future is in itself like an interim report. Given what I now know and believe, here is my judgement of what kind of action will be desirable. At this point he has stepped away from Aristotle. In fact, Aristotle hesitated over this, and sometimes speaks of *proairesis* as issuing in an action immediately, and as not being a judgement at all, and sometimes as being a judgement. And precisely for this reason Aristotle is confused.

Now I come to my disagreement with Davidson of a radical kind. I see the attractiveness of reducing "intending," but I think it is wrong. I think that to form an intention, or to have an intention — neither the one nor the other is to make a judgement that something is desirable, and specifically neither is to make a normative judgement of any kind. Here I have several distinct grounds of objection, even if I leave aside the grave doubts I have about the notion of judgement as he uses it — it appears to me to be used rather as Kant used the word "judgement," to mean something like a thought, though I am not sure.

My grounds of objection. First of all, just to go back to the first part of the paper — the reduction of intention in terms of want and belief — I do not think that you can make that reduction, on the somewhat banal grounds, I am bound to say, that not all the actions that I intend to perform are actions that I want to perform, in even the broadest possible sense of want, and however much wanting is qualified, restricted and complicated in the traditional Thomas Aquinas sort of way.

There are many cases of doing things, and of intending to do things, which one definitely does not want to do. This is one of the most important features about one's wants, desires, inclinations — and even about one's judgement that something ought to be done. The obvious case is fear. I think that the relations between fear and desire — between the fear of doing something and the desire to do it — are relations between two things on the same level. But I do not think that fear itself can be analysed in terms of desire. If, of course, it could, then you could preserve the traditional analysis, but I doubt that it can. And I think that otherwise it is true to say that such conflicts could not be redescribed appropriately in the way that the identification of intention and judgement would require.

So that kind of *akrasia*, or weakness of the will, which arises is a severe problem for the Aristotelian-Davidsonian view. But of course a more fundamental question is whether a pure intention — and we shall stick to pure cases — is a judgement. And is it a judgement "that..."?

I am going to argue that "intending to," like "hoping to" and "wanting to," is quite other than a judgement "that...".

There are two ways of arguing. One is to describe in acceptable terms the standard cases in which there seems to be a pure intention to act in a particular way, corresponding to a certain description, in particular circumstances envisaged. And then to show that there is certainly no all-in judgement, made by the subject in the light of his beliefs about the future, that acting in that way is desirable. That is, to describe situations in which it has been natural to say that there is a conflict between what one's actual intention is and one's own best judgement; for example, when someone cannot bring himself to do something.

There are indeed such cases, but this way of arguing seems to me to leave the question really up in the air, because it is perfectly open to Davidson to say — that is how we talk, but only because we have the myth of the will lodged in the centre of our language, and we have this myth for all sorts of historical reasons, and also for social reasons. For example, it is convenient to have this notion if we wish to exhort people to do things, or to get them to do things, or indeed to exhort ourselves to do things. But if we wish to make true statements, we should realise that this mythical notion is dispensable, and an argument from what you might call current speech is not significant and does not carry conviction. For common speech may well — in fact, certainly does — include, particularly in this sphere of the mind, all sorts of mythical entities, which have entered there for emotional, ethical and other reasons.

So that first way of arguing does not seem to me to be the proper one. The second and correct way of arguing would be — if only I could do it — to give a demonstration that practical reasoning, which is about what to do, issues in an intention to do something which is judged as right or wrong, and this is different from a judgement about something which is judged as true or false. That is the traditional way of arguing, and traditional ways are often good ways.

There are two bits of evidence I can give. The first is that it is sometimes necessary, or desirable, to perform an act which is forming an intention, rather than to have no intention at all. Just as sometimes it is important to decide, in the pure case of deciding — when one simply has to decide — like Eisenhower deciding on D-Day. This was a case of *tode ti* — press the button or not. No good Eisenhower saying, "Let's look up the maxims and find out whether it's a good thing to go today." The point is: there are all sorts of considerations — the action can be described as going when the clouds are over and there is no air cover — but he has to press the button one way or the other. That is pure deciding.

There are occasions when it is either necessary or desirable, I would say, not only simply to decide something, but also simply to form an intention. Yet I cannot find that this can be duplicated with judgement. I do not see what it means to say if there are equal reasons for course X and course non-X, then come to a judgement about whether X is desirable or not. It seems to me that in the case of intention there may be an act to be performed, which is forming the intention, and sometimes it could be important to perform that act even though the reasons are not sufficient for X or non-X, but the reasons are for performing that act. But there are never reasons for just believing. To me there are not. That is, again, a moral question. And I do not see what it means to say that you ought to come to a belief.

The second — and really traditional — bit of evidence is that there are countless activities in which we have to form intentions. This is the obsessional Greek figure of the artist-craftsman, the man who does not match his actions to a prescription. The Themistoclean politician, the man of flair, the man of taste, the games player, who forms intentions, knows what he is going to do, but he does not think in words at all. This is where the *tode ti* comes in. And if you are going to learn from such a person, you learn from him by watching him. You learn by imitation. He shows you how to do it. He knows exactly how to do it, wherever precision or getting things right are involved, or questions of syle. Take the pianist. "How do you intend to play it? Show me how you intend to play it. Can you describe it?" — "No." There exists no means of saying. If you ask a dancer how he will perform something, he can show you. That is why the question of particularity is fundamental. I think Aristotle saw that.

So I think there is a real difference between practical reasoning and theoretical reasoning. The games player, the dancer, indeed, has thought, but it is not verbal thought, and what it issues in is not a judgement.

Wadham College
Oxford

NATHAN ROTENSTREICH

HISTORICAL ACTIONS OR HISTORICAL EVENTS

I

The question we are about to analyse is whether or not the historical domain should be characterized as one of events or one of actions. We deliberately disregard, at least at the beginning of our analysis, the particularity of the historical domain in as much as the relation between dimensions of time goes: we deal only with the phenomenological features of the datum of history. We can put the question by employing the traditional distinction between *res gestae* and *historia rerum gestarum*, with a view of asking the question whether the *res gestae* are events or actions, or perhaps neither of the two.

The common feature of both actions and events lies in the fact that they can be described as belonging to what is called change. Change connotes shifts or regroupings in the given state of affairs or situations. Events can be understood as parts of the changes, and hence as particular shifts and transformations of a given situation; they can be understood also as outcomes of those shifts. When history as investigation or *historia rerum gestarum* is engaged in the deciphering of its subject matter, it encounters data like documents or institutions or else situations such as wars or unemployment. The data of historical investigation are in a sense accomplished events, or events which did find their manifestation in documents, relics of the past, or in situations, e.g. institutions, or states of affairs, e.g. unemployment. The accomplished datum can be seen as an event in the sense of being a finalization of a course of events. Situations or institutions are themselves continuous events or continuous actions. After all, parliament is not only the building but the sum total of its procedures and of the human beings populating the building and acting according to a constitution, procedures, habits, codes or rules. Hence, parliament is a continuous chain of events; the existence of the parliament is characterized by the fact that to some extent events happen in the parliament and thus changes occur in it. Still in a certain sense they do not change the

69

Yirmiahu Yovel (ed.), Philosophy of History and Action, 69–84. All Rights Reserved.
Copyright © 1978 by D. Reidel Publishing Company, Dordrecht, Holland.

parliament. The question of the line of demarcation between that which goes by the name of event and that which goes by the name of act or action is precisely the question which cannot be simply answered by pointing to the datum approached by historical investigation.

Let us comment now, in a preliminary way, about actions or deeds in general, from the point of view of their accomplishment and not from the point of view of the agent, since precisely the question of the agent is crucial within the historical context. In so far as every action is meant to posit, positing may mean placing something in a context or bringing something about. To move a table is positing it within a context, while to build the table as an artifact is to effect its existence (bring it into being). In this sense we have to distinguish, following both the Greek and the medieval distinctions, between acts referring to the actor himself and acts whose result lies outside the actor. It is well known that *praxis* in the Greek sense meant action bringing about the shaping of the actor, while *poiesis* brought about effects in the outside world, such as building bridges or houses. In so far as the self-referential character of acts goes, knowledge of an object is an act, since it brings about the awareness of the object or places the object within the horizon of the knower, and can be identified in Husserl's sense as *Selbsthabe*[1]. As against the self-referential character of acts, the accomplishment of objects, shaping their quality, creating conditions — all these are transitive acts, since they go beyond the scope of self-reference and thus beyond the scope of the person or actor himself.

We have already used the distinction between the agent or the actor and the act or the activity; though precisely that distinction is somehow problematic within the scope of history. While drawing this distinction we tacitly make several presuppositions: we presuppose the conception that every act exhibits a power used; and to do is to work and thus handle things. These descriptions imply an act of exhibiting one's power by setting them or positing them.

We adhere tacitly to an additional presupposition expressed in the saying: *operari sequitur esse.* Or, to put it differently, to do things presupposes reality or existence or presupposes the doer. The power vested in the deed — and this is our third presupposition when we take that common view — is that the energy of the will is the power exhibited or invested, and behind this energy is the willing person or agent. This is presupposed even when we do not perceive the energy but its outcome only, let alone the distinction between the agent and his will. Since acts or deeds change the state of affairs, we presuppose the existence of the state of affairs in respect to which the change occurs; the existence of the doer as distinguished from his deed is eventually part of the presupposition as to the existence of the state of affairs which is both the background and the cause of the deeds accomplished.

Already here the historical domain leads us to pose some questions as to these presuppositions: it is rather difficult to distinguish in the historical domain between the background and the cause, between the agent and his accomplishment, let alone between the deed and the will, finding its externalization in deeds or accomplishments.

II

There are probably several reasons for the fascination of history and philosophy of history with the question of the position of the individual and his role in history, or as the common description goes, with the position of heroes in history. One of the explanations for that fascination is that the transplantation of the common sense presuppositions about deeds and acts of positing vis-à-vis individuals in history seems to be easy or warranted. Let us refer here as an example to Collingwood's description of human action in history, focusing on Caesar's invasion of Britain. Every conscious act according to Collingwood, including acts in history, has two sides: it has a physical side which refers to the passage of Caesar and his army across the English channel. It has a second side consisting of thought which is specifically the intention or the plan entertained by Caesar to conquer Britain. An event or let us perhaps say here an act of Caesar's is, therefore, a unity of the physical aspect and the aspect of thought, or what is described as a unity of the inside and the outside. The outside aspect includes the agent's body as well as the equipment at his disposal like the ships of his army. In the aspect of inside, Collingwood distinguished two elements. He called them *causa quod* and *causa ut*, respectively. The *causa quod* of an act or perhaps of an event is the agent's estimate of his situation in which he acts or as he acts in it. This estimation, performed by the agent who is in this sense distinct from the act of estimation and all other acts concomitant with it, comprises the military estimation or the strategic evaluation of the situation, for instance, how many men he needs in order to accomplish what he planned. This aspect of *causa quod* precedes the subsequent elements of planning as well as his actual doing. As eventually the two aspects combine, one could make a case, which is not the case made by Collingwood, that all these distinctions are *post factum* constructs, once we presuppose that a historical event is a combination of the inside and outside aspects. We attempt to articulate the inside aspects by distinguishing within the scope of the inside either components coexisting, like estimation of the initial strategic situation and the planning for the men needed to bring about the effect; or we distinguish between the elements as consecutive elements, namely, conceiving the plan to conquer Britain as an objective or as an intention, whereby the directedness of Caesar towards that objective leads to the subsequent steps he is taking for the sake of his *causa ut*. In this sense *causa ut* is the overriding objective constructed in order to narrate the events or deeds which lead to the final act or else the narration presupposes that we know introspectively how we approach plans in our immediate situation and transpose that introspective knowledge to the historical agent or hero.[2]

Be it as it may, this is a simple situation, since we are concerned with individually delineated agents and many of the presuppositions pertaining to agents can be transplanted to the realm of history. There is even no need to question this transplantation because it is obvious that not all events with which history is concerned are related to biographical individuals. In this context we have to be reminded of Austin's caution: "All 'actions' are, as actions (meaning what?), equal, composing a quarrel with striking a match, winning a war with sneezing: worse still, we assimilate them one and all to the supposedly most obvious and easy cases, such as posting letters or moving fingers, just as we assimilate all 'things' to horses or beds."[3] We shall look now into some of the prevailing descriptions of actions in order to see whether they are applicable to the domain of history and thus attempt to clarify the basic issue in what sense history embraces events or actions.

If action is to be subsumed under the generic term "practice," and practice, to use John Rawls' description, is a form of activity specified by a system of rules, the system defines offices, rules, moves, penalties, defenses, etc. It is questionable whether practice in this sense can be applied to the historical realm and to historical action. In the first place one wonders whether historical action, like the emergence of Protestantism, or the French and the Bolshevik revolutions are specified by a system of rules. It is not precluded that *post factum* somebody could try to decipher the system of rules which gives structure to the activity like the renaissance of a religion or revolution. But it is — to say the least — questionable whether this is so in the terms of individuals and groups involved in the activity. To some extent we can even say that it is part and parcel of the situation to overrule the rules — not to cling to the ecclesiastic hierarchy, let alone to the existing social order. Somehow that description of practice is too much guided by the model or paradigm of a certain channel of activity like games, since games are guided by rules which an individual must learn before he can be a participant in the specific game and must observe them lest he is excluded from the activity of the game. When Rawls says that the rules are publicly known and understood as definitive, we again encounter a paradox:[4] history is a public realm and the actions and activities taking place within that realm are public by definition, at least in so far as their outcome goes, since there might be secret actions leading to historical results. But we may still wonder whether the position of an action within the public sphere is identical with an action characterized as being guided by public rules, or rules publicly known.

To what extent the current descriptions of actions and activities cling naively to the individual model can be seen from additional features usually attributed to actions. The first feature to be mentioned in this context is that of responsibility in the sense that actions, as related to agents, raise the question as to the responsibilities of the agents. Let us take a rather difficult and invidious example — of the guilt of the German people in the Nazi period. We know very well that the simple transposition of the notion of the individual in his personal sphere does not apply to the historical sphere, unless we refer again specifically to individuals, like Hitler or Eichmann. Responsibility implying the attributability of an action as well as accountability takes a different form when applied to groups of people, since vis-à-vis groups we cannot point to an explicit will or decision as implied in action and thus serving as the groundwork for responsibility. Attitudes of consent, even of passive consent, are contributing to the total historical situation, though will as initiating an action cannot be presupposed, or at least cannot be pointed to. In the attitude of consent we can discern a kind of adherence to an action initiated by a person or by a group of persons; and here, too, we have to distinguish between an expressed consent and a tacit consent. Moreover, we can and probably have to attribute responsibility to a group not from the point of view of the agent implied, but from the point of view of the magnitude of the result — and the Nazi era and the question of guilt is a case in point. A consent which does not lead to events of catastrophic orders of magnitude is an attitude which historically may not count a great deal. From the event as an outcome we regress to the activity and to those responsible for the activity. Hence, in the sphere of history when we disregard individual agents, we cannot pinpoint an individual agent, and the activity of action springing from the agent. We reconstruct the agent from the event and point to a sort of continuity from the event to the agent without describing or delineating the boundaries of the agent.

An additional feature usually mentioned in the context of the description of activity is that of mental action, as setting ourselves to do something, that is to say, to bring something about. It is well known that in this context the question arises of the distinction between intent and purpose, or the distinction suggested by Austin between acting intentionally, deliberately and on purpose. In so far as intention is concerned, let us recall the distinction between consciousness and goal-directedness. We can probably say that within the historical context goal-directedness appears e.g. as the renaissance of a certain religion or a revolution or a victory in a war. But the outcome of that goal-directedness goes beyond the goal initiated by the historical action which lacks, and necessarily so, the intention to bring about all the results of the action; one cannot be aware of all the results, since they may lie ahead of the individual agent or the group and still be, even when we call this hindsight, traced to the action. The distinction between intention and goal is rather significant for the historical sphere: implied in that distinction is the difference between intention or intentionality, belonging to the consciousness of individuals, and goals which by the very fact that they can be defined create a kind of trans-individual focus. Many human beings, as agents, be their intentions what they may, may share, as we put it, in the goal, and direct themselves towards the goal. They meet, as it were, in terms of the goal while their intentions and motivations may differ.

Moreover, within the sphere of history the trans-personal locus of the goal may initiate directedness, though directedness as such is not necessarily the initial step. Let us take a simple example: when we start from the position of the agents by way of intentionality or even goal-directedness, many human beings might be inspired by attitudes of protest, dissatisfaction, *malaise*, crises, expectations, etc. In this sense their attitudes can be described as goal-directed: their goal might be to express their bitterness, or even to undermine the present system which in their eyes is accountable (whatever this may mean) for their misgivings. The goal of a new social system, or of utopian communities to be formed parallel to the existing system, is a goal which as such can initiate a new goal-directedness or, as it happens ever so often in history, one goal-directedness takes advantage of another goal-directedness, utilizing its energies and reinforcing itself. Here, too, we have to distinguish between goals set by individuals, who can entertain goals in their intentionality, as against certain delineated conceptual nuclei, like systems or modes of existence and life, whose trans-individual status attracts individuals without assuming any kind of continuity from consciousness, intentionality to goal-directedness. But what is even more significant: the trans-individual status of goals evokes trans-individual actions which can be pointed to. These actions can be listed neither with psychic events nor with bodily events. They are, to use Max Scheler's expression, psycho-physically indifferent. Scheler used that description for the nature of the person, but *a fortiori* it can be used more properly for the nature of the historical action and the historical agent, if the distinction between the two is to be maintained at all. Parallel to that statement is the distinction, again suggested by Scheler, between functions and acts. He lists with functions seeing, hearing, testing, etc.; also all sorts of attention, observation, etc. He lists as acts all these attitudes in which something is meant (*etwas "gemeint" wird*).[5] What we do find in the historical sphere, precisely because of the goal-directedness, is that the directedness reinforces the entertainment of goals and goals create the directedness out of their own resources. Thus, an inter-subjective realm is implied which can be reduced neither to functions nor to actions as mental activities implying the component of will or willing. The fact that we use the expression "actions" connotes the occurrences taking place, and because human beings are involved, we again tend to transpose the descriptions which may or may not hold good for actions of individuals onto the inter-subjective level of history. But we are probably victims here of what might be called *individumorphism*, if we introduce a term parallel to the well-known anthropomorphism.

We have already referred several times to the component of will in actions of individuals. About practice Oakeshott says that it is the exercise of the will; practical thought is volition; practical experience is the world *sub specie voluntatis*. Oakeshott is consistent, because the stress he lays on the exercise of will leads him to the statement that the self, engaged in practical experience, is what is separate or else unique and self-contained. This position can be maintained only when we suggest a far-reaching chasm between the mode of practice and the mode of history. History is to be listed within the broad scope of alteration of existence. It is not merely a program for action but is action itself, to use again Oakeshott's statements. Practice and history imply and depend upon something "to be" which is "not yet." History is practice and we can speak of historical practice and historical action. But as long as we confine practice to the exercise of will, we are somehow at a loss, and because of our individumorphic description of action, we are looking for a trans-individual will. Either we find that will in a sort of *Volksseele*, or will of the proletariat, and thus maintain a consistent description of action, or else we do not find the component of will and see history only from the point of view of *praeteritorum* in Oakeshott's sense. Thus, we see history only from the point of view of dependence upon the past and not from that of occurrences en route and their results.[6] But once we bring to prominence the distinction between the inter-subjective character of history which, by definition, cannot contain components like will or intentionality characteristic of individuals, we have to make a distinction between the phenomenology of history, including historical actions, and a certain theory of action which at the best is applicable in the sphere of individual agents and not in a sphere of trans-individuality. The characteristics of the trans-individual sphere lead us to define certain foci of that sphere. If the focus is national self-determination, the agent is a people. If the focus is the share in the "national cake," the agents are those who are interested or those whose goal-directedness lies in the national income and its distribution. It is precisely because of that trans-individuality that the historical sphere is characterized by the coexistence of different goals and foci, and consequently by a coexistence of agents defined or delineated from the point of view of the different foci.[7]

III

Our previous reference to goals as factors creating the inter-subjective realm of history could possibly be interpreted as if we suggested a cause or a prime mover for the very establishment or emergence of the historical sphere. But this is not so, since the inter-subjectivity is not created out of sources outside itself, be they the goals or, as sociologists tend to emphasize, values, etc.

Solidarity, to which sociologists refer, characterized by the institutionalization of shared value-orientations, is but one of the expressions of the infrastructure of inter-subjectivity which as such can be focused or reinforced by shared values but is not created by them.[8] The historical sphere originates out of itself, and there is no extra-historical cause creating history, or the first historical deed, as Marx put it. Inter-subjectivity is related to as an awareness of those involved in the context and it implies that reality does not begin with themselves. From the historical point of view, it does not follow from people's awareness of being placed in the middle of time that they are aware of the past or their predecessors' existence: The notion of *Vorwelt* does not occupy, from the point of view of the awareness of inter-subjectivity and along with this of the historical realm, a more primary position than does the notion of what might perhaps be called, for the sake of symmetry, *Folgewelt* or *Nachwelt*, that is to say, the reality of the future and in the future.[9]

The reference to the preceding world as well as to the succeeding one is essentially a certain interpretation of the openness of reality which, as we have seen, is the ontological presupposition of any attitude which introduces changes into reality and brings about events or results. Once that openness is presupposed it becomes more closely interpreted as an openness in terms of time; the past and the future indicate the specific vectors of the openendedness. The further interpretation is imposed on the past from the point of view of the events encountered or interpreted. But were it not for the very possibility to go beyond the present, the rigidity or closedness of the past could not be discerned. Once human beings find themselves embraced as it were by a broader reality, by the openness of reality in general, and by the trans-personal or trans-individual status of time, the alleged subjectivity has already been broken through, since individuals reflect upon themselves as referring or relating to spheres outside themselves. In this sense transpersonality is the ontological precondition for trans-subjectivity or intersubjectivity. Hence it can be said that even an individual agent cannot be historically a prime mover, but only an interpreter or an agent for the focusing and the materialization of conditions, situations, directions, and the like. The doom of trans-subjectivity looms large even vis-à-vis individual historical agents, that is to say "great" historical individuals. A historical action is from this point of view never a new beginning; it is an action in so far as it brings about a certain course of events, but it is an event in so far as in the action things come to exist. Thus the concept of events related to *evenio* is applicable in this context, because it implies the notion of coming, coming out, coming along. Hence we may perhaps coin an expression like *activent* which combines both the aspect of action and that of event. If we refer to the notion of action at all, we may take advantage of the distinction suggested by Arthur C. Danto: "That is, if there are any actions at all, there must be two distinct *kind* of actions: those performed by an individual M which he may be said to have *caused* to happen, and those actions, also performed by M, which he cannot be said to have caused to happen. The latter I shall designate as *basic actions*." [10]

The lack of a primary historical fountainhead which we tried to explain by the very dimension of time can be explained correspondingly by looking also into the aspect of content. Historical actions presuppose the day-to-day infrastructure of human existence, mainly the infrastructure of the public realm, even when that realm is not audible or visible. It is often invisible because by and large it can be said that human existence in the public realm proceeds without being reflected upon. The day-to-day events are referred to only in critical situations. It is not only, as Dewey said, that a hitch in workings occasions emotion and provokes thought. At certain turning points the infrastructure of reality gains historical meaning and significance because certain problems become prominent. This is the nature of an economic crisis in the sense that work, earning, interaction between human beings—all these are presupposed. But certain problems emerge out of the context which make the smooth proceeding or course impossible or, to put it differently, call for a certain deliberate intervention in the course of events. The infrastructure is not created by the action; it conditions the action, because an attempt to come to grips with an economic crisis is bound to differ from an attempt to come to grips with the crisis in the curriculum of a school. Action in the strict sense of the term is future-directed because it is meant to bring about changes in the situation, but it is past-directed just as well, because the infrastructure to be changed has been read carefully and the programmed action adequately defined and carried out.

Let us take another rather topical example: busing in the American school system could become a program of action and an initiation of action only because the existence of buses is presupposed. But this existence is not confined to the vehicles in the physical sense; it comprises the facts or events that people ride in buses, that buses are meant to overcome distances in the geographical sense; buses as instruments for overcoming geographical distances become eventually instruments for overcoming social distances. Here, too, the infrastructure is of a social or inter-subjective character. That character cannot be limited to the value aspect or to the goal component. It is a kind of a totality, and historical changes, be they called events or actions, are essentially extractions of certain components of the infrastructure by way of making them foci of action. In this sense a focus of action becomes an event because of its involvement in the infrastructure on the one hand and its impact on the course of events or actions on the other. The grounding of the focus of action in the infrastructure reinforces the position that there is no new beginning in history. It also reinforces the fact that the impact of events transcends the intention. This is so since the event is by its very essence involved in the course of reality or else in the course of time. An event or even a cluster of events cannot therefore fully control either reality or time. If we use the two terms intention and motive in the sense suggested by G.E.M. Anscombe — "A man's intention is *what* he aims at or chooses; his motive is what determines the aim or choice;"[11] — we realize that from both aspects reality is sweeping the agent along: sometimes his motives become irrelevant by the very step towards transpersonalization which is characteristic of historical actions or events, and sometimes his intentions become obsolete. This is so because what he aims at or chooses lies within his individual horizon, but a historical event or an outcome of an action becomes, by its very nature, interwoven with other events or with the broad reality over which he has no control and cannot have control. Hence, even when we introduce Max Weber's notion of social action into the context of our analysis, we shall still have to express some doubts whether that notion does justice to the complexity of the historical realm.

Max Weber describes social action as action related to the behaviour of others. As such it includes both action proper as a deed, as well as failure to act and passive acquiescence. Since the emphasis is placed on the relation to the others, social action in that description may be oriented to the past as well as to the present or to the expected future behaviour of others.[12] One could easily assume that historical action is a social action in the first place or even *par excellence*, since it involves inter-action and is related to or implied in what goes on between various peoples. To put it differently, historical action is oriented to the behaviour of the others since it is embraced by the sphere which is public or common; different peoples are placed in that sphere before the action proper begins. Yet Max Weber's description of social action is too limited to do justice to the complexities of history and historical action. Let us take as an example one quoted by Weber himself, who says that religious behaviour is not social if it is simply a matter of contemplation or of solitary prayer. To cling to that example, we have to ask in the first place: what sort of prayer is a solitary individual utterance? Is the individual uttering a prayer which he received from tradition, e.g. by using the prayer-book? To be sure he uses it within the confines of his own individual existence. He may use the same prayer as another individual or as church-goers do who are with others and interact with them. If social action connotes the present or momentary interaction with the other, the attitude of the individual or his behaviour in the case quoted is not social. But if sociality or social action connote an involvement in a sphere which is a common ground for individuals, even when here and now they are solitary, the whole shape of the situation changes. Interestingly enough, when Weber speaks about the orientation to the past, he quotes the example of an individual who may be motivated by revenge for a past attack. He thus quotes an example which points rather to the immediate impact a past situation has or may have on the emotions of the individual involved. But when we speak of the realm of history, there is no personal involvement in the sense quoted in the as it were 'existential' impact of the past act on one's present response; there is more of an anonymous involvement of many individuals in a past, as well as a sort of deliberate or non-deliberate selection of events from the past remembered or reinstituted by those living in the present. The social character of the past serves as a reservoir, as a background, as a score for individual selections, as principles of actions or norms, etc. Hence it can be said that the social action as described by Weber is based on a model of linear relationship between co-present individuals, which can again perhaps be described also as a horizontal relationship. But precisely the position of the historical realm as well as the inter-action between the dimensions of time and human beings involved in those dimensions are of a different character. The inter-action is not given since the individuals are not co-present; the past is brought back to the present, the future is anticipated. Thus, individuals extend the network of their relationship in the directions prescribed by the dimensions of time which in turn are interpreted by them as containing contents of different meaning or impact.

In so far as we take Weber's description as a model of social action, we are bound to arrive at a paradoxical conclusion: the inter-action between human beings within the historical realm is not a social action proper. To avoid this paradoxical conclusion, we have to extend the meaning of social action to include inter-action between human beings, be the context of that inter-action, both in terms of time and in terms of meaning, lodged in the present or transcending it. This is rather significant from the point of view of our attempt to describe the nature of action in history as well as the inter-relation between actions and events. Actions occurring in the present, if they are of a historical character, do occur against the background of given circumstances which, historically speaking, are events or results of actions initiated in the past. A historical actor or agent is aware — be the actual, topical awareness focused or not — that he acts in certain circumstances. Were it not for the fact that he conceives the circumstances as historical, that is to say, as results of actions, he would not initiate his own action. He would take the world or reality as totally closed, and thus as preventing the intervention in the course of reality. The conscious or unconscious presupposition of any action, including historical action, is that reality is not closed. A historical agent, be the agent an individual or a group of individuals, presupposes history, that is to say, the constant shift from action to results or events, or the perennial possibility to initiate actions which will result in events.

The locus of the action is here and now. This applies to the other end as well, namely, that the historical agent assumes that his action will result in an event, and become a historical event proper, to be discerned in the future or by a future observer. We find here, as a matter of fact, a constant shift from actions to events. What a historical action is can be gauged by the historical events or by those actions which become events. The evaluation of an action as an event follows the principle that *wirklich ist was wirksam ist oder war* or, to put it differently, we come back from the results to the actions which initiated them.

If this shift from action to events is characteristic of the historical sphere, then we reiterate our previous comment, namely, that underlying the historical realm and the historical action occurring in it is the continuous awareness that we are in the midst of time, or that reality does not begin with ourselves.[13] Every historical action, accompanied by that awareness, may bring about an anti-egocentric evaluation of historical actions and agents. History is an anti-egocentric realm *par excellence*. Moreover, the shift from action to events and from events to their becoming the background for action — this perennial shift characteristic of history may lead us to a further conclusion related to the well-known distinction mentioned before of history as *res gestae* and history as the narration of *rerum gestarum*. History as *res gestae* is a forward-looking action occurring against the background of given events, that is to say, of results of actions which occurred previously. History, as a narration of *rerum gestarum*, is an attempt to look at events as results of action, or to find the causal or hermeneutic relationship between events which are the point of departure of our interpretation or observation and the actions which resulted in the events. Historical action proper as an occurrence or as an activity presupposes events, while historical narration presupposes actions. Historical occurrences are characterized by actions experienced, in which historical agents are involved against the background of events; historical events presuppose actions and they are historical since the presupposed actions occurred previously and are not and cannot be experienced by the observer in the present. The present is the locus of action, and the events which are the starting point of the investigation are lodged in the present as well. The events do not occur in the present, but they can be traced from the position of the present to the past as the locus and background. The distinction lies therefore in the parallel distinction between the locus and the point of departure, though the two perspectives are correlated.

An additional comment is apposite in the present context. History is perpetually recreated, and the shift from actions to events and the reconstruction of actions from events epitomize the character of the historical realm. It follows from this that history presupposes itself: the public realm, for instance, institutions or languages, are not created by a summing-up of individual deeds or voices. The public realm, being reshaped, is presupposed in the first place as are changes occurring within it, though they may bring about significant or radical innovations. Whatever applies to the circularity of the public realm applies also to the circularity of history and historical action. A historical action presupposes the historical realm. That presupposition can be terminologically and phenomenologically pointed to by applying the concept of events. Hence we may say that actions presuppose events, and events can lead to action; both components or correlates are embraced by the common sphere of history on the one hand and they keep recreating that common sphere on the other.

From the preceding analysis we may draw several conclusions as to the nature of history in general. In the first place it has to be said that history is a sphere and not a particular content. What is historical or not can therefore not be decided from the point of view of the substance of an action or an event, but from the point of view of the place, position, or impact of the action or event. Moreover, history in the spheric and not substantive sense, is a process of incorporation or integration of substantive actions and events into its own motion or continuity. History presupposes substantive contents like scientific events, political acts or technology as an order, etc. The substantive contents become historical events within the limited spheres delineated by the contents, namely events in the history of science or politics or technology. They may become events in the broader scope of history maintaining their substantive meaning by having an impact beyond the boundaries delineated by that meaning. The Theory of Relativity becomes an event not only in the history of science but in history at large because of the impact it had on the atomic bomb, and through the atomic bomb on the course of world history. Since there is no primary substantive aspect to history, what becomes historical is a *post factum* assertion.

The second conclusion is this: since historical meanings are meanings which gain impact, historical events are essentially radiating occurrences similar to the sense used by William Stern in his theory of values, namely *strahlende Werte*. To put it differently, they are events in so far as they have effects. But once we introduce the metaphor of radiation into the scope of our analysis, we may say against the present-day experience, and without being overly sarcastic, that historical events might be radiating in the neutral sense and might be radiating in the sense attributed to nuclear energy. The impact might be neutral, benign or malignant. The emphasis placed on the aftermath of events which in turn is related to the fact that events lack a substantive meaning, opens the door to the evaluation of historical events. The primary evaluation is the very assessment of the fact that events equal impact. That assessment in turn can lead to subsequent assessments and evaluations as to the nature of the impact — whether it was for the benefit or harm to subsequent generations, or what sort of substantive meaning the event contained from the aspect of the particular sphere to which it belongs, as distinguished from the aspect of the historical process.

Here, too, the distinction between meanings and impacts related to the analysis of action in history leads us, on the one hand, to a reconsideration of the interplay between action and events and, on the other, to reservations about a value-free interpretation.

The Hebrew University of Jerusalem

NOTES

[1] E. Husserl, *Erfahrung und Urteil, Untersuchungen zur Genealogie der Logik*, ed. Ludwig Landgrebe, Prag, Academia, 1939, pp. 235 ff.

[2] R.G. Collingwood, *The Idea of History*, ed. T.M. Knox, Oxford, Clarendon Press, 1946, p. 213; also his *An Essay on Metaphysics*, Oxford, Clarendon Press, 1940, pp. 292 ff; cf. the discussion in Alan Donagan, *The Later Philosophy of R.G. Collingwood*, Oxford, Clarendon Press, 1962, pp. 192 ff.

[3] J.L. Austin, "A Plea for Excuses," in *Philosophical Papers*, Oxford, Clarendon Press, 1961, p. 127. As to the question of non-individual agents, see my "On the Historical Subject," *Studi Internazionali di Filosofia* 4 (1972): 15 ff.

[4] John Rawls, "Two Concepts of Rules," *The Philosophical Review* 64 (1955): 3 ff.; see also Thomas Morawetz, "The Concept of a Practice," *Philosophical Studies* 24 (1973): 209 ff.

[5] Max Scheler, *Der Formalismus in der Ethik und die materiale Wertethik; Neuer Versuch der Grundlegung eines ethischen Personalismus*, Bern, Franke Verlag, 1954, p. 398.

[6] Michael Oakeshott, *Experience and its Modes*, Cambridge University Press, 1933, pp. 296-298, 273, 118.

[7] Several surveys of the contemporary literature on action are available. See, for instance, Glenn Langford, *Human Action*, London, Macmillan, 1971, and the extensive bibliography at the end of the book.

[8] *Toward a General Theory of Action*, ed. Talcott Parsons and Edward Shils, Cambridge, Mass., Harvard University Press, 1951, p. 193.

[9] Alfred Schütz, *Der sinnhafte Aufbau der sozialen Welt, Eine Einleitung in die verstehende Soziologie*, Wien, Julius Springer, 1932, pp. 236 ff.

[10] "Basic Action," in *Readings in the Theory of Action*, ed. Norman S. Care and Charles Landesman, Bloomington, Indiana University Press, 1968, p. 95.

[11] "Intention," in *The Philosophy of Action*, ed. Alan R. White, Oxford University Press, 1968, p. 147.

[12] I follow here Max Weber's *Wirtschaft und Gesellschaft* in its English translation, *The Theory of Social and Economic Organization*, by A.R. Henderson and Talcott Parsons, rev. and ed. with introduction by Talcott Parsons, London-Edinburgh-Glasgow, William Hodge, 1947.

[13] See my "Ontological Status of History," *American Philosophical Quarterly* 9 (January 1972): 49 ff.

EDDY M. ZEMACH

EVENTS

I

In a number of papers published over the last few years Donald Davidson has advocated an ontology which admits events as full fledged, real particulars. Events, in his view, are in no sense reducible to, or even secondary to, individual things. The category of events, he says, is "a fundamental ontological category" (IOE, p. 232). [1] "The assumption, ontological and metaphysical, that there are events is one without which we cannot make sense of our most common talk... I do not know of any better, or further, way of showing what there is" (CR, p. 703).

Davidson's main argument for this view is that his theory offers a satisfactory solution to Kenny's problem of the variable poliadicity of adverbs. The problem is, roughly, this. From a sentence like

(1)   Sebastian strolled in Bologna at 2 AM quietly

one would like to be able to derive

(2)   Sebastian strolled quietly
(3)   Sebastian strolled in Bologna
(4)   Sebastian strolled at 2 AM
(5)   Sebastian strolled quietly in Bologna

etc. In general, we can intuitively see that if a sentence S which includes the *genuine* adverbs (excluding 'apparently,' 'allegedly,' and similar non-genuine modifiers) $A_1 \ldots A_n$ is true, then any S', which is exactly like S except that some of the adverbs $A_1 \ldots A_n$ do not appear in it, is also true. However, on the classical PM analysis no such S' is logically derivable from S.

Davidson's solution to this problem is twofold. First he construes 'Sebastian strolled' as an existentially quantified sentence, saying that there occurred at least one event of Sebastian strolling. Then the adverbs are construed as regular (adjectival) modifiers attributing properties to the said event or events. Thus, the logical form of (1), Davidson's style, is

Yirmiahu Yovel (ed.), *Philosophy of History and Action*, 85–95. *All Rights Reserved.*
Copyright © 1978 by D. Reidel Publishing Company, Dordrecht, Holland.

(1D)   (Ex) [Strolled (Sebastian, x) & In (Bologna, x) &
            At (2 AM, x) & Quiet (x)].

The coveted result of simple, mechanical detachment of adverbs has
certainly been reached: p & q logically implies p.

There are, however, several highly questionable points in this account.
First of all, can adverbs be construed as modifiers of event terms? E.g., if

(6)   Sebastian ate carefully

is analysed as

(6D)   (Ex) [Ate (Sebastian, x) & Careful (x)]

we would seem to be saying that the event x was careful, rather than what
we want to say, i.e., that Sebastian was careful. We need, therefore, some
rule to the effect that 'careful' here means 'executed with care.' What this
rule might be is difficult to say since, obviously, we do not want to say that
for every F and every x, if x is an event 'Fx' is to be read as 'x is executed
with F-ness.'

A second problem is mentioned by Davidson, but left unsolved. It has to
do with a feature common to adverbs of manner and to attributives, i.e., that
these terms are relative to the terms they modify. Davidson's own example
(LFA, p. 82) is this: If Sue tells us that she has crossed the channel in fifteen
hours, we would say, 'it was slow.' But if we are then told that she swam
across, we would say, 'it was fast.' Since the swimming *was* the crossing the
analysis of the above would be

(7D)   (Ex) (Ey) [Swam (Sue, x) & Crossed (Sue, y) &
            Fast (x) & Not fast (y) & x = y]

and we have a contradiction. A possible solution is to say that the crossing
is not identical with the swimming (they are two distinct events). But this
cannot be maintained by Davidson who holds, e.g., that writing one's name,
signing a check, and paying one's gambling debts are all one and the same
event. It is clear that this objection can be raised with respect to almost
every event which sustains several descriptions.

A third objection is even more serious than the previous ones.
Supposedly, (1D) is to be read as follows: 'Some x was strolled by
Sebastian, and that x was in Bologna, it was at 2 AM, and it was quiet.' We

are supposed to understand that the x in question is a certain event, i.e., Sebastian's stroll. But this is nowhere said. If 'strolled' has its usual meaning, the said x could very well be Sebastian's dog. Davidson relies here on the first conjunct of (1D) to specify what x is. To do this, however, is to use a single operator (the term 'strolled') in two irreconcilable roles. It is supposed to be both (a) a one-place predicate saying which kind of entity x is (a stroll, rather than, e.g., a swim or a dog), and (b) a two-place predicate saying what is the relation between Sebastian and x. But this is impossible.

If Davidson is right, and we have a right to expect 'Sebastian strolled' to be a logical consequence of (1), then we also have every right to expect 'x is a stroll' to be a logical consequence of (1D). But if 'S' in 'S(Sebastian, x)' is an *unstructured* predicate (reading, say,'− is a stroll by −'), 'x is a stroll' does not follow from (1D). Hence Davidson's reasons for rejecting the traditional analysis of action sentences also weigh against his own.

In a later paper Davidson has attempted to correct this flaw. His reason was that Sebastian can stand in more than one relation to the stroll x: "there are endless things he can do with a stroll besides take it: for one, he can make sure... that someone else takes it" (EEE, p. 343). Thus Davidson now separates the one-place predicate from the relation-word. Instead of the D form above we are now offered what Davidson has earlier called (IOE, p. 219) the "ornate" form:

(1R)   (Ex) [Stroll (x) & Took (Sebastian, x) & In (Bologna, x)
        & At (2 AM, x) & Quiet (x)].

But this move, however necessary, is quite fatal. The second conjunct of (1R) states that there is some x such that Sebastian took that x. However, to present 'a took b' as having the logical form 'T(a,b)' is to use the classical, rather than the Davidsonian, method of analysis. If Davidson is right, then 'a took b' has the logical form '(Ex) T(a,b,x).'

The point is that 'T(a,b)' is itself an action sentence saying what a did with respect to b. As such, it is subject to the Davidsonian analysis and should be presented as '(Ex) T(a,b,x).' This becomes clearer when we examine the other relations which can exist between a and b. As we have seen above, Davidson suggests the following example for a relation between a and b: a made sure that someone else takes b. Let us refer to this relation as 'P.' Now 'P(a,b)' certainly is an action sentence; it says that a certain person performed a certain action with respect to a certain entity. Therefore it must be construed as having the logical form '(Ex) P(a,b,x).' If P and T are equally relations between a and b, 'T(a,b)' should also be represented as '(Ex) T(a,b,x).'

One cannot argue that only 'P(a,b)' and not 'T(a,b)' is an action sentence, and thus 'a took b' need not be represented as '(Ex) T(a,b,x).' True, if a is the agent and b the event which is his action it would normally be strange to say that the agent's performing his action b is itself another action, c. But here we must remember that on Davidson's view the event b is an *entity*, an individual, and what 'a took b' says is that a brought about the existence of b. And while it is plausible to say that a's V-ing does not involve any other action over and above this V-ing itself, it is *not* plausible to say that a's bringing about the existence of b does not involve any other action over and above the entity b itself. No entity, with the possible exception of God, is identical with the action of bringing about its own existence. (It seems that if something is identical with the action of bringing about its own existence, it would necessarily exist.) Thus a Davidsonian ontologist must say that the 'x' in '(Ex) T(a,b,x)' is not any more superfluous than the 'x' in '(Ex) P(a,b,x).'

In fact, the reasons that made Davidson reject the binary predicate form for action sentences such as 'Shem kicked Shaun' should count against 'T (Sebastian, x)' as well. For Sebastian may take his stroll *regularly*, *carefully*, *deliberately*, *reluctantly*, *intermittently*, etc. All these adverbs apply *not* to the stroll itself but to the manner in which Sebastian took it. Davidson must, therefore, by his own lights (if 'Sebastian took a stroll' is to be a logical consequence of 'Sebastian took a stroll reluctantly'), use a three-place, rather than a two-place, predicate in order to formulate 'Sebastian took a stroll.' Therefore, (1R) must be rejected by Davidson and its first two conjuncts should be replaced by

(1S)   (Ex) (Ey) [Stroll (x) & Took (Sebastian, x, y)].

But (1S) is inadequate and misleading in exactly the same way that (1D) was inadequate and misleading. The term 'took' as used in (1S) illegitimately amalgamates a one-place predicate designating the kind of event y is with a three-place predicate designating the relation between x, y, and Sebastian, exactly as 'strolled' in (1D) illegitimately amalgamated 'is a stroll' and 'took.' Hence (1S) should be rewritten as

(1T)   (Ex) (Ey) |Stroll (x) & Taking (y) & Performed
            (Sebastian, x, y)|.

It can be seen that the third conjunct of (1T) again uses only the PM form of analysis, and ought to be recast, like (1R) before it, in the proper Davidsonian form. Thus (1T) gives way to

(1U)   (Ex) (Ey) (Ez) |Stroll (x) & Taking (y) & Performed
            (Sebastian, x, y, z)|.

It is obvious now that (1U) is also unsatisfactory, for the same reasons that (1D) and (1S) were unsatisfactory, and so on and so forth *ad infinitum*. The regress is vicious, since every formulation we may reach will be inadequate.

Davidson's analysis, therefore, fails. But it fails on more than one count. Davidson's intended solution to the problem of variable poliadicity fails completely if we try to apply it to adjectives, where exactly the same problem exists. E.g., it is reasonable to expect that

(8)   Jane is a good secretary

will logically imply (as it cannot under standard formalization)

(9)   Jane is a secretary.

If, however, we use Davidson's method, we shall get

(8D)   (Ex) |Secretary (Jane, x) & Good (x)|.

The nearest reading of (8D) is probably this: There is a state of affairs of Jane being a secretary and that state of affairs is good. (8D) does, therefore, imply (9). But it demands an additional ontological price: we have to countenance states of affairs in addition to events. Even if we pay this price, however, this method of analysis will fail. First of all, Jane may be a talented secretary, but no state of affairs (e.g., that of Jane being a secretary) can be talented. Secondly, the state of affairs of Jane being a secretary may be good (e.g., for some other reason) even though it is false that Jane is a good secretary.

II

Before I offer my solution which, I hope, is both frugal and efficacious, I must argue that (8) implies not only (9) but also

(10)   Jane is good.

This result, I know, has traditionally been objected to on the grounds that, on it, everything turns out to be good, since everything is a good something (trivially, everything is a good example of itself). There is, however, a long philosophical tradition of espousing precisely this tenet and, I think, for a good reason. If 'x is good' is analysed as 'x is good *qua* f' then (provided we give a clear analysis of '*qua* f' locutions) it is *true* that every x has some f such that x is good *qua* f. It can be easily seen that the same goes for all the other attributives as well. Although attributives (e.g., 'good,' 'heavy,' 'big,' 'fast,' 'small,' 'cheap,' 'deep,' 'wide,' etc.) apply to different kinds of things on the basis of different criteria, they are still *univocal* terms and I see no reason why we should not regard them as expressing properties (attributive properties, as distinguished from purely predicative properties) and capable of generating classes. I believe, therefore, that (when 'G' is an attributive term and 'f' a variable ranging over purely predicative properties) 'Ga' should be construed as '($\exists$f) a is G *qua* f.' Note that 'not (Ga)' should be interpreted, not as 'a is not G as an f,' but rather as 'a is G as no f,' i.e., 'there is no f such that a is G as an f.' A good secretary, a good road, and a good apple are, all of them, good, although the criteria for something being good as an apple are not identical with the criteria of being good as a road or as a secretary. More importantly, saying of something that it is bad does not imply that it is not good; if a is bad as something then there is something *qua* which a is not good; but this does not mean that there is nothing *qua* which a is good. Also note that the above analysis does not apply to attributives which deny, rather than modify, their predicatives. Since there is no known syntactical way to distinguish genuine modifiers from spurious ones (e.g., 'alleged,' or 'half way') this distinction ought to be made semantically.

It seems that the best interpretation of adverbs of manner is to construe them as attributives. If Sebastian walked quickly at PT then, at PT, he was quick *qua* walker. We may still say that, at PT, Sebastian proceeded very slowly (we expected him to run, not to walk). In the same way, Micky may be a small animal (small *qua* animal) but a big mouse (big *qua* mouse). Let us say that sentences which include attributives (i.e., are of the form 'x is g *qua* f') have *multiple* predicates. (8), e.g., has the *binary* predicate 'good secretary' and should be represented as

(8')   GS (Jane, PT)

and (2) should be represented as

(2')   QS (Sebastian, PT).

Now in order for a, *qua* F, to have the attributive property G, it must also have some purely predicative property H which is sufficient for the attribution of G-ness to objects considered *qua* F. I therefore suggest the following definition of binary predicates:

Def. I: GF(a, PT) ≡ (∃h) {P(h) & □(x) (pt) {(h(x, pt) & F(x, pt))

$$⊃ G(x, pt)| \& h(a, PT) \& F(a, PT)\}$$

Read: a is GF at PT iff there is a purely predicative property h (thus, 'h' cannot be any expression which includes 'G' itself or any attributive synonymous with 'G') such that, necessarily, whoever has both h and F at a certain time and place has G at that time and place (the necessity operator guarantees that even if all GFs are GKs, 'GKa' will not follow from 'ha' and 'Fa') and a has both h and F at PT.

Applying Def. I to (8') yields, as required, both (9) and (10). The same is true of all adverbs of manner. E.g.,

(11)   Joe ran quickly

would be represented as

(11')   QR(Joe, PT)

which now yields, quite mechanically, that at a certain time and place Joe ran, that (there and then) he was quick, and that he had, there and then, some property (e.g., proceeding at a rate of 9 miles per hour) such that, necessarily, anyone who has it when and where he runs is quick.

The same analysis applies to predicates of higher multiplicity. Consider, e.g.,

(12)   Spots is a strong old dog.

(12) does not merely say that Spots is old and strong, but that, *qua* dog, he is old (if x is fourteen years old then if x is a man x is young but if x is a dog x is old) and *qua* an old dog, he is strong (any young dog can jump this fence, but if an old dog does this he is strong). Thus the proper representation of (12) is

(12')   SOD (Spots, PT).

(12') has a *trinary* predicate. Using the already defined binary predicates, trinary predicates can be defined as follows:

Def. II: $HGF(a,PT) \equiv (\exists i) \{P(i) \& \Box(x) (pt) \lfloor (i(x, pt) \& GF(x, pt))$

$\supset H(x, pt) \rfloor \& i(a, PT) \& GF(a, PT)\}$

In the same manner any n-ary predicate can be defined.

I do not claim the above analysis applies to all adverbs and adjectives; what I claim is that it applies to attributives and adverbs of manner. Now what about (1) and the adverbs 'in Bologna' and 'at 2 AM' in it? I answer that these are not attributives and should not be regarded as parts of multiple predicates. Consider the following test: If Sebastian strolled quietly then Sebastian was quiet as a stroller, but perhaps not, e.g., as a thief. But if Sebastian strolled in Bologna then Sebastian was in Bologna regardless *qua* what he was there. (1) is not to be represented as

(1')   QIAS (Sebastian, PT).

The analysis offered above applies to it in another way. It is to be represented as follows:

(1'')   QS (Sebastian, PT) & PT = Bologna at 2 AM.

('PT' is used as a marker indicating a spatio-temporal zone).

If the above analysis is satisfactory, I have shown how the problem of variable poliadicity can be solved without postulating the existence of events. Clearly, I have not tried to perform anything as grandiose as Davidson's semantic project. If he were successful, there is no doubt that his solution, with its Tarskian underpinnings, would have been much superior to mine. I think, however, that he did not succeed, and thus there is a place for more modest undertakings, i.e., logical analyses of ordinary language sentences showing how the inferences which we consider intuitively right are logically justified.

III

Our world is a spatio-temporal continuum. Thus if events exist out there they must take up space. This, indeed, is what Davidson believes. He claims that events have spatial locations, saying that "the location of the event at a moment is the location of the smallest part of the substance a change in which is identical with the event" (IOE, p. 228). This definition can be understood in three ways.

(1) The last clause may be understood as identifying a certain *substance*. The definition would then be, "the location of the event x is the location of the smallest part of y (when y is the substance whose change x is)." But this is surely nonsense, and Davidson could not have meant it. What part of y is the smallest part of y? Its tiniest electron?

(2) The last clause may be understood as identifying a certain spatio-temporal part z of the substance y, i.e., that part whose change *is* the event x. I take it that Davidson would not identify the event x with z itself, because this will amount to saying that there are *no* events (they would be merely parts of objects). Also, x cannot be identical with z because several distinct events can occur in z. (Davidson's own example for this, in LFA, pp. 116-117, is that "during exactly the same time interval John catches cold, swims the Hellespont, and counts his blessings.") Therefore, the definition intended by Davidson must be, "the location of the event x is the location of z (when z is the smallest part of y which can host x)." But this is both baffling and uninformative. The definition is baffling because it requires that several real entities (the object z, the event x, and possibly other events) have exactly the same location and yet be nonidentical. Moreover, we are asked to believe that x and z, which are at the same place, cannot causally interact according to any known law of physics. This is, to say the least, very suspicious. Real entities compete for place and physically interact. Secondly, the definition is hightly uninformative. To say that the location of x is at the smallest part of y which can host x is to say that x is located where x is located. But this is a mere tautology. It evades the real difficulty, i.e., how to identify changes with events. What changes, in which objects, are identical with the coronation of Queen Elizabeth, or with her marriage? Are the changes in my nervous system part of the event of my raising my arm? Changes in what objects (air molecules? oceans? the sun?) constitute the event, A Drop of Two Degrees in the Temperature?

(3) Perhaps the above definition can be made more informative by substituting 'is necessary for' for 'is identical with.' The definition will then be, "the location of the event x is the location of the smallest spatio-temporal part of the world whose change is necessary for x to occur." But this

definition is useless. If physical necessity is here meant, the event of my raising my arm is located (*inter alia*) in the bodies of my parents, certain changes in which were necessary for my existence and, hence, for my raising my arm. In fact, it is a law of physics that every change necessarily brings about changes all over the world. Thus the location of all events is identical, i.e., the entire universe throughout time. On the other hand, if logical necessity is here meant, the location of all events is again identical, i.e., nowhere, since *no* actual change is logically necessary for any other (only *types* of events can stand in logical relations).

There is one example which Davidson brings in order to elucidate his view and demonstrate its feasibility. But this example only helps to confuse the issue even further. Davidson quotes a passage from the *Scientific American* in which a seismologist writing about explosions and other seismic events mentions the *location* of such events, and of distances measured *from* them. However, when the seismologist tells us that "a seismic event can be located" with great accuracy what he means is that *the starting point* of this event can be accurately located. Using this sense of 'location,' one may say that John's house was destroyed by an earthquake located some fifty miles away from it. As long as this peculiar use of words is clearly understood, there is nothing wrong with it. But Davidson could ill afford to use it for his ontological purposes. Is the event of raising my hand located in my brain? Could the event which destroyed John's house be located fifty miles away from the house? Is it true that a soldier fighting in Vietnam is not *in* the war at all, since he is not at the time and place where this war has originated? The idea is preposterous. I conclude that Davidson has not given any definite sense to the expression, 'the location of an event,' and has failed to give an argument for regarding events as real constituents of this world.

Events, I believe, do not exist, and certainly do not exist in space. The very idea that events occupy space is extremely strange. Let us suppose that we have succeeded in identifying the location of my raising my arm as the area of this arm at that time. Does this *event* contain, then, bones, muscles, and blood vessels? If events are real constituents of the world, do they have weight, mass, or atomic structure? We can give the dates of World War II, but can those philosophers who wish to "identify events with space-time zones" (E.J. Lemmon in his comment on LFA, p. 99) also specify its size and volume? True, very often we say things like, 'the meeting is held in room 204' and thus seem to assign a location to an event. But a close scrutiny reveals the difference between this statement and genuine spatio-temporal determinations. If there is a table in room 204 we can say which part of the room is filled up by this table. But if there is a meeting taking place in room 204, it would be ridiculous to ask which part of the room is completely filled by the meeting. Does it encompass the chairman's shoes, his nose, or his kidneys? The only way out of this nonsense is to construe 'the meeting is in room 204' as saying that the *people* participating in the meeting are in room 204. Events do not exist and do not occupy chunks of space-time, but individuals which take part in them certainly do.

But how can individuals take part in events, if events do not exist? There is an easy answer: Statements about events and changes in (three-dimensional) individuals can be eliminated in favour of statements about the properties of four-dimensional individuals. It sounds paradoxical, but it is literally true that we need not acknowledge the existence of events because statements about them can be replaced by statements about events. However, the last occurrence of the term 'event' is, of course, not the ordinary language term used by Davidson, but the term 'event' as used in relativity theory contexts, i.e., areas in the four-dimensional continuum.

The Hebrew University of Jerusalem

NOTE

[1] Davidson's articles referred to in this paper (using the following abbreviations) are:
(LFA) "The Logical Form of Action Sentences," in *The Logic of Decision and Action*, ed. N. Rescher, Pittsburgh, University of Pittsburgh Press, 1967, pp. 81-95, 115-120.
(CR) "Causal Relations," *Journal of Philosophy* 64 (1967): 691-703.
(IOE) "The Individuation of Events," in *Essays in Honor of Carl G. Hempel*, ed. N. Rescher, Dordrecht, Reidel, 1969, pp. 216-234.
(EEE) "Eternal vs. Ephemeral Events," *Noûs* 5 (1971): 335-349.
(This is *not* a complete list of Davidson's writings on this subject.)

ELAZAR WEINRYB

DESCRIPTIONS OF ACTIONS AND
THEIR PLACE IN HISTORY

I

It is generally accepted that the word "history" has a two-fold meaning. On the one hand, it refers to the course of past events which historians study. On the other hand, we use it to denote the written accounts of these events, namely, the products of historical inquiry. Philosophy of history which deals with history in the former sense is sometimes called "speculative," while philosophy of history in the latter sense is called "analytical" or "critical."

There are some philosophers — it would be convenient to call them "Collingwoodians"[1] — who think that the objects of historical study are not mere events, but rather *human actions*. Collingwood himself wrote:

He [the historian] is investigating not mere events (...) but actions...He must always remember that the event was an action, and that his main task is to think himself into this action, to discern the thought of its agent.[2]

One of the two definitions by which Walsh tried to distinguish the above-mentioned meanings of "history," characterizes it as the "totality of past human actions."[3] Dray is certainly also a Collingwoodian. He says:

[T]he objects of historical study are fundamentally different from those, for example, of the natural sciences, because they are actions of beings like ourselves.[4]

Now it would only be reasonable to suppose that this nature of the historical subject-matter would be reflected in what historians do. Granting that they try to provide descriptions, explanations and, perhaps, interpretations, if the Collingwoodian standpoint is accepted, it must be admitted that the historian's main task is to describe, explain and interpret past human actions. The questions to be posed now are, therefore, whether descriptions and explanations of actions are essentially different from descriptions and explanations of events which are not actions, and how the supposed distinguishing characteristics of descriptions and explanations of actions affect the writing of history.

97

Yirmiahu Yovel (ed.), Philosophy of History and Action, 97–111. All Rights Reserved.
Copyright © 1978 by D. Reidel Publishing Company, Dordrecht, Holland.

The Collingwoodian view is that history is an inquiry *sui generis*, and its products are radically different from the products of other kinds of inquiry just because they deal with human actions. The Collingwoodians usually approach the problem of the uniqueness of history *via* explanation: the occurrence of action explanations is the characteristic feature of history. But obviously, in order to supply an action explanation the historian always needs an action description as an *explanandum*. Collingwood himself even thought that the adequate action description would certainly serve as its appropriate explanation. This is what is meant by his famous words: "|w|hen he |the historian| knows what happened, he already knows why it happened."[5] The Collingwoodians acknowledge the fact that what the historian has as his datum is not always an action description. But their point becomes especially clear when they argue, that even if the initially given description does not appear to be an action description, the historian is expected to re-describe the event in terms of human actions. Dray remarked that events such as the spread of European civilization are normally explained in a 'piecemeal' fashion which involves the detailed examination of the activities of individuals and groups.[6]

In this paper some aspects of action descriptions will be examined and conclusions will be drawn from these findings in respect of the nature of history (in the analytical sense of the term).

II

It often happens that by doing certain things we bring about other things. Brutus stabbed Caesar, and by stabbing him he brought about Caesar's death. If this is true, then both

> Brutus stabbed Caesar.

and

> Brutus killed Caesar.

are true descriptions of what Brutus did. It seems that Caesar's death was an effect of Brutus' stabbing of Caesar. In "Brutus killed Caesar" we "puff out," so to speak, the act of stabbing to include one of its effects, namely, the death of Caesar. On the other hand, we may "squeeze down" the action to include only the movement of Brutus' hand. This feature of our language of action descriptions, whereby a man's action can be described as narrowly or broadly as we please, has been called by Joel Feinberg "the accordion effect."[7] However, my point of departure will be the interesting discussion of this phenomenon in a paper by Donald Davidson.[8]

In order to explain what exactly is involved in the accordion effect I shall employ a useful distinction made by von Wright. According to him, the thing done is the *result* of an action, and the thing brought about is the *consequence* of the action.[9] If A opens a window, then the window opening is the result of A's action. The connection between the action and its result is described by von Wright as intrinsic, logical. That the result occurs or materializes is a necessary condition for the truth of the action description. Had the window ultimately not opened, it would not be true to say that A opened it. At most he tried to open it. His attempt consists of some actions, but not of that action of which "opening the window by A" is a true description. On the other hand, a consequence of an action is an effect of its result.[10] A change in the indoor temperature is a consequence of the act of opening the window, when it is caused by the fact that the window opens. By the same token, Caesar's being stabbed was the result of the action described by "Brutus stabbed Caesar." The death of Caesar was the effect of his being stabbed and a consequence of Brutus' act of stabbing Caesar. Thus, *x is an effect of y* is a relation between events; *x is the result of y* and *x is a consequence of y* are relations between events and actions.

The accordion effect may now be described in the following linguistic rules:

(a) Given a description D_1 of action x of which r is the result and s is a consequence (i.e., r is a cause of s), it is possible to formulate a description D_2 of action y such that s will be the result of y.

(b) Given a description D_1 of action x of which r_1 is the result, it is possible to formulate a description D_2, of action y, such that r_1 will be a consequence of y (the result r_2 of y is a cause of r_1).

As far as I can see, this formulation of the accordion effect thesis expresses Davidson's view in the technical terms of von Wright. Feinberg spoke of squeezing down and stretching out the action itself, but this way of speaking implies that the described action is always one and the same. I think that this view is mistaken. The term "accordion" will be used here for denoting a stretch of events and the question whether or not all these events can be identified as a single action is for the moment left open. By following rule (a) a description which covers a larger stretch of events is added to a given set of descriptions. Rule (b) authorizes the introduction of a description which covers a smaller stretch of events. Rule (a) is, thus, a rule for puffing or pulling out the accordion and rule (b) for pressing or squeezing down the instrument.

A question may now be raised: are there any limits for the puffing out and squeezing down of accordions? Of course, only action descriptions may be added to a given action description, and only such descriptions that are true of what the agent did. It is now widely held that pressing down has such limit. There are actions whose results are not the consequences of other actions. These are those actions which we do not perform by doing something else. They were called "basic actions" by Danto[11] and "primitive actions" by Davidson.[12] The latter suggests that primitive actions are only and always bodily movements, those actions which do not involve any events beyond our skins. Such movements are, according to him, necessary conditions for attributing agency. Unless there is a primitive action at the limit of squeezing down the accordion, we will not have the accordion effect of agency.

However, what Davidson has to say on the limits of the puffing out is but disappointing. He says, in fact, that "the possibilities for expansion are without clear limit."[13] Of course, "without clear limit" does not mean "limitless." But he also says that "once he [the agent] has done one thing (...) each consequence presents us with a deed."[14] (The term "deed" is here vague; I assume that it means "action.") In other words, all the effects of our actions are actions; or more accurately: every event (or state of affairs) which is a consequence of what is an action under one action description, is a result of what is an action under another action description.

The usual objection to such unqualified expansion of accordions is raised by pointing to those cases in which A causes x to happen by getting B to do x.[15] And this objection is sometimes rejected as irrelevant, because in these cases, if B does x intentiallly, then transitivity of causality also breaks down. To support this view, the legal principle is cited that intentional action negates, counteracts, causal connexion. Hart and Honoré, who state and explicate this principle, suggest at various places in their book that the methods of determining questions of causation in history are not unlike the methods employed in law.[16] The role of the historian thus is similar in important respects to the role of the lawyer and the judge. This has been taken by Dray to mean that free will cuts causal chains in history, as in law. [17] However, Hart and Honoré made an important distinction which might not have received due attention from Dray. They distinguished between *attributive* and *explanatory* uses of causal terminology. [18] In legal contexts the use is primarily attributive. In history, it seems to me, the use is principally explanatory. The historian does not respect the principle that free will counteracts causal connexion, and this is so because the explanatory use of causal terminology does not necessitate adherence to this principle. So in history, at least, this principle cannot be used as a criterion for limiting the expansion of accordions.

III

One mark of agency is, according to Davidson, the accordion effect. But he suggests another mark as well:

A person is an agent of an event if, and only if, there is a description of what he did that makes true a sentence that says he did it intentionally. [19]

He maintains that it is possible to supply different descriptions of the same action, and that no event is an action unless there is at least one description under which the action is intentional. Thus

Oedipus killed the old man who stood in his way.

is a description of an action which is identical with the action described by

Oedipus killed his father.

but only according to the former description was the act of Oedipus intentional. The existence of this description is a sign that what is described by the latter description is also an action.

When this criterion of agency is combined with the criterion of the accordion effect something very interesting results. Davidson argues that the different descriptions associated with the same accordion (i.e., those descriptions which are added to a given action description according to rules (a) and (b) and are true of what the agent does) correspond to a single action, which is nothing but the bodily movement, that is to say, the primitive action which is at the limit of squeezing the accordion. These descriptions are only different descriptions of the same action. The differences are between aspects of descriptions, not between aspects of actions.

When we take this Identiy Thesis [20] into account, the following explication of the concept of action results:

An event is an action if, and only if, (a) under some descriptions it is a bodily movement, and (b) under some descriptions it is intentional.

Intentionality of actions does not serve, in this view, as a criterion for the limits of puffing out the accordion. We may trace the consequences of what an agent does indefinitely into the future, and all these consequences may be described as his actions, though not as his intentional actions.

IV

I think that the Identity Thesis of Actions is mistaken, in so far as it means that different descriptions which pertain to the same accordion are always of the same action. Davidson's argument for this Thesis presupposes the following dilemma: any two descriptions which pertain to the same accordion are either descriptions of the same event or descriptions of wholly distinct actions. On the first horn of the dilemma the only possibility is that both descriptions are of the same primitive action, for otherwise they would be of events which have different space-time zones, and therefore cannot be identical (according to what seems a plausible necessary condition for event-identity). From the second horn — that we have here two actions — it follows that any given accordion consists of a multitude of distinct actions, the number of which increases with the puffing out of the accordion. This seems to Davidson to be incompatible with the normal approach to responsibility. I have some doubts on this point. But I will concentrate my criticism upon the argument which Davidson adduces in favour of the Identity Thesis. Using the example of Queen Gertrude who poured poison into the ear of Hamlet's father, he supplies the following premises:

(1)   The moving of her hand by the Queen on that occasion was identical with her doing something that caused the death of the King.

(2)   Doing something that causes a death is identical with causing a death.

(3)   There is no distinction to be made between causing the death of a
         person and killing him.

From these he infers:

(4)   The moving of her hand by the Queen is identical with the killing
         of the King by the Queen.[21]

In premise (1) there is an analysis of the killing in terms of event causality.
The result of the moving of her hand by the Queen is said to be the cause of
the King's death. Premise (2) equates what is described in language of event
causality with something described in terms of agent causality. For the
description "causing a death" is usually obtained from sentences of the form
"A caused the death of B" which is the standard form of attributing
causality to agents. Moreover, only when "causing a death" is thus
obtained, does premise (3) become plausible. It seems to me therefore that
by translating event causality into agent causality, Davidson subtly begs the
question. For formulations in terms of agent causality are obviously not
susceptible to the fine distinctions available by analysis of agency in terms of
event causality.

There is, however, a way of escape from the horns of this dilemma. It is
possible for one event, e, to be part of another event, f; in that case e and f
are neither identical nor wholly distinct. The relation between them is the
part–whole relation. I do not see why we cannot say that

> Brutus stabbed Caesar.

described an event which is part of the event described by

> Brutus killed Caesar.

The space-time zone of the latter event includes that of the former as its
parts. Understandably, Brutus could not be responsible for two actions, the
stabbing and the killing, but only for one: the killing which included the
stabbing as its part. Had Caesar remained alive after the events of March
15, 44 B.C., Brutus would have been responsible only for stabbing Caesar.

V

Davidson himself confesses that his view is surprising.[22] This, of course, does not disqualify it. But if it is counterintuitive, and if there is a more plausible solution, we would rightly prefer the latter.

Von Wright's insight has been that the result of an action is intrinsically related to the action. The description

A opened the window.

is a description of the window opening as much as it is a description of some movements of A's body. Descriptions of events are descriptions of what happens to the objects which are involved in these events. That actions are events seems to me undeniable. Action descriptions give thus account of what happens to the objects involved in those actions, and unless the action in question is primitive, it always involves a change in the state of an object, be it a window or Caesar. Descriptions which result from puffing out an accordion do not describe just a primitive action, but also more and more consequences of that action.

One basic idea about actions is that actions are controllable. An important difference between what happens to us and what we do is that we cannot prevent the occurrence of what happens to us, whereas when we act, when we do x, we can refrain from doing x and instead do something else, y. If I spill the coffee because you push my hand, I cannot be called the agent of the spilling.[23] And this is so because in that case I cannot help spilling the coffee.

How do we control our actions? Let me use another fruitful idea of von Wright. He says that "the performance of an action is...the putting in motion of a system."[24] This means that when we act we presuppose the existence of an at least partially closed system, the behaviour of which is changed by our interference. So in order to do something, it is necessary for us to foresee what will happen to the system if we interfere with its natural course. When we act successfully, our foresight is justified to a considerable degree. It seems to me that what happens to the system is under our control, and thus an action of ours, only if it has been foreseen by us. It is within our power to make happen only those stages of the system which we are able to foresee.

Some philosophers have argued that what an agent does (in contrast to what happens to him) is what he would say he is doing when asked: "What are you doing?"[25] This awareness of what one does, which appears to these philosophers to be a necessary condition for acting, may be identified with what I call here "foresight." (Awareness is not, of course, a sufficient condition for acting because one might be aware of what happens to one.) When an agent is asked what he is doing, his answer will naturally be an action description, formulated to include a reference to as many consequences of the action as the agent pleases. First person action descriptions are governed by the rules for pulling out and pressing down of accordions, the same as those for third person action descriptions. But the agent cannot supply an action description which includes a reference to a consequence of his action unforeseen by him at the time of his acting. The limit of the agent's ability to expand an accordion is identical with the limit of his ability to foresee the behaviour of the system he sets in motion.

It seems clear to me that what I am not aware of doing is not my intentional action. It may therefore be said that actions the results of which are unforeseen consequences are unintentional actions. A says something to B, by which B is offended. This is a clear case of the accordion effect, so we may say that A offended B. We may also realize that A was not aware of the fact that his words were offensive. It is then true that A's offending B was unintentional and beyond A's control. Of course A could have been more careful in his words in the first place. But not realizing that his words would offend B, A had no reason not to utter what he wanted to say. A could not have acted otherwise had he wanted to, because he could not have wanted to do what he was not aware of.

VI

The basic idea that what happens to us is not our action because it is beyond our control may be extended to cover not only cases when, for instance, I spill the coffee because you push my hand, but even all unintentional actions. This means that unintentional actions are not really actions at all. It is true, of course, that whenever we "perform" an unintentional action there is "another action" which is intentionally done by us. Davidson's view is that the intentional action and the unintentional one are identical.[26] The action, e.g., the killing of his father by Oedipus, is unintentional under this description and intentional under another one that speaks of the killing of the offensive man. The Oedipus case is not, however, a case of the accordion effect. In sections IV and V some serious objections to Davidson's version of the Identity Thesis have been advanced in so far as this Thesis is applied to accordions. I argued that it is wrong to suppose that when a description D_2 is added to a given description D_1 according to the rule for puffing out accordions (rule (a) of sec. II), then D_1 and D_2 are of the same action. *A fortiori* D_1 and D_2 do not describe the same action when what is described by D_2 is unintentional under D_2. While in the Oedipus example both descriptions are at least of the same event, in accordions we do not even have identity of events. Unintentional consequences are nothing but effects of results (in von Wright's terminology) of intentional actions. But such unintentional consequences cannot be described as results of actions because according to such descriptions the actions would be unintentional and, as we have seen, intentionality is a necessary condition for being an action.

According to Davidson's conception an action may be intentional under one description and unintentional under another. I suggest the following terminology: we may say of certain *events*, that they are actions under some of their descriptions and mere events under others. What happened to Oedipus is such an event. It just befell him that he killed his father. The same mode of speaking is to be applied to accordions. Some descriptions may describe a series of events as intentional actions, while others, that describe longer series of events, describe them as mere processes. My point is not, however, just terminological. A serious weakness in Davidson's account of the accordion effect thesis is removed when we take foresight as a criterion for delimitation of accordion expansion.

When we speak of the accordion effect of *agency*, we must delimit the expansion to what is intentionally done; and what is intentional is in turn determined by what the agent foresees will happen as a consequence of his acting or, in other words, by what he is aware of doing.[27] We may pull an accordion out beyond the boundaries of intentionality as long as causation permits us to do so; but we will not get the accordion effect of agency.

VII

We are now in a position to answer one of the questions raised at the beginning of this paper, namely: given that historical events are human actions, to what extent does this fact determine the basic features of written history? My conclusion has been that events, or series of events, are actions only under certain descriptions. If this is so, then the mere fact that the subject-matter of historical inquiry consists of actions does not mean that historians must always supply action descriptions. It might be objected that I try to decide a philosophical issue by narrowing the meaning of the term "action," and procedure of this kind is, of course, illegitimate. My answer to this objection is that the Collingwoodians themselves use this term to denote only intentional actions. By "action" they mean only an event the appropriate explanation of which is by reasons.

If what I have said about the necessity of foresight and intentionality is right, then historical descriptions are action descriptions only if what happened is described in them as the historical agents saw it. This immediately rules out any description in terminology unknown to the agents. Alasdair MacIntyre expressed this idea very clearly by saying that "an agent can only do what he can describe" and therefore "to analyse the ideas current in a society is also to discern the limits within which action necessarily moves in that society."[28]

Does the historian always have to ask himself whether the descriptions he supplies are such that they could have been supplied, at least in principle, by the historical agents? Must he supply only descriptions which are similar to what these agents were aware of doing? Is it necessary for all historical descriptions to be couched only in the terms and concepts of the historical agents themselves? There are good reasons to believe that the answer to these questions is negative on the whole.

The accordion effect is extensively at work in history. The historian's original insight may be shown by saying of a historical hero that by doing one thing he brought about something else. In this way the importance of the personality in question can be assessed.

Skinner described many cases of expansions of accordions in the history of ideas.[29] Some historians, for instance, say of Machiavelli and Rousseau, that by writing what they did, Machiavelli laid the foundation for Marx, and Rousseau provided the philosophical justification for the totalitarian as well as the democratic national state.[30] Skinner argues that descriptions such as "Machiavelli laid the foundation for Marx" cannot be action descriptions, even though from the grammatical point of view they appear to be so, because they are not descriptions "which the agent himself could at least in principle have applied to describe and classify what he was doing."[31] Such expansions of accordions are therefore in Skinner's view meaningless. However, according to the analysis of the accordion effect sketched here we may accept much expansion of an accordion as legitimate in history, as long as we realize that the resulting descriptions need not be action descriptions. They are meaningful, but not as action descriptions.

VIII

I will now advance four reasons why I think the view that history should be an attempt to see the past as it appeared when it was present is mistaken or, at least, only very partially true; this view means, as we have seen, that the historian must, whenever it is possible, describe historical events only by action descriptions.

(1) Perspective is an essential feature of history. Danto's "Narrative Sentences" are just those written in a perspective, that is to say, in the light of what happened since the occurrence of the events described. Danto emphasized that "narrative sentences are so peculiarly related to our concept of history that analysis of them must indicate what some of the main features of that concept are."[32] Take one of his examples for a narrative sentence:

Petrarch opened the Renaissance.[33]

A historian might wish to say:

With his ascent of Mount Ventoux Petrarch opened the Renaissance.

But as Petrarch did not intentionally open the Renaissance, "his ascent of Mount Ventoux" is an action description while "his opening the Renaissance" is not. Yet such narrative sentences are typical of history. The characterization of history as an attempt to see the past as it appeared when it was present has been taken from the historian Llewellyn Woodward who observed that as far as history is really such an attempt "the idea of historical perspective is misleading."[34] Woodward seems to think that the historian is confronted with exclusive alternatives here. But he also thought that historians must know "what happened next" — in other words, they need perspective.[35]

(2) Hayek and Popper's insight was that almost all social institutions are unintended and unforeseen products of human actions, and that the function of social sciences is just to reveal the laws which govern the production of

unintended consequences.[36] In so far as historians are primarily concerned with past social life, their descriptions will not be action descriptions.

(3) The historian William Langer declared that psycho-history is the "next assignment."[37] Many historians have since come to the same conclusion. Descriptions of events in psychoanalytic terminology are, by definition, such that they would not have been recognized by the historical agents as descriptions of what they were doing.

(4) Any event description in terms of a theory or a conceptual scheme, alien to the participants of the described event, cannot be an action description. For obvious explanatory purposes the historian frequently wants to use some theoretical vocabulary for his descriptions. As such a vocabulary was almost never at the disposal of the historical agents, descriptions in its terms cannot be identified by them as describing what they did.

I conclude that the analysis of the concept of action descriptions, together with some considerations regarding the nature of history and the general aims of the historical inquiry, yield conclusions very unfavourable to the Collingwoodian views. Even if it is true that history is the "totality of past actions," this does not mean that written history contains or must only, or principally, contain action descriptions. In many cases it is in the historian's interest to supply a description under which what is done is unintentional. I argued that such descriptions are not action descriptions at all.

The Hebrew University of Jerusalem

NOTES

* Some of the ideas in this paper were included in my "Causation and Human Action in History" (unpubl. Ph.D. Thesis, Jerusalem, 1973 [in Hebrew]). I have profited from discussions with my supervisors, Prof. Y. Arieli and the late Mr. E.I.J. Poznanski.
[1] They are so called by William H. Dray, *Philosophy of History*, Englewood Cliffs, N.J., 1964, pp. 12, 14.
[2] *The Idea of History*, Oxford, 1946, p. 213.
[3] *An Introduction to Philosophy of History*, London, 1951 (3rd ed. 1967), p. 16. On p. 60 Walsh expresses some reservation, but his general outlook remains Collingwoodian through the book. There is, however, some evidence that he has changed his mind; cf. his "Colligatory

Concepts in History," in *Studies in the Nature and Teaching of History*, ed. W.H. Burston and Thompson, London, 1967.

[4] *Laws and Explanation in History*, Oxford, 1957, p. 118.

[5] *The Idea of History*, p. 214.

[6] *Laws and Explanation in History*, p. 142.

[7] "Action and Responsibility," in *Philosophy in America*, ed. Max Black, Ithaca, N.Y., 1965.

[8] "Agency," in *Agent, Action and Reason*, ed. R. Binkley, R. Bronaugh and A. Marras, Oxford, 1971.

[9] *Explanation and Understanding*, London, 1971, pp. 66-68, 87-89.

[10] *Ibid.*, p. 88.

[11] "What We Can Do," *Journal of Philosophy* 60 (1963): 435-445; "Basic Actions," *American Philosophical Quarterly* 2 (1965): 141-148.

[12] "Agency," p. 10f.

[13] *Ibid.*, p. 22.

[14] *Ibid.*, p. 16.

[15] J.E. Atwell, "The Accordion-Effect Thesis," *The Philosophical Quarterly* 19 (1969): 337-342; see Davidson, *ibid.*, p. 16, note 10.

[16] *Causation in the Law*, Oxford, 1959. The similarity of the lawyer's and the historian's causal language is indicated on pp. 2, 8, 10, 11, 21.

[17] *Philosophy of History*, p. 57f.

[18] *Causation in the Law*, p. 22f. They think, however, that in history as in law, causal terminology is used for both purposes (p. 59).

[19] "Agency," p. 7.

[20] It has been called so by Alvin I. Goldman; see his *A Theory of Human Action*, Englewood Cliffs, N.J., 1970, p. 2.

[21] "Agency," p. 22.

[22] *Ibid.*, p. 23.

[23] *Ibid.*, p. 5.

[24] *Explanation and Understanding*, p. 68.

[25] See G.E.M. Anscombe, *Intention*, 2nd ed., Oxford, 1963, pp. 44, 48; Stuart Hampshire, *Thought and Action*, London, 1959; J.L. Austin, "Three Ways of Spilling Ink," in *Philosophical Papers*, 2nd ed., Oxford, 1970, pp. 283f.

[26] "Agency," p. 7.

[27] See also von Wright, p. 89.

[28] "A Mistake about Causality in Social Science," in *Philosophy, Politics and Society* (2nd Series), ed. Peter Laslett and W.G. Runciman, Oxford, 1962, p. 59f.

[29] "Meaning and Understanding in the History of Ideas," in *History and Theory* 8 (1969): 3-53.

[30] *Ibid.*, pp. 11, 23.

[31] *Ibid.*, p. 29.

[32] *Analytical Philosophy of History*, Cambridge, 1965, p. 143.

[33] *Ibid.*, p. 169.

[34] "The Study of Contemporary History," *Journal of Contemporary History* 1 (1966): 4.

[35] *Ibid.*, p. 5.

[36] Friedrich A. von Hayek, "The Results of Human Action but not of Human Design," in *Studies in Philosophy, Politics and Economics*, London, 1967, pp. 96-105; Karl R. Popper, *The Poverty of Historicism*, London, 1961, p. 65.

[37] "The Next Assignment," *American Historical Review* 63 (1957-58): 283-304.

PART TWO

THE PHILOSOPHY OF HISTORY
FROM KANT TO SARTRE

YIRMIAHU YOVEL

KANT AND THE HISTORY OF REASON

Is rationalism compatible with the modern historical outlook? This is perhaps the most challenging problem left over by the rationalists of the Enlightenment to their modern successors. As a fair generalization it may be said, that the philosophers of the Age of Reason — starting with Descartes and following Plato — had seen reason as eternal, non-temporal, unbound by cultural and sociological factors. Even the limits of reason (when admitted) were to be understood *sub specie aeternitatis*. This led to viewing history as a contingent, empirical affair, having no rational import in itself. Whatever is *Geschichte* is thereby mere *Historie*. It consists in the simple accumulation (or recounting) of facts that, *per se*, neither disclose a rational pattern nor are relevant to the growth of rationality. Indeed, the very notion of growth in rationality could have, at best, only a quantitative but not a qualitative sense. Individual men could, indeed, become more rational, as they complied with the fixed and eternal norms of rationality which, as such, were independent of man's actual thinking and practical attitudes. But only concrete rational beings belonged to the world of becoming, whereas reason itself was pure being. It was an eternal truth — immovable, *an sich*, and without change.

The nascent historicism of the 18th century challenged this classic view. The problem was not just to admit the rational import of history, but to supply it with a systematic ground. And this suggested a re-appraisal of the nature and status of rationality. For history to have a rational significance, reason itself — so it seemed — should be construed in a way as to allow for its possible historization.

It was certainly Hegel who offered the most comprehensive (and far-reaching) theory in this respect. In essence, Hegel made the historization of reason a necessary moment of its ascent to the status of eternal truth. Seeking to explain the possibility of absolute knowledge, Hegel made it depend upon the process of the becoming of reason, and upon the dialectical *Aufhebung* of this becoming. In this way, the growth of rationality was presented as constitutive of its rational character.

115

Yirmiahu Yovel (ed.), Philosophy of History and Action, 115—132. All Rights Reserved.
Copyright © 1978 by D. Reidel Publishing Company, Dordrecht, Holland.

Even before Hegel, the conflict between rationalism and historicism has arisen within the philosophy of the Enlightenment itself, finding a most interesting expression in Kant's system. Kant was concerned, on the one hand, with the pure and transcendental forms of human reason. But, on the other hand, he did not conceive of them as fixed and ready-made but as constituted by the rational subject. In that Kant introduced what may be called his "Copernican revolution of rationality" — a revolution which affects Kant's view of the nature of reason, no less than his special doctrines of knowledge and ethics. This revolution rejected the Platonic model of reason and suggested the systematic ground that, eventually, could account for the historization of reason. In fact, Hegel's own theory relied on the same basic revolution. Reason, for Hegel, has a becoming, because it is the product of the rational subject, who constitutes himself through his historical development. And thus the anti-Platonic theory of rationality was logically necessary for Hegel's concept of a history of reason. But, on this crucial point, Hegel did not put forward an absolutely new principle; he only developed more coherently (and on a comprehensive scale) an idea that Kant already expressed implicitly and without a dialectical logic.

Against this background, it should no longer be surprising that Kant did, in effect, introduce an explicit concept of a "history of reason," a history which is itself rational (or "transcendental") and not empirical. This concept is usually overlooked or explained away by Kantian critics, who find it embarrassing. It seems to be at odds with the "pure" character of reason, and — I may add — also with Kant's theory of time. And yet the concept of the "history of reason" is genuinely Kantian. It pervades Kant's philosophy of ethics and religion; it underlies his theory of scientific revolutions and the history of philosophy; and it has its systematic roots in his meta-philosophy. The extent to which this concept is incompatible with Kant's theory of time — and has a problematic relation to *empirical* history — is an inner difficulty of the system which does not justify dismissing the concept altogether. Systematic difficulties arise also in well-established Kantian concepts, such as the "thing-in-itself" or "schematism," which no serious Kantian critic would dream of overlooking despite their problematic status.

Therefore, in the following discussion I shall accept the *prima facie* legitimacy of the concept of a history of reason and ask about it two questions, one *quid facti* and one *quid juris*. First I shall ask to what extent this concept actually functions in Kant's critical system and what are its major expressions. And, secondly, supposing that it does in fact function in the system, we must ask how the use of this concept can be *justified* in terms of Kant's own theory of reason.

I. THE HISTORY OF REASON: *QUID FACTI*

Kant's overt statements, including his official essays on history, do not exhaust the role which rational history actually plays in his philosophy. To recognize this role one must make recourse to a reconstructive analysis, reading the texts against the inner logic and necessary commitments of Kant's position, and putting together the ingredients of a philosophy of history that emerges from them. Having followed this method in a number of studies on Kant's practical philosophy,[1] I shall have to be somewhat dogmatic in this part of my paper, answering the question of *quid facti* by listing the main areas on which Kant's concept of a history of reason comes to bear.

Generally speaking, the history of reason has two main expressions in Kant: one is the history of reason reshaping the world, and the other is the history of reason becoming known and explicated to itself. The first aspect of the history of reason is mainly practical; it is the process whereby human reason imprints itself upon the actual world, reshaping its empirical organization in light of its immanent goals and interests. In this practical sense, rational history is an open-ended process, moving toward an infinitely remote ideal. The second sense of the history of reason is mainly theoretical (using "theory" in the broad sense, which includes the theory of morality as well); it is the process whereby human reason gradually explicates its latent paradigm, articulating its essential concepts, principles and interests, and bringing them to light within a coherent system. This aspect of the history of reason is in principle *finite*; it culminates in scientific revolutions, which elevate the various theoretical disciplines (logic, mathematics, physics, and, eventually, philosophy itself) to the level of valid science, and thus, in fact, abolish their history and give them a final, immutable form.

Let me elaborate a little on both aspects of the history of reason, respectively.

(1) *The History of Praxis: Reshaping the World*

The Highest Good. Kant was interested in history primarily as a moral task rather than as a cognitive object. History is the domain in which human action is supposed to create a progressive synthesis between the moral demands of reason and the actual world of experience. This synthesis should not be confined to singular acts and particular results, but should aim at the whole range of human practical experience. It thus must serve as a principle of *totalization*, whereby the basic shapes of the moral, political and cultural world are gradually transformed.

The highest totality toward which this process is oriented is called by Kant "the highest good in the world." To make coherent sense, this rational ideal should be construed as the regulative idea of history and, correspondingly, the special imperative which Kant formulates: "act to promote the highest good in the world," can properly be called the *historical* imperative. On the other hand, the rational goal of the Highest Good (the total moral end of humanity) also expresses the supreme interest of reason; and thus rational history is not only integrated into Kant's critical system, but is even related to its very architectonic.

The Philosophy of Religion. This conclusion is further corroborated by Kant's philosophy and critique of religion — which is, in fact, a latent philosophy of history. According to Kant there can be many faiths and churches but only one religion. This is the religion of reason, which the many historical faiths express in varying degrees of vagueness and empirical distortion. The one true religion is basically identical with Kant's moral theory — especially with that part which sets the goal of establishing a moral *totality*. The history of religion is thus a latent mode of the history of reason in two respects. On the one hand it is the process in which the rational principle of morality is gradually breaking through the diverse historical creeds, until it attains clear explication as a pure system of practical reason. But, on the other hand, even after the true nature of religion is known in theory, the task of rational religion is not done, but still lies ahead in future history. This task is to establish the "kingdom of God on earth" — a metaphor expressing the secular moral ideal contained in the Highest Good. In this way the history of religion is a moment of rational history in general, moving to the same moral totality.

The "Cunning of Nature." Alongside this view — in a way as its rival — we find Kant's well-known theory of the dialectic of political history. According to this theory, nature itself — even without the rational will — is working according to a hidden design, bringing about political progress by means of violence and passion. It is through wars, exploitation and calculated self-interest that new political institutions (domestic and international) are created, which in effect serve the goals of reason and freedom. This is the main thesis of Kant's explicit essays on history, such as the *Idea for a Universal History* and *Perpetual Peace*, and it also occurs in Par. 83 of the *Critique of Judgement*. Because these texts put forward a principle of blind, natural teleology — which may be called the "cunning of nature" — they are usually interpreted as dogmatic and therefore as incompatible with Kant's critical philosophy. This is a strong claim which, however, calls for three important modifications. First, the principle of the cunning of nature undergoes in the *Critique of Judgement* a radical transformation in its methodological status. It is now conceived only as a "reflective" teleological judgement, and thus it becomes compatible with the demands of a critique of reason. A reflective judgement is distinguished by Kant from a constitutive one, in that it has no ontological import. Although certain types of phenomena — like living organisms, or the development of culture — cannot be fully intelligible unless we subsume their mechanical explanations under a second-degree order of teleology, this second degree organization is necessary only subjectively — but cannot count as an objective feature of the phenomenon itself. In admitting the use of telic forms in certain types of phenomena, we do not thereby commit ourselves to the existence of an external intender, who had created these phenomena by design, nor to the ontic make-up of the object at hand. Indeed, the use of a reflective teleological judgement is not accompanied by any ontological commitment whatever, although, on certain grounds explained by the *Critique of Judgement*, it should necessarily be used. This topic is well known with respect to Kant's philosophy of living organisms; but it applies equally to his principle of natural dialectic — the one we named the Cunning of Nature.

Secondly, even as a reflective judgement, the cunning of nature applies only to a narrow aspect of the historical goal. It does not cover the whole range of historical progress, but only the external field of "legality," i.e., politics and jurisprudence. The crucial aspect of history, however, is the creation of an ethical community, defined by the quality of the *inner* attitudes of its members to each other; and with respect to this side of the ideal, the cunning of nature is irrelevant and of no avail.

Finally, ever since the Enlightenment, the cunning of nature does not enjoy an exclusive status even with respect to political progress. Once the requirements of practical reason have been clearly explicated (in Kant's own critique of reason), the political world, too, must and can be transformed by the *rational* will. At this stage of the development, the two apparently rival principles — the cunning of nature and the rational will — become complementary rather than mutually exclusive. But the rational will has the primacy in this relation, because it alone can generate genuine moral progress, and because morality has precedence over politics in Kant's theory, serving as the crux of the historical goal, of which rational politics is only the external embodiment.

(2) *The History of Theory: The Self-Explication of Reason*

The History of Philosophy. Further evidence of the genuine position held by the concept of a history of reason in Kant's system refers to the process in which human reason actualizes its theoretical potential and becomes known and explicated to itself. This includes the history of the sciences, and especially of philosophy. At the end of the *Critique of Pure Reason* Kant introduced the concept of a transcendental history of philosophy which he actually named "the history of reason." This concept is further developed in his posthumous *Lose Blätter*; in the chapter on the "Architectonic" in the *Critique of Pure Reason* itself; and in the two prefaces to this major work. Kant offered there a theory of scientific revolutions and a model of the history of philosophy which bears a striking resemblance to that of Hegel.

Kant conceives of reason as an interested or "erotic" activity moving towards a systematic explication of itself. Underlying this process is a latent paradigm (or "schema") which all philosophical systems have been gradually realizing. All the important doctrines in the history of philosophy are thereby tacit members of one systematic whole, each stressing some particular "interest of reason" and special aspects of the final pure system. This one-sidedness produces antinomies between the historical systems, leading to their subsequent breakdown. The collapse of historical systems leaves out, however, a multitude of particular concepts, principles and categories which gradually accumulate until they find a new systematic organization. According to Kant this process is finite; like the other theoretical sciences, philosophy is expected to undergo a final revolution, creating the ultimate system, which resolves the antinomies among the historical systems and finally actualizes the latent paradigm of reason in full. This revolution will for the first time constitute philosophy-as-science and bring to an end the historical process in which one can only philosophize and not yet "learn philosophy." (This is similar to Hegel's idea that the final system abolishes philosophy as the "love of knowledge" and transforms it into actual knowledge.)

To give a first-hand impression of Kant's idea of the history of reason, I shall quote a few sentences from the chapter on the "Architectonic."

Systems seem to be formed in the manner of vermin, through *generatio aequivoca*, from the mere confluence of assembled concepts, at first imperfect, and only gradually attaining to completeness.[2]

This confluence is not, however, a mere aggregate but a *latent organic system*. All historical doctrines, Kant adds,

have had their schema, as the original germ, in the *self*-development of reason alone. Hence…*they are one and all organically united in a system of human knowledge, as members of one whole* (ibid., italics added).

Hence the historicality of this process:

only after we have spent much time in the collection of materials in somewhat random fashion, *at the suggestion of an idea lying hidden in our mind*, and after we have, indeed, over a long period, assembled the materials in a merely technical manner, does it first become possible for us to discern the idea in a clearer light and to devise a whole architectonically, in accordance with the ends of reason (*KrV*, A 834/B 862, italics added).

Kant says it is "unfortunate" to have to go through this historical process but, as we shall see, we must also conceive of it as inevitable because of the *finitude* of human reason. Recognizing that our reason is finite, includes, among other things, the recognition that it must have a "becoming" of its own.

In summary, Kant presents reason as having a development and a historical goal. It gradually becomes explicated or known to itself in a progressive movement, and it is also supposed to reshape the actual world according to its precepts and practical goals, thus promoting the Highest Good. From these viewpoints, the concept of rational history not only belongs to the critical philosophy but — as the Highest Good — it is even the supreme goal around which the system is architectonically organized.

II. THE HISTORY OF REASON: *QUID JURIS*

The results we attained are somewhat surprising. They suggest, among other things, a closer affinity between Kant's philosophy of reason and that of Hegel, and they raise a question concerning Kant's own view of reason as "pure" and transcendental. Therefore, having laid down the case for the history of reason in terms of *quid facti*, I must now ask the question *quid juris*.

Since Kant did not develop his idea sufficiently, it would be too much to expect to find a fully systematic justification for it. It would be more plausible to predict that the concept of the history of reason would invoke inner antinomies in Kant's system – as I shall show later on. But it would also be an oversimplification just to dismiss the concept at the outset because of its embarrassing appearance. Instead, we must first try to find as much systematic grounds for it as we can in Kant's own theory of reason – even if these grounds are not sufficiently developed to amount to a full and coherent theory.

To construe Kant's conception of reason we have to draw on three main sources. One is Kant's discussion of the "Architectonic of human reason" – a major text for understanding his meta-philosophy. The second source is Kant's principle of the Copernican revolution, not only in its bare formulation but in the way it is actually worked out in Kant's ontology, ethics, aesthetics (the theory of the sublime), etc. This idea is central to Kant's critique of reason and includes both his re-interpretation of reason and his account of its finitude. Finally, the whole range of the Kantian corpus must count as an additional source, in so far as it is saturated with allusions to the functions, interests, tasks and even "needs" and "aspirations" of human reason. The following analysis will draw from all these sources.

In order to identify the meta-philosophical grounds in which Kant's concept of a history of reason can be anchored, we have to consider four main topics: (1) Kant's Copernican revolution in rationality (his *constitution* theory of reason); (2) the *finitude* of human reason; (3) the conception of reason as a system of *interests*; and (4) the *"architectonic" unity* of reason. All four subjects are interrelated with respect to our problem, but for the purpose of analysis I shall focus on each of them separately before bringing them together again.

(1) *The Copernican Revolution in Rationality*

Spontaneity and Subjectivity. Kant conceives of reason mainly as a spontaneous activity, not as a mere set of forms. Even the objective side of reason — its concepts, principles, etc. — must be construed as subjective functions by which the human mind (the Ego) structures itself as well as its experience. This *dynamic* conception of reason is radically different from that of Plato and, indeed, it breaks away from the whole classic view of the *logos* as fixed and independent, governing the mind and the world as a *Ding an sich*. For Kant, whatever is rational depends on the thinking subject. Reason cannot be divorced from the actual operation of thinking — or from the practical attitudes of the mind — but is formed by them while also forming them. To be sure, Kant does not mean by this the psychological process of thinking, as an empirical event, but the so-called "transcendental" functioning of the mind. But, as such, the dynamic feature of reason belongs to its very definition.

Autonomy and Constitution. This idea is closely connected with Kant's concept of autonomy and with his constitution theory of rationality. As autonomous, human reason must abide only by those universal rules which it sets up by itself, and in which it can recognize the explication of its own subjective structure. Any other attitude will be "heteronomous" and thereby non-rational. This view of autonomy is based upon Kant's constitution theory of rationality, i.e., on his Copernican revolution as it affects his view of the nature of reason itself and not only of knowledge or ethics. According to this theory, reason cannot be conceived of as a system of universal norms that subsist in themselves, but has to be seen as constituted by the human subject. The objective side of reason, as a set of principles, is thus dependent on its subjective side, that is, upon the spontaneous activity of the rational Ego, who explicates his own structure in these principles and recognizes them as his own. This model of rationality lays down the conditions by which both our subjective attitudes and the objective norms themselves can gain rational status. No set of universal norms is rational in itself — only in so far as it is constituted by the subject and can be recognized by him as such. And, correspondingly, we become rational not by complying with a system of pre-established norms, but by setting up the norms with which we comply.

In this way, the very status of rationality is not ready-made but constituted, depending on the spontaneous activity of the Ego, and this supplies a systematic ground for assigning reason a historical "becoming" of its own. This becoming must, moreover, assume a specifically historical character because of the finitude of human reason.

(2) *The Finitude of Reason*

As a critic of reason, Kant was concerned with the finitude of human reason side by side with its autonomy. Moreover, an essential aspect of the autonomy of reason is its recognition of its immanent limitations. As finite, human reason is necessarily confronted with the problem of its own historization. It is not an *intellectus archetypus* in which there is no difference between the possible and the actual. Since it is finite, reason must inevitably suffer from a gap between its (limited) potential and its actual articulations; and it thus faces the problem (or the task) of gradually closing this gap. Reason does not immediately possess the full, though limited, scope which it can in principle attain, but must be actualized in a progressive move of self-explication; and thus, again, human reason is subject to a history or a becoming of its own.

The finitude of human reason and its autonomy jointly account for the fact that Kant must admit the concept of an ascent of rationality, not as compliance with externally fixed rules, but as the *self*-explication of the human mind.

The finitude of human reason has also a direct bearing on our next topic — the interests of reason (although this issue has in Kant also an independent standing).

(3) *Reason as Interest*

Kant describes reason primarily as a system of interests. Its basic feature is teleological activity, pursuing its own "essential ends" (or, immanent tasks). This goal-oriented activity is what the "architectonic" of reason basically means. By this Kant does not mean a technical symmetry between the different parts of the system, but a dynamic harmony of interests. To say that reason is architectonic is to say that it is a system of rational interests that complement one another within an organized hierarchy. Rational activity is thus a goal-setting activity. It is directed to the attainment of ends which are not given to it from without, but are set or projected by reason itself.

This idea is best known from Kant's moral philosophy, but it is equally present in all the other branches of his system — including his definition of reason as such. In saying that reason is architectonic or teleological, Kant puts forward the autonomy of the rational interests, and lays down a necessary condition for rationality in general. Rationality cannot, by definition, be only instrumental. It does not consist in the maximization of certain desired values, whose desirability derived from sources other than reason — such as utility, passion, happiness, piety, social benefits or technological efficiency. This is for Kant the main difference between reason and what may be called mere intelligence. Intelligence is basically instrumental and pragmatic; it uses rational means in order to further ends which are accidental from the viewpoint of reason itself, since they are always taken from the outside. Reason, however, uses its instrumental means in order to further its essential, not its accidental, ends: and these essential ends are set or projected by the rational subject.

We may express the above by saying that reason is a *self-sufficient* teleological system. It sets forth its immanent tasks while serving as a means for attaining them. Moreover, reason is supposed to be sufficient onto itself even in so far as the motivational power is concerned. Again, this idea is best expressed in Kant's theory of action, but also applies to reason in general. In saying that reason can be "practical," Kant means, among other things, that it is endowed with sufficient motivational power to realize its own prescriptions regardless of any other interests. Since it is fundamentally an *interest*, reason can generate the motivating principle needed for its actualization.

Logos and eros. By defining reason in terms of its interests and immanent tasks Kant ascribes to reason not only a dynamic nature but, indeed, an "erotic" aspect. Kantian reason is not mere *logos*, but a fusion of Plato's *logos* and *eros*. Plato drew a fundamental distinction between the rational and the motivational aspect of the mind. Reason in itself is the pre-established goal of the mind to which its erotic principle aspires. Kant accepts the basis of this theory with two modifications. First, the rational goal is not prescribed in advance but rather projected, or constituted, by the activity which pursues it. And consequently, it is reason itself that has the erotic side, that is, the aspect of aspiration and becoming. This is why, in effect, as we look at the Kantian texts, we find that they are studded with expressions that amount to a real erotic glossary of words which Kant consistently uses of reason. Reason is not only endowed with "ends," "tasks" and "interests"; it also has "needs," "satisfactions," "aspirations," "strivings" and "affection"; it has a "vocation," a "destiny," a "calling" and an "appellation," and needless to say, it has "requirements," "claims" and "pretenses" — which Kant portrayed as concrete attitudes. Many of these expressions should certainly be understood as metaphors; but metaphors for what? The answer, I suggest, is that they are metaphoric expressions of certain aspects of the *interest* of reason which, in itself, is no longer a metaphor in the same sense[3] but rather a systematic concept. It belongs to Kant's meta-philosophical account of the architectonic of reason and thus supplies a ground for assigning reason a processuality of its own and, eventually, a history.

Despite the clear evidence, Kantian scholarship has tended to disregard the "interested" character of reason — perhaps because of its anti-historical bias. It is symptomatic that even a serious lexicographer like Rudolf Eisler, in his well-known *Kant-Lexikon*, virtually passed over the abundant wealth of dynamic (or, erotic) predicates which Kant attaches to reason; and even the crucial concept of *Interesse der Vernunft* is mentioned by him in extreme brevity, almost as something to get rid of. (By contrast, the computarized *Kant-Index* started by G. Martin renders the number of occurrences of "interest" in Kant's works as over 700, many of which have reference to reason.) Eisler was so hasty to do away with the entry on *Interesse der Vernunft* that he did not even quote the occurrence of this term in such central chapters as the "Antinomies" and "The Primacy of Pure Practical Reason."

The necessary relation between interest and reason is made unmistakably explicit when Kant says that an interest "can never be attributed to a being which lacks reason."[4] An interest is not a mere impulse but the consciousness of an impulse and the ability to serve and promote it by taking one's reflective distance from it. In this sense, an interest is fundamentally a rational phenomenon pertaining only to rational beings. But interests can either be autonomous or heteronomous according to the origin of their goals. A sensuous interest is heteronomous, in that it uses the mediation of reason to promote ends which are accidental to reason;

whereas a proper interest of reason is directed towards the promotion of rationality itself, i.e., to an essential end of reason.

At this point we should relate the interested character of reason to the foregoing points, i.e., the finitude of reason and its subjective constitution. These two points give the idea of the architectonic, as a teleology of reason, a distinctively Kantian sense.

First, we have seen that Kant ascribes interests only to rational beings. But, equally, he says that only finite beings have interests (*KpV,* 79/82), thus restricting the concept of interest to finite rational beings — Kant's typical characterization of man. It is because we are finite that our rationality assumes an interested character. Reason sets itself its immanent goals, not as actually accomplished but in the form of a lack or a privation, and makes the pursuit of these goals a rational requirement in itself. This point also introduces a distinction between an "interest" of reason and an "end" of reason. Until now we have used these concepts interchangeably, but now their difference has to be stated. The concept of end does not necessarily indicate a lack or a privation. It is a teleological concept, whose function is retained even after it has been actualized. The teleological form is absorbed into the final product — say, the system of reason — and preserved in its subsisting organization. Therefore, had we been infinite creatures, in whom the archetypal model of rationality is immediately realized in full, we would still have retained the teleological form of our reason. An interest, on the other hand, is related to the *gap* that exists between the abstract goal and its actuality, between the archetypal model of rationality latent in our minds and its full explication. In this way, the finitude of reason sheds further light on what we called the erotic aspect of reason, explaining both its motivational principle[5] and its indispensable historization.

Secondly, as "interest" has to be understood with respect to finitude, so "essential ends of reason" must be conceived in relation to its autonomy. By the Copernican revolution it is clear that the immanent goals of reason must be understood as projected by the rational subject (who explicates his own structure in them), and not as merely discovered or assumed by him, as ready-made goals. Earlier philosophers also spoke of inherent ends and immanent rational goals, but they gave them a "dogmatic" status. An immanent rational goal by definition indicates that it should be pursued for its own sake. But who assigns it this value-status, as something to be pursued *per se*? According to Kant's theory of rationality, the answer must again be: the human subject, as he explicates his own subjective structure. One cannot coherently say that one ought to pursue a goal for its own sake but that this attitude itself is somehow prescribed to us from without. In this case we will not pursue the goal for its own sake but for the sake of satisfying whoever prescribed this attitude to us. In this way, Kant's constitution theory of rationality affects his interpretation of the old notion of inherent ends. Strictly speaking, there are no inherent ends if by this we mean that the end actually inheres in an object as a *Ding an sich*. There certainly are ends which are teleologically sufficient, but not because they are such in themselves, but because they are constituted (or projected) as such by the rational subject who envisages them. If reason itself is subjectively constituted, so are its values and final ends.

(4) *The Architectonic Unity of Reason*

What are the specific interests of reason? Kant distinguishes between two types of rational interests which may be called "regional" and "cross-regional." All these interests are modes of pursuing rationality for its own sake, not for the sake of extraneous values. The regional interests correspond to the specific uses of reason – in knowledge, moral actions (and also in aesthetics). The cross-regional interests are at work in all the regions, laying down further rational requirements. These are, for instance, the *critical* interest of reason (cutting through all the regions); the *metaphysical* interest of reason (which operates in ethics as well); its interest in *totalization* (which operates in the various "Dialectics" of the system); and, finally, the *architectonic* interest of reason, which seeks the harmonious unity of all the others. Kant accepts as a first postulate that reason can achieve systematic unity by its ideal "schema." All its interests are, in principle, harmonizable, in subordination to a supreme end which, however, does not abolish their respective autonomy.[6]

In so far as the different interests of reason have not attained full explication, they may produce conflicts and antinomies – as the history of philosophy (as well as moral history) had shown. But all are mutually compatible in principle and, therefore, the supreme architectonic end of reason is to actualize and bring to light its fundamental unity. It is precisely in this way that Kant accounts for the birth of his own critical system and for the philosophical programme which underlies it. Kant found an unresolved antinomy between the metaphysical and the critical interests of reason which took the form of the opposition between dogmatic rationalism and sceptical empiricism; and his major problem in the *Critiques* is to resolve this antinomy, creating a critical metaphysics that could, finally, count as science. In this Kant believes that his system will bring the whole history of reason to an end — in the theoretical sense — and thus abolish its historicality. But in so doing it will also have to harmonize the cognitive and the practical interests of reason — a result attained in Kant's doctrine of the Primacy of Pure Practical Reason.

Even without elaborating this point to its full scope, we already see that the historicality of reason becomes inevitable from the viewpoint of the architectonic unity of reason — even though on the other hand, when the unity is finally achieved, the history of reason is transcended. This might seem to be a proto-Hegelian idea, did it not have a typically Kantian corollary. According to the Primacy of Pure Practical Reason, even after the history of theory has been consummated, the history of *praxis* is still open. The supreme interest of reason — under which the whole system of reason is subsumed — is the creation of the moral totality, named the Highest Good; and this is an infinitely remote utopia, defining the perspective of future history. In this way, the architectonic unity of reason, when attained, brings the history of theory to a close, while opening an infinite perspective for the history of *praxis*.

THE HISTORICAL ANTINOMY

Having shown the role which Kant's concept of the history of reason plays in both his substantive and his meta-philosophical doctrine, I shall now indicate its major difficulties. I might call them the "historical antinomy" and the "problem of historical schematism," respectively.

The historical antinomy is produced in relation to Kant's theory of time. For reason to be a historical principle it must be embodied in actual time. Yet time, according to Kant's Transcendental Aesthetics, is merely a "form of intuition" that cannot apply to reason at all, only to empirical data categorized by the forms of the understanding. Both theories, however, are necessary for Kant's philosophy to be what it is. They both stem from Kantian presuppositions, the denial of which would incur an intolerable systematic price. For this reason, in showing that the concept of history of reason is indispensable to Kant's theory, I have not at all shown that it is

ultimately coherent. Quite the contrary, despite its logical roots in one part
of Kant's philosophy, it stands in obvious incompatibility with another
essential part of his philosophy, i.e., the theory of time.

However, asserting the existence of an antinomy implies that both
principes are equally necessary to Kant; and this was all I wished to do (and
all that a reconstructive analysis of the text can yield). There can, to be sure,
be made a distinction between processuality and time — as earlier
philosophers have distinguished between *duratio* and *tempus*. Using this
device one might say that Kant must admit of *duratio* in reason but not
necessarily of *tempus*. Yet this solution seems to me to be much beyond
what can be attributed to Kant without stretching his theory too far.

The second difficulty does not constitute an antinomy but an
unbridgeable *dualism*. Although Kant must admit of a non-empirical history
of reason he cannot explain its relation to *empirical* history. Being finite, and
being related to thinking subjects, reason is operating "in" and "through"
empirical creatures, all of whom participate in the world of experience.
Human reason does not have a history which is independent of Plato,
Descartes or even Robespierre; it is carried out by concrete men and is
supposed — in the field of *praxis* — to affect the organization of the
empirical world. How can a bridge be built between the history of reason
and empirical history? I think that Kant has no sufficient answer (and
cannot have one). But this, again, is no justification to disregard the genuine
place which rational history has in his system. Had we dismissed as
illegitimate all the concepts that cause Kant trouble — or even only those
related to his dualism — we would, indeed, not have much left.

KANT AND HEGEL

Finally, since my discussion of Kant has brought to light many similarities
between his theory and Hegel, I wish to conclude by pointing out the main
differences.

It goes without saying, that Kant's conception is only rudimentary with
respect to Hegel's, and that Kant did not admit of a dialectical logic as a
way to reconcile rationality and empirical history. This latter point
accounts, I think, for the fundamental dualism in Kant's position, which led
most of his critics to opt for pure reason and dismiss its history. In a sense,
if a choice has to be made, I think they have made the right one; but I

contest that such a choice is necessary. As long as we deal with interpretation, a better and more faithful method is, I think, to show the inner difficulties without resolving them in a one-sided way. These difficulties arise from the fact that Kant, contrary to Hegel, did not view the history of reason as necessarily mediated by empirical history. Hegel, indeed, saw reason as constituted not by the pure Ego in his transcendental history, but by the concrete subject immersed in the *empirical* process of his historization. Therefore, whereas for Kant empirical history is a challenge and a difficulty vis-à-vis the history of reason, for Hegel empirical history is the medium (or, the "moment") in which alone the history of reason can take place.

This also explains the second major difference. For both philosophers the history of reason implies it becoming explicated and known to itself. Yet the self-explication of reason applies in Kant only to the subject, not to the object; whereas in Hegel it is equally the self-explication of both, including the object (the world, the absolute) who actualizes his rationality and becomes self-conscious in history. Kant could not accept this daring view, among other things, because he rejected the dialectical logic that underlies it. Therefore, he viewed reason only as belonging to the subject, and the history of reason was for him the self-explication of the subject alone who, subsequently, imprints his rational forms upon the object as well rather than explicating them from the object itself.

It may well be that Hegel presented not only a more comprehensive and developed theory, but also a more coherent one. Yet Hegel achieved this result by a number of unacceptable presuppositions, especially that reason was infinite and had even actualized itself in history. For this reason, his more coherent theory is attained at the price of being, ultimately, false. Kant's great achievement seems to me to be his realization of the finitude of reason, and any further correction of his stand should be made upon the basis of this recognition, rather than upon its rejection.

Finally, however, there is a crucial presupposition which Hegel and Kant share. This is the idea that the history of reason can in principle be sublated by attaining a final, immutable system. In contrast, I think that it should follow from the "erotic" aspect of reason and its self-structuring activity, that rationality is an open-ended enterprise, capable of permanently transcending the forms and structures it assumes. Reason should not be equated with some latent, pure and final paradigm, that awaits explication once and for all. Rather, as the reflective articulation of our actual experience, it must be conceived, first, as embedded in all the forms of our knowledge and opinion and, secondly, as an ever self-transcending activity finding no rest in a "pure" system. The history of reason has no end, except — one might say — in the end of man himself.

The Hebrew University of Jerusalem

NOTES

[1] Completed in my *Kant and History*, Princeton University Press (in press).

[2] *Kritik der reinen Vernunft*, A 835/B 863 (henceforth: *KrV*; quoted by the pagination of the original first (A) and second (B) editions); *Critique of Pure Reason*, tr. N. Kemp-Smith, London, 1970.

[3] It might be a metaphor in a deeper sense in which the substantive "reason" itself is a metaphor, or in which such concepts as "ground" or "basis" are metaphoric. But this is a different issue altogether.

[4] *Kritik der praktischen Vernunft, Kants gesammelte Schriften*, Berlin, 1913, 5:79; *Critique of Practical Reason*, tr. L.W. Beck, New York, 1956, p. 82 (henceforth: *KpV*).

[5] See *KpV* on "The Incentives of Pure Practical Reason."

[6] This harmony is governed by the Primacy of Pure Practical Reason which makes the practical interest superior to the others. The supreme end round which the system is organized is the supreme practical end and thus, as we have remarked above, the historical ideal is placed not just within the system but in fact at its "architectonic" centre.

CHARLES TAYLOR

HEGEL'S *SITTLICHKEIT*
AND THE CRISIS OF
REPRESENTATIVE INSTITUTIONS

How can we learn from history? We can think of history as a repository of examples which illustrate the laws and regularities governing human behaviour, or the rise and fall, survival and destruction of societies. And we can study it with a view to discovering these laws, or in a less nomologically-oriented way, we can read it in order to extract maxims of effective action for ourselves. Something like this was Machiavelli's use of history.

But this way of using history cannot help us very much today. Or perhaps we might say that we are in a position to see how little help it has ever been. For we are very much aware of the unprecedented. The unprecedented nature and predicament of our civilization has been so dramatized and banalized, that we are tempted to look on the human past as lying on the other side of an irreversible mutation.

Of course the very dramatization of our unprecedented predicament, examplified in a work like Toffleer's *Future Shock* for instance, may irritate us to such a degree that we lose sight of the underlying truth. Those who talk about the flashier, more spectacular aspects of our civilization today — the tremendous growth in population, the immediate accessibility of everywhere to everywhere provided by communications technology, the growing pressure of industry on certain ecological limits — are often lamentably ignorant of history. But it remains true that these more spectacular aspects of the unprecedented have come about through more fundamental cultural mutations which have laid the basis for modern civilization.

By 'cultural mutation' I mean a change at once in social discipline, social arrangements and self-understanding which brings about a new human possibility. Examples relevant to our civilization are, for instance (1) the "inner-wordly ascesis" of the early Calvinist sects which has been very

Yirmiahu Yovel (ed.), Philosophy of History and Action, 133–154. All Rights Reserved.
Copyright © 1978 by D. Reidel Publishing Company, Dordrecht, Holland.

important in the development of modern society whether or not it was as closely and exclusively tied to the development of capitalist production as Weber thought. This brought with it an unprecedented organization and discipline of everyday secular life, along with new social forms and a new conception of the human predicament. In an important way we are still living with the outgrowth of this discipline of the everyday and secular. The Puritan sects also produced a new kind of militancy, and this was part ancestor of (2) another mutation, this one belonging to the twentieth century, the creation of an organization of dedicated revolutionaries, capable not only of overthrowing a shaky social or political order, but of taking over and remaking a society from the top down. In doing this the Bolsheviks surprised perhaps most of all themselves, and they inaugurated, without having intended to, a new genus of political system, that of a society under the tutelage of a vanguard party. This involved new social forms and disciplines bound up with a new conception of human possibilities and human aspiration. The few historical parallels which come to mind—such as the Jesuits in Paraguay—just serve to stress its unprecedented nature. (3) The bolshevik precedent has then been taken up in a number of variants which can be considered as significant mutations on their own in some cases. This is particularly evident with the Chinese revolution, but may also come to light with some new third world regimes.

The fact that modern, industrial civilization is so much the outgrowth of certain important historical mutations makes the examination of history as a repository of examples a hazardous and ultimately unrewarding project. I want to consider in this paper a pattern of developments which is more and more forced on our attention in the developed North Atlantic world. There appears to be a loosening of the disciplines and restraints on which liberal, industrial societies have relied to function in recent decades. This appears to be an important underlying cause of the present very rapid rate of price inflation, for instance. It is unlikely that inflation can be explained by such purely "economic" factors as variation in the money supply (American deficit and Euro-dollars) or sudden shifts in resource prices (the oil crisis), important as these undoubtedly are. It has a lot to do as well with an income scramble, a kind of inter-group economic Hobbesism, often bizarrely and incongrously dressed up in the most empathic rhetoric of social solidarity, that of the socialist left.

But this loosening of previously accepted disciplines can be seen in more than the current inflationary crisis; it also emerges in the pattern of "dropping out" which is becoming more frequent in advanced societies, in greater "permissiveness" of *mores*; and it goes along with a change in the images and aspirations by which people define themselves. The inflationary spiral may have a special significance only in this, that it threatens to introduce us into an accelerating and self-heeding process of breakdown; since the frustrations which exacerbate inter-group Hobbesism are increased with each disruption of the productive process, and the escalating economic scramble cannot but produce greater and greater disruptions.

Now historical analogies come readily to mind. In particular, the Hellenistic period or the Roman Empire have been cited. And it is undoubtedly instructive to think of our age in the light of these parallels. But the disciplines of the *polis*, or of republican Rome, which dissolved in these periods, are of course so utterly different from those under threat today, that only the most tentative and general lessons can be drawn. The Machiavellian use of history will very evidently yield little fruit.

But there is another use of history which becomes very germane once one has accepted the reality of cultural mutation. For the nature of this mutation is such that one can only understand what emerges from it by bringing to light how it came about. A new human possibility involves a new web of self-defining images and concepts. Man is a self-interpreting animal, in the sense that he does not become capable of sustaining a hitherto unattainable discipline or mode of life — e.g., conforming his work life to the regularities of industrial production, or maintaining certain institutions of self-government — without altering his conception of human life, of his motives, aspirations and possibilities. This is not to say, of course, that some change in "ideas" brings about a change in human possibility; just that this latter mutation, however it comes about, is accompanied by a change in self-definition as its indispensable vehicle.

But a definition of human possibilities can only be made by contrast. So that new human possibilities are essentially if not exclusively defined by the negation of what they supersede or have to overcome. The modern identity of an autonomous subject of knowledge and rational choice, capable of studying his world and himself with the disciplines of science and planning his future accordingly, can only be understood by contrast with the weaknesses and temptations of superstition, animistic thought, the abdication of responsibility to charismatic authority, which moderns attribute to their opponents and forebears and see as the standing dangers they must guard against. The revolutionary identity must similarly define itself against superstition, religion, false consciousness and the sense of inexorable fate.

In their more widespread formulations, of course, these self-definitions end up distorting and seriously misidentifying the alternatives and temptations they must guard against. But they remain defined by polemical contrast. In order to understand them more deeply, we have to recover a more faithful and discerning account of the contrast; and this must usually involve bringing to light again the historical transition in which the contrast was established. In other words, because a given set of human possibilities is sustained by a self-definition, and self-definitions essentially involve polemical contrast, historically new human possibilities carry their histories within themselves, so to speak, usually in distorted form. In order to understand them more fully, perhaps in order to resolve some dilemmas which men have encountered in living them out, we have to recover the transition which brought them into being.

And this is another use of history than as a repository of examples: the study of history as the clarification of contemporary human possibilities through their genesis. This is the Hegelian use of history one might say — although hardly in a proprietary sense since Hegel is not alone in this; not perhaps even in the sense of a paradigm, since it is certainly not a condition of this kind of learning from history that one accept a necessary and rationally-defined direction to the chain of historical transitions. But this use is Hegelian in the sense that Hegel is one of the earliest and greatest of its practitioners, and that his reflections remain of great importance and relevance today.

I

I cannot try to make good this thesis in its whole extent. But I would like to concentrate in this paper on one contemporary phenomenon which we are trying to understand with the help of history, and certain Hegelian concepts which most naturally encompass this phenomenon insofar as we can speak of it in Hegelian terms. I want to look at the fragmentation of social discipline in advanced Atlantic societies which I mentioned above; and to see it in relation to the Hegelian concepts of *Sittlichkeit* and alienation.

The notion of *Sittlichkeit* has been variously translated, as 'social ethics,' or 'objective ethics,' or just as 'ethics' (in contrast to *Moralität* — 'morality'), but all these can mislead, and I prefer to leave the word in the original. The nub of the idea is familiar enough. Men's ethical obligations are *sittlich* when they hold in virtue of a larger social existence in which men find themselves.

As against the obligations of *Moralität*, which enjoin us to realize unfulfilled and perhaps even unrealizable ideals, with *Sittlichkeit* the gap between *Sein* and *Sollen* is made up; what we are enjoined to realize already is, since we are enjoined to continue the life of a community which is already in existence.

What underlies the notion that there can be such a thing as a *sittlich* ethical obligation, and one that is even higher than the obligations of *Moralität*, is a conception of men's relation to society in which they are seen as set in a social life which is essential to their status as subjects of ethical action in the fullest sense; that outside of this community, men would not be ethical subjects, or only in the reduced form of *Moralität*. This is what underlies the Hegelian term 'substance' applied to society. This is the *sittliche Substanz* on which individuals depend. It is also what underlies Hegel's attribution to society of the status of subject, as is conveyed in a notion like *Volksgeist*. True, Hegel says that this is a "philosophic concept";[1] and it is mistaken to think of Hegel's *Volksgeister* as subjects in the same sense as individuals are subjects. But part of the sense of this term is that individuals only attain an important dimension of their existence as subjects—the ethical—by participating in a larger life, that of a community, and which in this sense can be seen as the locus of the kind of existence as attribute to subjects.

I would like to look briefly at what is involved in this cycle of ideas of ethical substance, *Sittlichkeit*, and the corresponding notion of alienation, turning later on to see what bearing it might have on our attempt to understand what we are going through today.

First, let us see why Hegel wanted to speak of a spirit which is larger than the individual. What does it mean to say that the individual is part of, inheres in, a larger life? and that he is only what he is—e.g., an ethical subject—in virtue of doing so?

These ideas appear mysterious because of the powerful hold on us of atomistic prejudices, which have been very important in modern political thought and culture. We can think that the individual is what he is in abstraction from his community only if we are thinking of him qua organism. But when we think of a human being, we do not simply mean a living organism, but a being who can think, feel, decide, be moved, respond, enter into relations with others; and all this implies a language, a related set of ways of experiencing the world, of interpreting his feelings, understanding his relation to others, to the past, the future, the absolute, and so on. It is the particular way he situates himself within this cultural world that we call his identity.

But now a language, and the related set of distinctions underlying our experience and interpretation, is something that can only grow in and be sustained by a community. In that sense, what we are as human beings, we are only in a cultural community. Perhaps, once we have fully grown up in a culture, we can leave it and still retain much of it. But this kind of case is exceptional, and in an important sense marginal. Emigrés cannot fully live their culture, and are always forced to take on something of the ways of the new society they have entered. The life of a language and culture is one whose locus is larger than that of the individual. It happens in the community. The individual possesses this culture, and hence his identity, by participating in this larger life.

When I say that a language and the related distinctions can only be sustained by a community, I am not thinking only of language as a medium of communication; so that our experience could be entirely private, and just need a public medium to be communicated from one to another. Rather the fact is that our experience is what it is, is shaped in part, by the way we interpret it; and this has a lot to do with the terms which are available to us in our culture. But there is more; many of our most important experiences would be impossible outside of society, for they relate to objects which are social. Such are, for instance, the experience of participating in a rite, or of taking part in the political life of our society, or of rejoicing at the victory of the home team, or of national mourning for a dead hero, and so on. All these experiences and emotions have objects which are essentially social, i.e., would not be outside of (this) society.

So the culture which lives in our society shapes our private experience and constitutes our public experience, which in turn interacts profoundly with the private. So that it is no extravagant proposition to say that we are what we are in virtue of participating in the larger life of our society — or at least, being immersed in it, if our relationship to it is unconscious and passive, as is often the case.

But of course Hegel is saying something more than this. For this inescapable relation to the culture of my society does not rule out the most extreme alienation. This comes about when the public experience of my society ceases to have any meaning for me.

Far from wishing to deny this possibility, Hegel was one of the first to develop a theory of alienation. The point is that the objects of public experience, rite, festival, election, etc. are not like facts of nature. For they are not entirely separable from the experience they give rise to. They are partly constituted by the ideas and interpretations which underlie them. A given social practice, like voting in the ecclesia, or in a modern election, is what it is because of a set of commonly understood ideas and meanings, by which the depositing of stones in an urn, or the marking of bits of paper, counts as the making of a social decision. These ideas about what is going on are essential to define the institution. They are essential if there is to be *voting* here, and not some quite other activity which could be carried on by putting stones in the urns.

Now these ideas are not universally acceptable or even understandable. They involve a certain view of man, society, and decision, for instance, which may seem evil or unintelligible to other societies. To take a social decision by voting implies that it is right, appropriate and intelligible to build the community decision out of a concatenation of individual decisions. In some societies, e.g., many traditional village societies throughout the world, social decisions can (could) only be taken by consensus. An atomistic decision procedure of this kind is tantamount to dissolving the social bond. Whatever else it is it could not be a *social* decision.

Thus a certain view of man and his relation to society is embedded in some of the practices and institutions of a society, so that we can think of these as expressing certain ideas. And indeed, they may be the only, or the most adequate, expression of these ideas, if the society has not developed a relatively articulate and accurate theory about itself. The ideas which underlie a certain practice and make it what it is, e.g., those which make the marking of papers the taking of a social decision, may not be spelled out adequately in propositions about man, will, society, and so on. Indeed, an adequate theoretical language may be as yet undeveloped.

In this sense we can think of the institutions and practices of a society as a kind of language in which its fundamental ideas are expressed. But what is "said" in this language is not ideas which could be in the minds of certain individuals only, they are rather common to a society, because embedded in its collective life, in practices and institutions which are of the society indivisibly. In these the spirit of the society is in a sense objectified. They are, to use Hegel's term, "objective spirit."

These institutions and practices make up the public life of a society. Certain norms are implicit in them, which they demand to be maintained and properly lived out. Because of what voting is as a concatenating procedure of social decision, certain norms about falsification, the autonomy of the individual decision, and the like, flow inescapably from it. The norms of a society's public life are the content of *Sittlichkeit*.

We can now see better what Hegel means when he speaks of the norms or ends of society as sustained by our action, and yet as already there, so that the member of society "brings them about through his activity, but as something which rather simply is."[2] For these practices and institutions are maintained only by ongoing human activity in conformity to them; and yet they are in a sense there already before this activity, and must be there, for it is only the ongoing practice which defines what the norm is our future action must seek to sustain. This is especially the case if there is as yet no theoretical formulation of the norm, as there was not in Hegel's view in the Greek city-states at their apogee. The Athenian acted "as it were, out of instinct" (*VG* 115), his *Sittlichkeit* was a "second nature." But even if there is a theory, it cannot substitute for the practice as a criterion, for it is unlikely that any formulation can entirely render what is involved in a social practice of this kind.

Societies refer to theoretical "value" formulations as their norms rather than to practices, when they are trying to make themselves over to meet an unrealized standard; e.g., they are trying to "build socialism," or become fully "democratic." But these goals are, of course, of the domain of *Moralität*. *Sittlichkeit* presupposes that the living practices are an adequate "statement" of the basic norms, although in the limit case of the modern philosophy of the state, Hegel sees the theoretical formulation as catching up. Hence we see the importance of Hegel's insistence that the end sought by the highest ethics is already realized. It means that the highest norms are to be discovered in the real, that the real is rational, and that we are to turn away from chimeric attempts to construct a new society from a blue-print.

Hegel strongly opposes those who hold

that a philosophy of state...[has]...the task of discovering and promulgating still another theory...In examining this idea and the activity in conformity with it, we might suppose that no state or constitution had ever existed in the world at all, but that nowadays...we had to start all over again from the beginning, and that the ethical world had just been waiting for such present-day projects, proofs and investigations.[3]

The happiest, unalienated life for man, which the Greeks enjoyed, is where the norms and ends expressed in the public life of a society are the most important ones by which its members define their identity as human beings. For then the institutional matrix in which they cannot help living is not felt to be foreign. Rather it is the essence, the "substance" of the self.

Thus in universal spirit each man has self-certainty, the certainty that he will find nothing other in existing reality than himself.[4]

And because this substance is sustained by the activity of the citizens, they see it as their work.

This substance is also the universal work [*Werk*], which creates itself through the action of each and all as their unity and equality, because it is Being-for-self [*Fürsichsein*], the self, the act of doing [*das Tun*] (*PhG* 314).

To live in a state of this kind is to be free. The opposition between social necessity and individual freedom disappears.

The rational is necessary as what belongs to substance, and we are free insofar as we recognize it as law and follow it as the substance of our own essence; objective and subjective will are then reconciled and form one and the same untroubled whole (*VG* 115).

But alienation arises when the goals, norms or ends which define the common practices or institutions begin to seem irrelevant or even monstrous, or when the norms are redefined so that the practices appear a travesty of them. A number of public religious practices have suffered the first fate in history; they have "gone dead" on subsequent generations, and may even be seen as irrational or blasphemous. To the extent that they remain part of the public ritual there is widespread alienation in society — we can think of contemporary societies like Spain, which remains officially Catholic while a good part of the population is rabidly anti-clerical; or communist societies, which have a public religion of atheism, even though many of their citizens believe in God.

But the democratic practices of Western society seem to be suffering something like the second fate in our time. Many people can no longer accept the legitimacy of voting and the surrounding institutions, elections, parliaments, etc., as vehicles of social decision. They have redrawn their conception of the individual's relation to society, so that the mediation and distance which any large-scale voting system produces between individual decision and social outcome seems unacceptable. Nothing can claim to be a real social decision which is not arrived at in a full and intense discussion in which all participants are fully conscious of what is at stake. Decisions made by elected representatives are branded as sham, as manipulation masquerading as consensus. With this redefinition of the norm of collective decision (that is, of a decision made *by* people, and not just for them), our present representative institutions begin to be portrayed as an imposture; and a substantial proportion of the population is alienated from them.

In either case, norms as expressed in public practices cease to hold our allegiance. They are either seen as irrelevant or are decried as usurpation. This is alienation. When this happens men have to turn elsewhere to define what is centrally important to them. Sometimes they turn to another society, for instance a smaller, more intense religious community. But another possibility, which had great historical importance in Hegel's eyes, is that they strike out on their own and define their identity as individuals. Individualism comes, as Hegel puts it in *VG*, when men cease to identify with the community's life, when they "reflect," that is, turn back on themselves, and see themselves most importantly as individuals with individual goals. This is the moment of dissolution of a *Volk* and its life.

What happens here is that the individual ceases to define his identity principally by the public experience of the society. On the contrary, the most meaningful experience, which seems to him most vital, to touch most the core of his being, is private. Public experience seems to him secondary, narrow, and parochial, merely touching a part of himself. Should that experience try to make good its claim to centrality as before, the individual enters into conflict with it and has to fight it.

This kind of shift has of course been instantiated many times in history, but the paradigm event of this kind for Hegel occurs with the break-up of the Greek city-state. Thus in the Greek *polis*, men identified themselves with its public life; its common experiences were for them the paradigm ones. Their most basic, unchallengeable values were those embodied in this public life, and hence their major duty and virtue was to continue and sustain this life. In other words, they lived fully by their *Sittlichkeit*. But the public life of each of these *poleis* was narrow and parochial. It was not in conformity with universal reason. With Socrates arises the challenge of a man who cannot agree to base his life on the parochial, on the merely given, but requires a foundation in universal reason. Socrates himself expresses a deep contradiction since he accepts the idea of *Sittlichkeit*, of laws that one should hold allegiance to; he derives this from universal reason as well. And yet because of his allegiance to reason he cannot live with the actual laws of Athens. Rather he undermines them, he corrupts the youth not to take them as final, but to question them. He has to be put to death, a death which he accepts because of his allegiance to the laws.

But now a type of man arises who cannot identify with this public life. He begins to relate principally not to the public life but to his own grasp of universal reason. The norms that he now feels compelling are quite unsubstantiated in any reality; they are ideas that go beyond the real. The reflecting individual is in the domain of *Moralität*.

Of course, even the self-conscious individual is related to some society. Men thought of themselves qua moral beings as belonging to some community, the city of men and Gods of the Stoics, the city of God of the Christians. But they saw this city as quite other than and beyond the earthly city. And the actual community of philosophers or believers in which they worked out and sustained the language by which they identified themselves was scattered and powerless. The common life on which their identity as rational or God-fearing individuals was founded was or could be very attenuated. So what was most important in a man's life was what he did or thought as an individual, not his participation in the public life of a real historical community.

The community of the wise, as that of the saints, was without external, self-subsistent existence in history. Rather, the public realm was given over to private, unjustified power. This is Hegel's usual description of the ancient period of universal empires which succeeded the city-state, particularly the Roman empire. The unity and fulfillment of *Sittlichkeit*, lost from this world, was transposed out of it into an ethereal beyond.

What then is Hegel saying with his thesis of the primacy of *Sittlichkeit*, and the related notion of the community as "ethical substance," a spiritual life in which man must take part? We can express it in three propositions, put in ascending order of contestability. First, that what is most important for man can only be attained in relation to the public life of a community, not in the private self-definition of the alienated individual. Second, this community must not be a merely partial one, e.g., a conventicle or private association, whose life is conditioned, controlled and limited by a larger society. It must be co-terminous with the minimum self-sufficient human reality, the state. The public life which expresses at least some of our important norms must be that of a state.

Thirdly, the public life of the state has this crucial importance for men because the norms and ideas it expresses are not just human inventions. On the contrary, the state expresses the Idea, the ontological structure of things. In the final analysis it is of vital importance because it is one of the indispensable ways in which man recovers his essential relation to this ontological structure, the other being in the modes of consciousness which Hegel calls "absolute spirit," and this real relation through the life of the community is essential to the completion of the return to conscious identity between man and the Absolute (which means also the Absolute's self-identity).

Obviously these three propositions are linked. The third gives the underlying ground of the first and second. If man achieves his true identity as a vehicle of cosmic spirit, and if one of the indispensable media in which this identity is expressed is the public life of his political society, then evidently, it is essential that he come to identify himself in relation to this public life. He must transcend the alienation of a private or sectarian identity, since these can never link him fully to the Absolute.

This is the complex of ideas which lies behind the Hegelian use of terms like "substance," "essence," "*Endzweck*," "*Selbstzweck*," in speaking of the community: First of all, that the set of practices and institutions which make up the public life of the community express the most important norms, most central to its members' identity, so that they are only sustained in their identity by their participation in these practices and institutions, which in their turn they perpetuate by this participation. Secondly, that the community concerned is the state, that is, a really self-sufficient community. And thirdly, that this community has this central role because it expresses the Idea, the formula of rational necessity underlying man and his world.

II

In what way do these Hegelian notions of *Sittlichkeit* and alienation help us to understand the malaise in contemporary society? Not principally, I would claim, because they enable us to see a parallel between our age and that of the Hellenistic or Roman empires. And certainly not because of the truth of Hegel's third claim, that the law state embodies the Idea, and hence is grounded ontologically. The very fact that this law state seems to be suffering break-up would have made this thesis seem implausible even to Hegel.

Rather what we can extract from Hegel's conceptual web here are two related notions: (1) that the practices and institutions of a community can be seen as expressions of certain fundamental common notions about man, society and their relation to each other, as well as in some cases expressions of the relations of man to nature, or to the sacred. This "expression" may exist alongside a "theoretical" mode of expression (or modes of expression) in some commonly accepted philosophical formulations; but it may also exist before any philosophical formulation, and may in an important sense say something more about the common ideas and values of a people than any philosophical theory, even where one exists.

(2) It is of crucial importance whether or not men define their identity at least in part by the values and ideas expressed in their common, public institutions, and by the way they are expressed there. For otherwise participation in these institutions will not be essential to their identity, and if it is not, then these institutions, and the polity they define, is likely to be in peril.

I should try to make a little clearer what is involved in the notion of "identity" as used here. A human subject is the subject of evaluation in a strong sense; that is, he not only evaluates different goal objects or potential outcomes as preferable or undesirable, but also evaluates different desires, or desired modes of life as in some way higher or lower, more or less fulfilling, more or less worthy, more or less integrated, or whatever through a host of evaluative languages which are available. A human agent is the subject of 'second-order desires' to use Harry Frankfurt's term.[5]

But contrary to the view put forward by Sartre and to those of such Anglo-Saxon philosophers of ethics like Hare, this kind of evaluation cannot be *ex nihilo*. Evaluation takes place within a horizon formed by certain paradigm actions or modes of life, or by some fundamental evaluative distinctions, some basic moral language which we think of as unchallengeable, or in some other such way. The ultimate context of such evaluation cannot be thought of as having chosen itself uncontextually.

On the contrary, it defines for each one of us our identity. Our identity is thought of as the answer to the question who we are. But it is who we are as human subjects in the fullest sense, that is, subjects of strong evaluation, which is relevant. And this is defined by what we experience as the ultimate context of our strong evaluations, our definitions of the higher and lower, more or less worthy, and so on. This can be thought of as our identity for the following reason: that outside of it we would lose our bearings altogether, and be unable to evaluate, to say any more "where we stood," to have a firm sense of what for us was a worthier or better, or praiseworthy or contemptible life.

Something is essential to our identity—say, a community, a set of institutions, loyalty to a given tradition—when we could no longer function as subjects of evaluation in the full sense if we were separated from the background of this community, these institutions, this tradition. If I say that belonging to some national group or cultural community is essential to my identity, I mean that my adherence to this national or cultural community forms part of the ultimate horizon of my evaluations; to set this adherence aside would at least partially cripple me as a subject of evaluation.

Now in this sense of identity men frequently define their identity by their common public institutions, and by the values and ideas that these express. When they cease to do so, these institutions are in danger. For the public institutions of any society require certain disciplines and sometimes sacrifices to be maintained. If men identify with them, these disciplines are gladly undertaken. But if not, they easily come to appear irksome and intolerable. Of course, men may accept certain disciplines because they judge the underlying goals and values positively, even though these do not shape their ultimate horizon of evaluation. I may obey the state, or give my allegiance to a certain polity because I judge it useful for instance, or the best available form of rough justice in present circumstances.

But this is a very fragile basis of allegiance. Not just because it is revocable; but also because in the case of certain institutional forms, more than just contingent acquiescence is required for them to function. In ancient empires, it may have been enough for the subject to accord a passive allegiance to the ruler. But in modern democratic polities much more than this is required. Contemporary institutions cannot function with just passive allegiance. If everybody obeys the law, but does not bother to vote, let alone participate more actively, a democratic polity rapidly ceases to be such; it would mutate into another form. The same would happen if people, faced with the legal obligation to vote, simply turned out in fulfillment of this obligation and cast their vote, say, for the party in power as a token of allegiance. In either case, the balance, tension — and uncertainty — required for democratic politics would disappear.

And in fact even the minimal allegiance can be threatened when it seems to go against strongly felt private or group interest; which is what we seem to be witnessing today.

My suggestion is that the present malaise in Western representative democracies can most fruitfully be seen in the language of Hegelian *Sittlichkeit* and the corresponding notion of alienation. This would mean that we understand their "stability," in the periods when they have been "stable" and unchallenged, in terms of widespread identification with the ideas and values they expressed in the manner in which they express them; and we understand the present slippage in terms of a change in identity. This would be a "philosophical" diagnosis in the sense that it involves our interpreting the underlying ideas and images of man, society, nature, etc., which are central to men's identification with the institutions in question. Just what did/do these institutions express, in virtue of which men identified with them? And hence what is threatening this identity now? This opens the way to a certain use of history to cast light on our present malaise, what we saw above as the genetic study of a present identity.

A bit of speculative meandering in this field will help illustrate what I am talking about, even if it falls lamentably short of answering the above questions. We can distinguish three modes of identity which have helped to sustain Atlantic democratic politics. One is the modern identity of man as a producer, that is, a being capable of transforming nature to suit his ends, and more, to engage in a progressively more and more far-reaching transformation. Men who see themselves this way tend to see society as a great collaborative enterprise in which human power becomes multipled many times through the combination of technology and social collaboration. There is a Marxist variant of this self-vision, in which the moving subject is the collective, social labour has society for its fundamental subject, and man is defined by his *Gattungswesen*. But in the "western" variant, the sense of control over nature which confirms the producer in this identity is meant to be at the disposal of the individual. This is one of the reasons why Western producers' societies are so consumer-oriented. Social labour is seen as a collaborative enterprise of free individuals, whose relations can be constantly shaped anew through negotiations and common decisions.

In this perspective, democratic institutions are the guarantors and part locus of this perpetual shaping of the common productive enterprise by the preferences and goals of individuals. The main concern of politics is the economy, questions of production and distribution, managing the economy fairly and towards growth. What may be eating away at this identity is the sense of doubt about the value of unlimited production and growth which is becoming more widespread in contemporary society. Or it may be as well that this self-understanding of society cannot but produce a set of continually-rising expectations on the part of individuals and groups which must encounter increasing frustration and hence engender increasing social tension and strain on the disciplines of society.

A second mode of identity which has often been intricated with the first is that defined by the main traditions of democratic thought in the West. It belongs to the dignity of man to be a fee, self-determining being, and not a mere subject. But to be such a free being is necessarily to live in a democratic polity where the citizen can determine who shall govern and on the basis of what laws through the exercise of the vote. Representative institutions on this view are essential to freedom in this sense of self-determination (not national but personal and group self-determination); and therefore have been the object of identification for people whose identity has been defined by this freedom.

Nothing is more evident than that this estimate of the value of representative institutions is under increasing attack in Western polities. Of course, this attack is founded itself on certain strands in the Western democratic tradition; most notoriously, the contributions of Rousseau and Marx. But whatever its justification, this questioning of representative institutions is one of the major forms of the contemporary malaise in Western societies.

For those who are in the radical succession of Rousseau and Marx, this is both to be welcomed and relatively easily explained. Representative democracy is in fact the façade behind which our societies have been ruled by a narrow élite, and in the nature of things will always be so. The present rejection of such institutions, of elections and Parliaments, is the inevitable product of an awakening, the inevitable maturation of the democratic movement, through time, education, agitation or prosperity, to the realization that this is so. But to those for whom these Rousseauian verities are a little less self-evident, the phenomenon will be harder to explain.

Perhaps it is that representative institutions can only seem responsive to electors when the scope of government is relatively restricted, when we expect them to decide a limited number of matters. But when society engages more and more in remaking the conditions of its own existence, and when therefore the scope of government begins to seem virtually unlimited, the number, complexity and interdependence of the issues decided takes them largely beyond the grasp of most people, and ensures that whatever the outcome, masses of citizens will feel dissatisfied and neglected. To live in an underdeveloped region of any Western polity today is to have a grievance not against God, fate, or climate, but against government and society.

Perhaps the steady escalation of individual and group expectation, mentioned in connection with the productive identity, has made it impossible to accept the relative satisfaction of demands, the relative sensitivity of representative institutions to their constituents. And this may have been exacerbated by the images of greater potency which our consciousness of technological change breeds, and the sense of greater immediacy which the electronic media generate. Nothing short of immediate and total redress seems commensurate with the powers of society and the claims of the protesters.

But perhaps, too, these factors, although present, are insufficient to explain the change which seems to be taking place in the sense of what constitutes a free, self-determining man. For the various protest movements which challenge the legitimacy of representative institutions do so in the name of another, often quite undefined, notion of more direct democracy — self-management, "participation," or whatever. Why this recurrence to the tradition of Rousseau? Is it just a screen whereby a greater reluctance to subordinate the goals of the group to the common interest dresses itself up in the "legitimating" language of democracy and freedom? Some degree of "dressing up" and rationalization there often is, without a

doubt. But this is not a sufficient explanation; for the question remains why
the reluctance to accept social discipline has grown, and why it needs just
this language to express itself. That there is more than one way of
rationalizing a breach in society's basic yardsticks of justice has been shown
by large corporations which for years have justified special tax concessions,
irresponsible pricing policies, bad labour conditions, etc. precisely on the
basis of the common interest they were violating rather than by some
alternative ideology.

To understand what is afoot in this contemporary challenge to representative institutions we have to get a clearer view of what lies behind
the rhetoric of contemporary protest. Just to set it aside as rationalization
begs all the important questions. We have to come closer to understanding
the self-interpretations, the notions of individual and society, of autonomy
and potency which underlie it.

This way of coming to grips with the present malaise of our society is an
interpretive one. It treats social inquiry as "hermeneutical."

Taking either of the above accounts of the identity underlying democratic
society as our basis, the aim would be to define more precisely the images
and ideas of man and society which were expressed in the institutions of
democratic society and with which men identified, and then to characterize
what new ideas, images and self-definitions are challenging and displacing
these. And the same procedures would apply if we were to examine a third
major basis of collective identity in the contemporary world — nationalism.
(Perhaps I do not need to repeat here the disclaimer I made earlier — but I
shall anyway: this in no sense entails that we are intending to *explain* the
change in social reality by the "introduction" of new ideas, whatever this
might mean; rather the claim is that the change cannot be properly
understood (in the sense of the *Verstehen* thesis) without such a clarification
of ideas and images; and that its being so understood is a necessary
explanation of an adequate explanation, whatever factors this explanation
brings into play as determinative: class conflict, technological change,
population growth, or whatever.)

This naturally leads us to refer to history in the genetic sense defined
above. For just as we cannot fully understand the new self-definitions
underlying, say, a protest movement without understanding the previously
dominant self-definitions which they are challenging, so we cannot grasp
these constitutive self-definitions of democratic society without studying

their genesis. For without this we will be unable to define adequately the polemical contrast which essentially characterizes them. The self-image of man as free and self-determining is defined by contrast to man as mere subject, the image of man as producer by contrast to a life of submission to the rhythms of nature, in which human powers remain occluded by superstition and the thraldom of animistic thought. Self-definitions must be understood polemically, and that means historically.

But this historical understanding is interpretive in the wide sense. For we are engaged not just in studying doctrines as laid down in texts – e.g., the philosophical tradition of democratic theory: Locke, Rousseau, Mill. The premiss of this kind of inquiry is that practices and institutions are also "expressions" of ideas and images after their own fashion; and that there may be no counterpart in philosophical prose for the ideas expressed in any given institutions or practices. So what is of prime interest for this kind of hermeneutic study of the present malaise is not so much the democratic tradition in theory, as the growth of the democratic identity (or identities) as we can trace it in the institutions and practices of democratic society by which men identified themselves. As a paradigm example of this kind of historical writing, in which explanation is shaped by genetic understanding which can also illuminate the present, I could cite E.P. Thompson's *Making of the English Working Classes*.

But of course, this kind of hermeneutical study is highly controversial among students of society. It is widely thought to be arbitrary, without an adequate method of intersubjective verification, vague, imprecise, in short unscientific. To answer attack with counter-attack, we might consider what resources are left to us in studying the present malaise once we set aside any hermeneutical approach.

Well, if we refuse to see institutions as *expressions* in any sense, one way we can look on them is as *instruments*, and this is the basis of a whole family of political and social theories, which go back to Hobbes and Locke (or Thrasymachus and Glaucon, if you will), and which are exemplified today by the vogue of "conversion" or input–output models in political science. If we see institutions as instrumental, then we will tend to account for declining allegiance to them in terms of their failure to satisfy (output failure).

But this is bound to be unsatisfactory. Failure to satisfy is itself what we want to explain. What we need to understand is why institutions which "satisfy" at one moment in time cease to do so later. Of course, there may sometimes be a quite adequate explanation in terms of the frustration of a need which we can independently identify, as when a given society is so organized that many of its members (e.g., Ethiopia) are reduced to starvation. But in cases like the modern Western polities, the non-satisfaction itself results from changes in the definitions and understanding of satisfaction on the part of the people concerned. This is what theorists gesture towards with relatively empty phrases like "the revolution of rising expectations." The adjective "rising" makes it sound here as though the change were merely quantitative. But on examination this is hardly a plausible view.

Consequently there is a recognition that people can withdraw allegiance from institutions because they change their "values" and the institutions no longer meet their "ideal" expectations. When we analyse the transition in this way, we are still not looking at institutions as expressions of ideas, but as realizations which carry out (or fail to carry out) certain ideas. The institutions are now seen as rejected not because of "output failure" but because they fail to realize certain norms or values.

But this account too can be distortive, since it requires that the norms be expressed independently of the institutions. Institutions are placed against norms to judge whether they conform or not. But this approach neglects that social norms can themselves only be understood in the context of institutions. I cannot have the ideal of a representative democracy in my mind without some however rudimentary notion of representative institutions. Now it can be of course that men define their norms largely in independence of *existing* institutions, and criticize what exists on the basis of what can be imagined. And much contemporary criticism of society is expressed as though it arises this way.

But this does not have to be so. Some ideals are not formulated explicitly. For instance, the notion mentioned above of society as an association of producers is rarely formulated; certainly it is not formulated in the minds of most people; it is implicit in certain practices and expectations. Yet it is not implausible to argue that many people evaluate and criticize society on the basis of it. Again one may criticize or at least disapprove of society on the basis of certain norms which are implicit in family life, although unformulated, or disapprove of one's family life on the basis of norms implicit in some outside, larger association.

To restrict ourselves to formulated norms, as the approach must do which separates norms and institutions (even though one may allow for unconsciously formulated ideas, rejecting still the truly implicit) cannot but impoverish our study, and blunt our understanding of what is afoot. Moreover, it only allows for the cases where the reality fails to meet certain norms, not for the cases where certain institutions express ideas incompatible with another view (as representative institutions do, for instance, for a follower of Rousseau). Nor can it allow for the contradiction which arises when given practices or institutions express contrary ideals (e.g., the practices of some contemporary communes of drop-outs, trying both to embody a way of life in close communion with nature and a closely integrated society and at the same time one founded on the most extreme liberty of self-determination).

But most of all, this approach cannot comprehend how institutions and practices can shape ideas; how certain ideas can receive an interpretation in the lives of people through the institutions under which they live. But this interpretation may be crucial to understanding social change. The general notions of freedom in the Western tradition have been given a certain gloss by democratic institutions, and also by the practices of consumer capitalist society. Just what this gloss is can only be recovered by a hermeneutical study of society, in which not just what men write and say, but also their practices and institutions constitute the "text."

A non-interpretive approach is impoverished because it can only see institutions as instruments or the realizations of certain ideas; but never as expressions. But in an important transition in which long-standing allegiances and disciplines are under attack, this kind of restriction is fatally narrowing. For we are dealing with what we called above "cultural mutation." To understand these large-scale changes in social discipline, institutions and self-understanding we have to see how these are linked, and this we can never do unless we see how institutions can express certain self-definitions.

But an interpretive study which tries to clarify the underlying self-definitions is necessarily historical. For a self-definition is clarified by what we have called polemical contrast and this in turn must be studied in historical transition. In studying society in this way we not only can but must learn from history, drawing from it not a repository of examples, but a clarifying account of genesis. This is as we saw a Hegelian use of history, and his work provides us with a web of concepts, including those of *Sittlichkeit* and alienation which remain illuminating and invaluable tools of contemporary self-understanding.

All Souls College
Oxford

NOTES

[1] *Die Vernunft in der Geschichte*, ed. J. Hoffmeister, Hamburg, 1955, p. 61 (henceforth: *VG*).
[2] *Die Philosophie des Geistes*, in *Sämtliche Werke*, ed. H. Glockner, Stuttgart, 1927–1930, Vol. 10, §514 (henceforth: *EG*).
[3] *Grundlinien der Philosophie des Rechts*, ed. J. Hoffmeister, Hamburg, 1955; *Hegel's Philosophy of Right*, tr. T.M. Knox, Oxford, 1942, Preface, p. 4 (henceforth: *PR*).
[4] *Phänomenologie des Geistes*, ed. G. Lasson, Hamburg, 1952, p. 258 (henceforth: *PhG*).
[5] "Freedom of the Will and the Concept of a Person," *Journal of Philosophy* 68 (1971): 5–20.

SHLOMO AVINERI

COMMENTS

Since I am very much in agreement with Professor Taylor about his general understanding of the importance of Hegel, and the importance of Hegel's conception of *Sittlichkeit* generally, I have decided to limit my remarks to the second part of his paper. This part attempts to understand the crisis of the modern democratic liberal bourgeois world in terms of the break-up of a traditional *Sittlichkeit* in Western societies. Here I am not in complete agreement.

Before raising my main point of dissent, however, I would like to make a distinction which is not by way of disagreement with Taylor, but relates to the difficulties which those coming from an Anglo-Saxon tradition may have with the concept of *Sittlichkeit*. Taylor spoke about two forms of obligations in contrasting *Sittlichkeit* with *Moralität*. Perhaps he would agree that we may bring out a distinction between the two concepts by suggesting that *Moralität* is based on obligations, while *Sittlichkeit* is based on duty, in the sense that duty is something that I have prior to my conscious acceptance of it.

The concept of duty is not as clear a concept as obligation, because the concept of obligation is, especially in the Anglo-Saxon tradition, connected with the will to accept an obligation freely, while duty appears to be a much more fuzzy concept. Perhaps, therefore, we should try to introduce the concept of duty as something pre-existing to one's conscious acceptance of this particular kind of obligation.

Now for my main point. It is that, although I basically agree with Taylor's description of the present crisis in Western societies, I am unsure whether I can go along with him in attributing it to the break-up of a traditional *Sittlichkeit* in Western capitalist society. For I wonder whether Western societies as we have known them since the middle of the nineteenth century — that is, basically democratic, liberal, consensual, capitalist, bourgeois societies — really have had anything that could be called *Sittlichkeit* in the Hegelian sense. The dominant impression conveyed by Taylor's paper is that there has been something like an accepted *Sittlichkeit*

155

Yirmiahu Yovel (ed.), Philosophy of History and Action, 155–158. All Rights Reserved.
Copyright © 1978 by D. Reidel Publishing Company, Dordrecht, Holland.

in the West for the last hundred or hundred and fifty years, say since the French Revolution, or since the stabilization of the Victorian order, and this is what is breaking up now. But it could be argued that what we see breaking up – and I am sliding into the political and historical as against the philosophical, and do it very consciously – is not something which has been there for the last hundred and fifty years, but is a very ephemeral phenomenon, a post-1945 phenomenon.

I think that very few intellectuals writing before 1945 would have said that the Western world had achieved that kind of equilibrium which we now say is breaking up. It was rather the case, in the nineteenth and early twentieth century, that there was never anything like a Hegelian *Sittlichkeit* applicable in the Western world, that indeed *Sittlichkeit* in the sense of an internalized societal ethics, if we try to translate this untranslatable German term, was always denied to the proletariat in the West. Nor did it belong even partially to the non-European world that was, until the middle of the twentieth century, under Western political domination. Whatever forms of Indian or African tribal *Sittlichkeit* or primitive *Sittlichkeit*, as Hegel would say, did exist, were certainly being broken up in the nineteenth and twentieth centuries. Thus, it seems to me to be in general an illusion to suggest that the West had this kind of *Sittlichkeit*.

There was only a very small part of Western society – I do not want to use Marxist terminology, saying it was the bourgeois classes or the capitalist classes – that was able to produce and maintain a very partial form of internalized *Sittlichkeit*. This it did at the expense of denying any form of *Sittlichkeit* to other sectors of European society, as well as to the totality of non-European society.

What happened after 1945 – between 1950 and the mid 1960's – was that there occurred a very unusual phenomenon in that the Western world was able – if I want to be topical, because of American aid and cheap oil prices – to create the illusion of an equilibrium, the illusion that the threats to democratic Western institutions, which before World War II had come from Fascism on the one hand and Communism on the other, were being contained. People spoke of the affluent society, the welfare state, the end of ideology – supposing that these pretty Western phrases really reflected a post-capitalist society to which the classical terminology of the class war and the class society no longer applied. It was apparently a new form of society and one which indeed possessed a *Sittlichkeit*.

Now, what is really breaking up is not a hundred and fifty years of history, but just this very unusual interlude of about twenty years that was raised by sociologists, political scientists and sometimes even philosophers into a new era, though what people have been writing about for the last fifteen years, about the end of ideology and a new kind of stabilized society, is very much like the kind of writing which Hegel attributed to his own time when he talked about the end of history.

I do not, therefore, disagree with the general tendency of this paper as regards our own picture of ourselves, our own understanding of our history, our own image of man which is so very important to our understanding of the processes which we are undergoing. I certainly agree with Taylor's understanding of what the disruptive forces in present-day society are. My difficulty, simply, is with the applicability of the Hegelian concept of *Sittlichkeit*. Hegel was basically mistaken, if I may say so, in suggesting that the nineteenth century had already achieved *Sittlichkeit*. Where things were going wrong was in the lower strata of society. He even had, I think, a good inkling of this, and therefore I attach very great importance to those passages in which he discusses alienation among lower orders of society, but his own system has no answer to that kind of alienation.

To use Hegelian language, I would say that the kind of limited *Sittlichkeit* that parts of Western societies were àble to achieve in the nineteenth and twentieth centuries was premised on its involving partial institutions and partial achievements. The unusual feature of the post-1945 era was an attempt to universalize this partial *Sittlichkeit*. But once an attempt is made to universalize it, it begins to fall apart.

So you can understand, I think, even in a Hegelian way of saying it, that the universalization of this sort of bourgeois *Sittlichkeit* creates within itself its own transcendence, its own contradictions. Of course, the rhetoric of the ideas of the liberal bourgeois West was always universal. Take the Declaration of the Rights of Man: "All men are created equal." But the possible application was *de facto* always partial, and there was always this tension between the universal promise of the liberal democratic revolution and its partial application within Western liberal societies. Once this rhetoric was taken seriously as a universal rhetoric, applying first to all strata of society in the West, applying secondly also to the Third World, then the thing burst. Its internal contradictions made it incapable of survival.

In addition, I would like to ask whether the conception of the Western form of society as one based on voting, on equal rights, lives up to the Hegelian idea of *Sittlichkeit*. Towards the end of his remarks, Professor Taylor made a comment which I wholly agree with as a very apt expression of the Hegelian view, namely, that to Hegel political institutions are not purely instrumental. Now, I think it could be said of the prevailing conventional wisdom of the West that it always saw its political institutions as instruments. In both its ideology and its practice, the egalitarianism of the democratic process has been viewed as an instrumental one. Hence, it has also been suggested that some societies, like Asian and African societies, could not achieve maximal aims of, say, economic expansion under forms of democratic institution; instead, military dictatorship or some sort of Fascism might be good for them, because it could achieve economic progress, national liberation, and those are the real aims, while democratic institutions are merely instruments.

Certainly in the United States context, the view of the political order as being purely instrumental was until very recently the predominant one, and therefore I do not feel that the democratic ethos of the West could be subsumed under the Hegelian concept of *Sittlichkeit*. To put it in a nutshell, a *Sittlichkeit* is not disappearing — it never existed. The promise, the rhetoric, the dream perhaps all existed — the reality did not.

What I feel is under attack is the inability of this partial system to become truly universal. When you truly universalize the liberal ethos of the West, its basic instrumental nature becomes clear and therefore it is unable to get out of people the kind of internalized belief that *Sittlichkeit* really necessitates. Further, it cannot be universalized socially, it is a system that can only serve limited ends. When the rhetoric overtakes the reality, a gap opens within Western societies, where you cannot give everything to everybody on a universalized level when the economy is beginning to shrink, where you do not have unlimited expansion. Nor can you really relate it to the non-European world, where those very limited European concepts do not have a reality, but certainly are dysfunctional in a developing society like an African one or some Asian ones.

The Hebrew University of Jerusalem

JACQUES D'HONDT

MARX ET LES LEÇONS DE L'HISTOIRE

SUMMARY. The very idea of a lesson implies that of history, demands a consciousness or knowledge of the past. The consciousness or knowledge of the past necessarily intervenes in present action.

The motives for negating the existence of the lessons of history therefore derive from the following. (1) The artificial isolation of the political domain. (2) The illegitimate restriction to a certain type of lesson—to precepts for individual or occasional use. (3) Complex motives, ones different from those alleged. One sometimes challenges the lessons of history because one understands them only too plainly, and they are distasteful (Lachelier). But such an attitude implies having recourse to the objectivity of history with a view to suggesting precisely its lack of objectivity. (4) One of the most customary arguments in favour of this negation takes into consideration the unique and irreversible character of historical development. It is again employing recourse to history against that history itself. One finds in Hegel this temptation to see in history a not very effective retrospective knowledge: "the bird of Minerva takes its flight at nightfall."

In Marx this knowledge acquires a much more marked prospective and directing role. (1) Marx produces historical works with a practical intention, as an educator of the proletariat and organizer of its action. (2) He appeals constantly to historical examples in order to orient present steps. (3) He puts a philosophy of history—historical materialism—at the basis of all his theoretical conceptions. (4) He proposes a historical explanation of the genesis and development of this historical materialism itself. This attitude implies a reversal of common opinions on this subject and assumes a paradoxical aspect for many observers. In order to adopt it, one must in fact submit to several theoretical demands. (1) The dialectic of the subject and the object. (2) The indispensable role of consciousness in events: without consciousness, no "lesson" of history would be evidently conceivable. (3) Conscious activity produces partially unconscious effects. It becomes alienated in an objective reality which emancipates itself from its tutelage, becomes autonomous and follows its own laws. (4) Historical changes comprise moments of rupture and "qualitative bonds," but ones integrated in a basic continuity.

History gives lessons only to the extent that it is capable of receiving lessons. Everything takes place as if the human past instructed and guided the present, as if from a global viewpoint, history were its own pupil.

Yirmiahu Yovel (ed.), Philosophy of History and Action, 159 −175. All Rights Reserved.
Copyright © 1978 by D. Reidel Publishing Company, Dordrecht, Holland.

Y a-t-il des leçons de l'histoire?

Cette question peut s'entendre diversement. Veut-on dire que l'histoire donne des leçons, comme un maître, ou bien qu'elle les apprend, comme un élève?

Il est particulièrement intéressant d'entendre la réponse de Marx à ces questions, à cause de l'immense influence actuelle de ce penseur.

LA SAGESSE DES NATIONS

Il semble bien que Marx recueille d'abord à ce propos un certain nombre d'idées admises. Qu'allègue-t-on, ordinairement, pour justifier la réalité d'un enseignement de l'histoire?

D'abord, peut-être, cet argument: la notion même de leçon implique celle d'histoire, elle réclame une conscience ou une connaissance du passé, et sa transmission au présent.

On n'enseigne jamais que ce que l'on a appris, directement ou scolairement, sauf dans le cas, tout à fait rare, d'une création immédiate dont le maître offrirait le spectacle instantané à ses disciples.

Pour qui n'accepte aucun transcendentalisme, et c'est évidemment le cas de Marx, il n'y a même de leçons que de l'histoire. D'où une connaissance, une réflexion sur des connaissances, pourraient-elles provenir, sinon d'une expérience ou d'une réflexion passée — à moins que ce ne soit d'une situation, d'une expérience ou d'une réflexion présente?

Pas de leçons sans histoire!

Inversement, on voit mal comment une conscience, ou mieux une connaissance du passé, de quelque ordre qu'il soit, pourrait s'instaurer, chez un individu ou dans une collectivité, sans exercer d'influence sur le comportement intellectuel et pratique de cet individu ou de cette collectivité. La conscience et la connaissance du passé comportent des lacunes, des défaillances, des erreurs, des illusions, mais telles qu'elles sont, qui donc leur échapperait, qui donc pourrait volontairement et efficacement les occulter? l'oubli n'obéit pas à une volonté arbitraire, et chacun agit, actuellement, selon l'expérience qu'il a acquise.

Il n'est point de savoir stérile.

Encore moins, bien sûr, pour qui admet la nécessité tendancielle des processus réels qu'il a détectés. Je ne puis enflammer une allumette en me cachant à moi-même les conséquences prévisibles de ce geste, avec ses possibilités et ses risques. La conscience ne prophétise que parce qu'elle recueille.

Mais tout cela n'implique pas que la connaissance du passé soit adéquate. Il suffit qu'il y ait un passé, et que la conscience que nous en avons influence nos attitudes présentes: l'histoire nous enseigne, plus ou moins utilement, plus ou moins objectivement, mais inéluctablement.

LES CAUSES DE LA CONTESTATION

Pourquoi donc certains philosophes en doutent-ils, cependant, quand ils ne le nient pas décidément?

Déjà, peut-être, parce que dans cette négation ils ne comprennent que l'histoire *politique*, détachée arbitrairement de l'histoire universelle. Ils isolent la vie politique des multiples autres aspects de la vie des sociétés, et aussi de la vie du monde.

C'est pour l'histoire politique seule que vaut leur refus, et il est compensé par une approbation d'autant plus naïve des enseignements du passé dans d'autres domaines, dont ils n'aperçoivent pas, ou ne reconnaissent pas, le caractère historique. Ils suivent docilement des préceptes d'hygiène ou de politesse, des règles de circulation ou de concurrence, des ordonnances de médecine ou d'administration, sans songer que tout cela leur vient du passé et leur a été transmis consciemment, non sans complications et incertitudes. Cet héritage familier capte leur confiance si facilement qu'ils en oublient que c'est un héritage, dont l'estimation dépend d'ailleurs de critères qui valent pour toute transmission historique. Si la connaissance du passé ne livrait pas de leçons, pourquoi donc lutterait-on contre l'alcoolisme, les excès de vitesse en automobile, l'esclavage, l'analphabétisme? Sans elle, nous agirions dans une spontanéité aveugle.

De plus, ils ne considèrent qu'un seul type de leçons, fort restreint: celles qui consisteraient en préceptes à usage individuel. Or, s'il est vrai, comme le pense Marx à la suite de Hegel, que de même que l'universel contient le particulier, le nécessaire implique le fortuit, alors la reconnaissance de lois historiques globales a pour conséquence que, par rapport à elles, les destinées individuelles présentent un caractère de fortuité relative.

Celui qui cherche à tirer son épingle du jeu considère une autre nécessité, une autre causalité, une autre finalité que celui qui vise la sauvegarde et le développement du jeu tout entier. Marx croit pouvoir tirer un riche enseignement de l'étude de la Commune de Paris. Mais cet enseignement ne peut profiter, à son avis, qu'au prolétariat. Il n'a d'utilité pour les prolétaires, considérés en tant qu'individus, que si ces individus acceptent de confondre leur destin personnel avec celui de leur classe sociale.

A Kugelmann qui s'effrayait des conséquences que pourrait avoir pour l'avenir le massacre d'une grande partie des "chefs" ouvriers, à la suite de la défaite de la Commune de Paris, Marx répondit en avril 1871: "Les Parisiens ont été placés devant l'alternative suivante: accepter le combat ou succomber sans combat. Dans cette dernière éventualité, la démoralisation de la classe ouvrière aurait été un malheur bien plus grand que la perte d'un nombre quelconque de 'chefs.' " [1]

Il est bien possible que quelques-uns des révolutionnaires concernés aient été d'un autre avis, au moment de leur mise à mort par les adversaires. Une relation dramatique se noue, dans l'histoire, entre les destinées collectives et les destinées individuelles, et le passé ne les éclaire pas de la même lumière.

De plus, la connaissance du passé n'atteint pas une certitude et une précision telles qu'elles permettraient de prévoir sans hésitation et de diriger sans aléas. Elle réserve d'ailleurs toujours sa place au hasard objectif.

Le même Marx qui a d'abord condamné le projet d'insurrection parisienne en 1871, puis qui a vivement critiqué la tactique appliquée et les fautes commises, magnifie l'entreprise après qu'elle a échoué, et il analyse minutieusement cette expérience dont pourront, selon lui, s'inspirer des tentatives ultérieures du même ordre.

En même temps, Marx met en valeur le caractère *relatif* des conjectures que l'on peut faire, concernant un devenir humain dont la nécessité n'a pas grand chose de commun avec le déterminisme absolu, et, selon lui, mystique, que Laplace avait naguère exposé. Il écrit à Kugelmann: "Il serait certes fort commode de faire l'histoire universelle si on n'engageait la lutte qu'à condition d'avoir des chances infailliblement favorables. Cette histoire serait d'ailleurs de nature fort mystique si les 'hasards' n'y jouaient aucun rôle." [2]

L'action humaine n'échappe jamais complètement au risque, mais on calcule le risque, et l'on choisit, parmi d'autres, l'attitude convenable. Il faut, pour cela, se servir utilement de l'expérience passée. Mais qui donc a jamais pensé qu'il suffisait de prendre des leçons de conduite automobile pour éviter ensuite infailliblement tout accident de la route?

En réalité, beaucoup de théoriciens omettent d'inscrire, au compte de l'histoire, des connaissances qui présentent un caractère politique indubitable, et qui leur sont si familières qu'ils croient ne les avoir jamais acquises, comme si elles étaient innées, ou *a priori*.

Chacun, à notre époque, sait que non seulement les individus sont mortels, mais aussi les classes sociales, les nations, les religions, les langues, les civilisations; que les frontières des Etats ne sont ni naturelles, ni immuables; que les hiérarchies connaissent avec le temps des pétrifications, ou des renversements, ou des métamorphoses. On pourrait dresser une longue liste de ces connaissances d'ample portée que seule l'expérience historique est capable de procurer.

Certes, on rencontre à chaque époque des gens qui n'ont rien appris, qui restent en retard d'une guerre, qui pensent dans un monde périmé. Et sans doute chacun doit-il, à cet égard, se juger lui-même avec modestie. Mais cela ne change ni n'efface la réalité: nous vivons et nous nous mouvons dans une multitude de traditions, souvent contradictoires entre elles, souvent confuses, et ce qu'elles nous transmettent nous soutient, même si nous le comprenons mal, et diversement, et absurdement. La médiocrité des élèves ne contraint pas le maître au silence. Il crie d'ailleurs parfois assez fort pour que les plus durs d'oreille finissent par l'entendre.

En notre ère du soupçon, nous sommes tentés de penser qu'en cette affaire il n'y a pire sourd que celui qui se bouche les oreilles. Il arrive, dans quelques cas singuliers, que les raisons alléguées d'une grande méfiance envers l'histoire ne coïncident pas avec les véritables motifs, tenus secrets, ou restés inconscients.

L'obstination négatrice de quelques uns dissimule une foi profonde, et peut-être excessive, en l'objectivité massive de l'histoire et des leçons. S'ils veulent lui retirer la parole, c'est parce qu'à leurs oreilles elle ne parle que trop!

Nous en trouverons le témoignage dans cet extrait d'une lettre de Lachelier à Boutroux: "et quand cela serait arrivé, il faudrait dire plus que jamais *que cela n'est pas arrivé*, que l'histoire est une illusion, et le passé une projection, et qu'il n'y a de vrai que l'idéal et l'absolu; (...) C'est la légende qui est vraie et l'histoire qui est fausse."[3]

L'indignation devant un fait historique déplaisant entraînait Lachelier peut être plus loin qu'il n'eût délibérément voulu. Car l'héroïsme de la négation implique une solide consistance de la chose, et le propos de Lachelier confirme, malgré son intention, l'objectivité d'un passé irrécusable.

La dénonciation du caractère prétendument illusoire de l'histoire se fonde sur un recours à cette histoire, et se retourne donc ironiquement contre son auteur.

Hegel lui-même s'abandonne à ce paradoxe, d'une manière partiellement lucide — ce qui suscite le doute sur la portée exacte de ses propos:

On renvoie les souverains, les hommes d'Etat et surtout les peuples à l'enseignement par l'expérience de l'histoire. Mais ce que l'expérience et l'histoire enseignent, c'est que jamais les peuples ni les gouvernements n'ont rien appris de l'histoire, ni n'ont agi d'après des leçons qu'on aurait pu en tirer. Chaque époque, chaque peuple a des circonstances si particulières, réalise une situation si individuelle, que c'est uniquement en elle et à partir d'elle qu'il faut prendre ses décisions (et précisément, seul le grand caractère sait faire ici ce qui est approprié). Dans la cohue des événements mondiaux, une maxime générale ne sert à rien, le souvenir des situations analogues dans le passé ne suffit pas...[4]

Comment la saisie d'un passé unique et irréversible pourrait-elle manifester quelque utilité dans la construction intelligente du présent et de l'avenir? Surtout si l'on admet, comme le fait Hegel, que les périodes historiques successives se séparent les unes des autres par des ruptures qualitatives, non pas radicales, certes, mais importantes!

En fait, Hegel répond lui-même implicitement à ces questions, d'une part en acceptant l'enseignement de l'histoire sur ce point, et d'autre part en fondant son opinion sur une compréhension du développement historique qui lui est propre et qu'il expose longuement: histoire considérée comme un processus; processus dialectique qui comporte des moments de fixation, de stagnation, et des moments d'accélération; constatation des phénomènes de rupture; unité de la continuité et de la discontinuité, etc.

Il faut avoir beaucoup étudié l'histoire, pour apprendre qu'elle constitue un processus nécessaire et nécessairement dialectique. Mais comment une acquisition théorique d'une telle ampleur resterait-elle sans effet sur la conduite de ceux qui en bénéficient?

Pourquoi Hegel s'intéresserait-il à l'histoire autrement qu'en "antiquaire," comme il le proclame, s'il n'envisageait pas un usage de ce savoir?

Il veut être le porte-parole de l'esprit mondial, et toutes les leçons qu'il prodigue ne sont que des leçons de l'histoire!

Il convient donc d'atténuer les présentations parfois excessives et exclusives d'une tentation à laquelle Hegel cède parfois, et qu'il a superbement illustrée par l'image de "l'oiseau de Minerve qui ne prend son vol qu'à la tombée du jour."

Quelles sont alors les conditions qui, si elles étaient réalisées, rendraient effectivement impossible toute influence du passé sur le présent et l'avenir humains, ainsi que sur les intentions humaines?

LES RUPTURES

La première serait une rupture absolue entre l'homme et le monde, ou, plus exactement, entre l'esprit et le monde. On reconnaît ici le principe de toutes les métaphysiques traditionnelles, qui ont su en développer diversement, de manière cohérente, les conséquences. Elles présentent alors une conception du monde qui comporte de grands avantages intellectuels, et qui, notamment, donne beaucoup de commodités pour l'élaboration d'une théorie de la connaissance simple et bien structurée. Tout le monde aperçoit la difficulté de leur réfutation éventuelle.

Elles ménagent d'ailleurs la justification d'une liberté humaine intégrale et elles autorisent l'espérance d'une immortalité de l'âme individuelle.

Elles rendent à la fois inacceptable théoriquement et insupportable pratiquement une action du réel, considéré comme extérieur, sur l'esprit humain, du moins pour ce qui concerne l'essentiel. Celui-ci se garde pur de toute contamination empirique: *Noli me tangere*! Et même si certaines doctrines concèdent que quelques aspects de l'esprit dépendent du monde, du moins la production proprement intellectuelle reste-t-elle une immaculée conception.

En tant que sujet spirituel, l'individu ne se trouve alors conditionné d'aucune façon, ni par le monde naturel, ni par le monde historique. Il ne peut être question, pour lui, d'obtempérer à des indications, des commandements, des mises en garde qui lui viendraient de quelque positivité que ce soit, habitude personnelle ou tradition collective: il n'a de leçons à recevoir de personne, et en tout cas pas de l'histoire. C'est plutôt à lui d'en donner, bien qu'il soit malaisé de comprendre comment il peut agir sur une réalité aussi radicalement séparée de lui. Celui qui refuse d'être touché par rien, comment pourra-t-il toucher quoi que ce soit? Faut-il oublier l'argile dont on a été pétri?

Cette thèse fondamentale de la séparation absolue de l'homme et du monde, et donc de l'homme et de l'histoire objective du genre humain, a trouvé, ces derniers temps, une forme nouvelle d'expression: la théorie de la rupture épistémologique radicale, développée et soutenue par des auteurs talentueux.

Elle constitue la deuxième de ce que nous pouvons appeler les "conditions d'impossibilité" de l'histoire.

Ne retenons d'elle que ce qui intéresse ici notre propos. Elle veut mettre en évidence que les connaissances et les activités humaines, concernant des objets très variés, comportent des structures similaires qui révèlent leur unité de composition épistémique.

Elle entraîne des conséquences importantes et bien connues: d'abord, il n'y a pas de rapport entre les divers systèmes épistémiques que l'on peut détecter, et donc aucune filiation, aucun passage de l'un à l'autre.

Ensuite, elle interdit le maintien de la représentation traditionnelle de l'homme, un être qui permanerait dans ou sous les constitutions épistémiques successives. Cet antihumanisme a acquis rapidement une grande popularité. Une de ses implications c'est que chaque conception du passé dépend de l'épistémie dont elle relève. Ce n'est pas l'histoire qui, dans certaines conditions, produit les épistémies successives, mais c'est l'épistémie dans laquelle on se trouve et dont on ne peut sortir, qui produit un certain type d'historicité et d'histoire. Notre propre archive donne à notre discours "ses modes d'apparition, ses formes d'existence et de coexistence, son système de cumul, d'historicité et de disparition." [5]

Pouvons-nous comprendre, dans ce dispositif, comment une épistémie peut ressaisir authentiquement les autres, alors qu'elle les soumet immédiatement à ses propres contraintes? Cette épistémie, c'est comme si elle tombait du ciel, sans origine ni genèse. Elle se pose comme commencement absolu.

Il n'y a plus alors d'histoire qu'à l'intérieur de chaque système de conditions, et constituée par lui. Cette épistémie de l'histoire compromet les chances de toute histoire de l'épistémologie. Elle se révèle par là profondément antihistorique: on a pu évoquer à son propos, et fort justement, un "transcendentalisme sans sujet" (Paul Ricoeur). Or ce que Marx rejette, et il scandalise par là, ce n'est pas le sujet, mais le transcendentalisme!

L'histoire ne serait pas non plus possible si le développement humain n'offrait pas une continuité. On pourrait dire, par opposition à la continuité épistémologique: une continuité phénoménale. Certes Marx, à la suite de Hegel, et peut-être même davantage que lui, a insisté sur les ruptures relatives, et sur leur importance. Elles représentent des moments décisifs du cours de l'histoire. Mais à condition qu'elles ne soient pas elles-mêmes en rupture radicale avec ce qui les précède et les prépare! Bonds qualitatifs brusques, elles résultent de lents accroissements quantitatifs, et l'histoire forme, en conséquence, une continuité de ruptures et d'évolutions, réalisant la formule abstraite que Hegel avait énoncée: "le lien du lien et du non-lien." Une révolution est un renversement, non pas un déménagement.

A défaut de toute continuité, nous aurions affaire à une rhapsodie, à un décousu, mais même à ce pot-pourri il serait difficile de refuser une unité de composition.

Il n'y aurait pas d'histoire, au sens ordinaire, si le politique ne détenait une spécificité propre et une continuité de développement. Ce qui n'implique nullement son autonomie absolue.

L'histoire de la philosophie, l'histoire de l'art, réclament elles aussi la spécificité de leur objet. On constate donc une discontinuité relative des objets considérés, mais pas une autonomie absolue: au contraire, ils exercent les uns sur les autres une influence mutuelle, et constituent un tout, le tout de l'histoire humaine, elle même comprise dans le "grand tout de la nature."

L'HISTOIRE INSTITUTRICE

L'attitude de Marx, devant cette problématique, ne fait aucun doute. Il a admis qu'il y a des leçons de l'histoire et cela implique des conditions de possibilité qu'il a indiquées à maintes reprises.

Marx a lui-même exercé le métier d'historien, et pas seulement celui de philosophe de l'histoire. Après avoir établi le matérialisme historique comme théorie générale, il a lui-même mis, si l'on peut dire, la main à la pâte. Dans ce travail, une intention pratique le guidait, et elle s'exprime clairement sous sa plume: il s'agit pour lui d'éduquer et d'organiser le prolétariat en lui expliquant ce qui est advenu dans le passé, afin qu'il ne retombe pas dans les mêmes erreurs, et qu'il imite les exemples d'action efficace.

Que l'on relise *La guerre civile en France*, ou *Le dix-huit Brumaire de Louis-Bonaparte*, on y trouvera des préceptes fondés sur la connaissance et l'analyse d'expériences échues. Non pas que Marx envisage toujours une histoire immédiatement didactique! Il insiste au contraire souvent sur le fait que la recherche théorique doit prendre ses distances à l'égard des projets d'application immédiate. Aussi bien, Engels et lui-même étudieront-ils l'histoire grecque, retraceront-ils l'histoire du christianisme primitif, l'histoire de l'Allemagne féodale, etc. La connaissance du passé se montre toujours utile, en fin de compte, mais pas nécessairement sous cette forme *de préceptes* applicables instantanément.

Toutefois Marx ne les dédaigne pas. Entre mille exemples, on peut citer quelques-uns des plus célèbres. L'étude de la Commune de Paris conduit Marx à des conclusions telles que celles-ci: une révolution prolétarienne ne peut réussir sans l'accord des classes moyennes, dont une grande partie est constituée par la paysannerie. Sans l'alliance avec la paysannerie, la révolution prolétarienne reste un "solo funèbre." Donc, si le prolétariat n'a pas noué cette alliance, il est vain de s'engager dans une révolution.

Autre enseignement tiré du même événement: la révolution ne doit pas changer l'Etat, tel qu'il est établi, mais le briser. Et puis, nous l'avons déjà vu, dans certains cas, mieux vaut un échec sanglant qu'une résignation décourageante.

Voilà des leçons que les disciples de Marx n'ont pas laissé tomber dans l'oubli.

Mais l'étude de l'histoire instruit aussi d'une autre façon: elle permet certaines prévisions.

Par exemple, contre l'avis de tous les économistes de son temps, Marx a maintenu la thèse selon laquelle tant que le système capitaliste persisterait, il connaîtrait des crises économiques. Après l'échec de la Commune, il a prétendu qu'il y aurait d'autres révolutions prolétariennes.

D'une manière plus précise, Engels, trente ans à l'avance, et contre l'opinion commune, prévoyait le déclenchement de la première guerre mondiale et certaines conséquences à ses yeux nécessaires:

Et enfin, il n'y a plus pour la Prusse-Allemagne d'autre guerre possible qu'une guerre mondiale, et, à la vérité, une guerre mondiale d'une ampleur et d'une violence jamais imaginées jusqu'ici. Huit à dix millions de soldats s'entr'égorgeront; ce faisant, ils dévoreront et tondront toute l'Europe comme jamais ne le fit encore une nuée de sauterelles. Les dévastations de la guerre de Trente ans, condensées en 3 ou 4 années et répandues sur tout le continent, la famine, les épidémies, la férocité générale des armées ainsi que des masses populaires provoquée par l'âpreté du besoin, le gâchis désespéré de notre mécanisme artificiel du commerce, de l'industrie et du crédit finissant dans la banqueroute générale. L'effondrement des vieux Etats et de leur sagesse politique traditionnelle, et tel que les couronnes rouleront par dizaines sur le pavé et qu'il ne se trouvera personne pour les ramasser; l'impossibilité absolue de prévoir comment tout cela finira et qui sortira vainqueur de la lutte; un seul résultat est absolument certain: l'épuisement général et la création des conditions nécessaires à la victoire finale de la classe ouvrière. [6]

C'était écrit en 1887. Cela s'accomplit en 1914-1918.

La prévision permet d'adapter les comportements. Elle montre que tout n'est pas possible, mais que ce qui est possible se réalise plus ou moins rapidement, plus ou moins heureusement. A quelle autre ambition pourrait prétendre une leçon?

Tout avertissement ne porte cependant pas fatalement ses fruits.

Marx et Engels ont très fréquemment mis en garde contre ce qu'ils appelaient le *"Personenkult."* En particulier, dans son *Introduction* à l'édition de 1891 de la *Guerre civile en France*, Engels précise les moyens d'empêcher la naissance et le développement de ce "culte de la personnalité," et, plus spécialement, les moyens pour la classe ouvrière d'assurer sa sécurité et sa liberté contre ses propres députés et représentants, ainsi que contre ses propres employés. Reprenant une terminologie bien connue, il explique que chaque serviteur a tendance à se métamorphoser en maître, et comment on peut empêcher ce renversement. [7] Il semble bien que cette leçon, retirée de l'expérience historique de la Commune de Paris, se soit perdue.

Mais il reste que Marx en appelait constamment aux exemples historiques pour orienter les démarches actuelles.

Comment pourrait-il en être autrement chez un penseur qui place une philosophie de l'histoire, le matérialisme historique, à la base de toutes ses recherches scientifiques et de toutes ses activités pratiques préméditées?

Comme l'a dit Engels, résumant brutalement une doctrine bien connue: "Toutes les vues théoriques qui surgissent dans l'histoire ne peuvent être comprises que si les conditions de vie matérielle de l'époque correspondante sont comprises et que si les premières sont déduites de ces conditions matérielles." [8]

Dans une telle perspective, l'histoire devient la science fondamentale, et le point de vue historique inspire toute démarche intellectuelle.

Aussi, de manière très cohérente — quelle que soit d'ailleurs la difficulté d'une telle entreprise — Marx a voulu rendre compte historiquement de la genèse et du développement de ce matérialisme historique lui-même.

Il l'a fait dans sa *Préface* à la *Contribution à la critique de l'économie politique* de 1859, et il a approuvé les articles qu'Engels a écrits, à la même époque, à ce propos.[9] L'idée générale, sur ce point, est celle qu'Engels présentera en raccourci dans l'*Anti-Dühring*:

La pensée théorique de chaque époque, donc aussi celle de la nôtre, est un produit historique qui prend en des temps différents une forme très différente et, par là, un contenu très différent. La science de la pensée est donc, comme toute autre science, une science historique, la science du développement historique de la pensée humaine.[10]

Le matérialisme dialectique et le matérialisme historique naissent à l'époque qui les rend possibles, et la convergence des recherches de théoriciens indépendants les uns des autres signale que, si l'on ose dire, l'époque attendait cette naissance.

JUSTIFICATIONS THÉORIQUES

Une telle vue des choses implique un renversement des opinions communes et prend, pour beaucoup d'observateurs, l'allure d'un scandale.

"Par l'étendue, le monde me comprend et m'engloutit comme un point. Par la pensée je le comprends." Cette formule de Pascal semblait déjà forte. Mais Marx en rajoute: ce point de pensée qui comprend le monde est lui-même un produit du monde, une partie, une différenciation parcellaire et éphémère de ce monde!

C'est la dialectique qui se charge de faciliter l'assimilation de ce paradoxe. Elle réussit peut-être ce tour de faire passer le sujet pour un enfant de l'objet, un enfant tyrannique qui malmène son père.

L'histoire qu'écrivent les historiens (*Historia*) est distincte de l'histoire effective (*Res gestae*), mais elle en est cependant, à certains égards, un produit, et elle consiste en un reflet plus ou moins adéquat du cours réel des choses. Ce reflet n'est pas passif: d'une part, comme toute chose au monde, et comme tout produit, il gagne une certaine autonomie, il s'autonomise (*Verselbständigung*), et d'autre part il entre en interaction avec son modèle: l'histoire réelle ne serait pas ce qu'elle est, si n'y intervenait la conscience des hommes, collective et individuelle.

Cette relation de l'histoire réelle et de la conscience historique comporte toutefois une dominante: l'histoire réelle. Et, bien sûr, avant que le genre humain, par la production, ne se fût engagé dans un processus historique concret, il ne pouvait naître d'historiens pour raconter. L'histoire produit et ensuite abolit le bénéficiaire de ses leçons.

Toutefois, si l'être, selon Marx, précède la conscience, la conscience disparaît dans la mort, en même temps que ses conditions naturelles.

On saisit alors le caractère relatif des leçons de l'histoire qui ne peuvent surgir que dans l'entre deux, et qui gardent toujours une portée et une validité subordonnées.

Autrement dit, il n'est possible de tirer des leçons de l'histoire que parce que celle-ci, en fin de compte, ne manque pas d'infliger une leçon à ceux qui n'ont pas su s'instruire auprès d'elle. La conscience a toujours le dernier mot, mais il peut être faux. L'histoire, elle, donne toujours le dernier coup, imparable.

Cela suppose que la conscience joue un rôle dans les événements. Sans elle, aucune "leçon" de l'histoire ne serait concevable, car les événements ne prennent une signification monitrice, indicative ou réprobatrice, que par rapport aux analyses et aux prévisions. Une telle exaltation du rôle de la conscience dans l'histoire ne peut surprendre chez un théoricien tel que Marx, puisque précisément, sans elle, aucune théorie ne présenterait d'intérêt. Celle-ci est, selon lui, un guide pour l'action, et il a toujours mis en garde, en ce qui concerne la vie politique, contre la spontanéité. L'homme, être conscient, organise intelligemment ses actions, et déjà le type d'action qui le définit comme espèce singulière et remarquable: le travail, la production.

Il n'est donc pas question pour Marx de nier l'existence du sujet. Au contraire, il s'y réfère fréquemment. Ainsi, par exemple, il écrit, dans les *Théories sur la plus-value*, qui forment le tome IV du *Capital*:

C'est l'homme lui-même qui est la base [*die Basis*] de sa production matérielle, comme de toutes les autres productions qu'il effectue. Donc, toutes les circonstances qui affectent l'homme, le sujet de la production [*das Subjekt der Produktion*], modifient plus ou moins toutes ses fonctions et toutes ses activités, et donc aussi ses fonctions et ses activités en tant que créateur [*Schöpfer*] de la richesse matérielle, des marchandises.[11]

Il est donc abusif d'attribuer à Marx une attitude "anti-humaniste," sinon en prenant le mot "humanisme" en ce sens obscur et exceptionnel que lui a imposé Feuerbach.

Mais alors, si l'homme, sujet de la production, et aussi de la production intellectuelle, entre en relation dialectique avec les circonstances et avec les résultats de cette production, il convient, pour que la notion de leçon garde un sens dans un tel contexte, que le monde des produits détienne lui aussi une autonomie relative. Si l'histoire, faite par les hommes, répondait immédiatement et limpidement à leurs intentions, ils la produiraient en y pensant et ils n'en tireraient ni n'en recevraient jamais de leçons.

En réalité, selon Marx, l'activité consciente suscite des effets partiellement involontaires et inconscients. En fabriquant ce qu'ils veulent, les hommes fabriquent en même temps autre chose, un surplus non désiré et peut-être indésirable. L'action s'aliène dans une réalité objective qui s'émancipe de sa tutelle, s'autonomise par rapport à elle, et suit ses propres lois. Cette doctrine générale de l'aliénation, héritée de Hegel et adaptée, soutient toute la théorie historique de Marx.

Il n'y aurait pas d'histoire, si elle n'était faite par les hommes. Il n'y aurait pas de leçons de l'histoire, si celle-ci obéissait immédiatement aux intentions humaines: il faut donc qu'elle prenne sa propre consistance spécifique, étrangère, ou même contradictoire à ces intentions. Elle se présente aux hommes comme une manifestation d'étrangeté (*Fremdheit*), souvent surprenante et déroutante. Mais l'analyse révèle qu'ils ont eux-mêmes créé cette étrangeté, sans le savoir ni le vouloir, dans une aliénation de leurs projets et de leurs actions (*Entfremdung*).

L'impression d'étrangeté ressentie devant l'histoire résulte de multiples constatations. Elle n'est jamais plus vive que lorsque le cours de l'histoire semble "perdre la tête," renverser les institutions et les valeurs qu'il avait lui-même sanctifiées, s'emballer comme un cheval fou, dans les périodes de crise et de révolution. Ce qui était sagesse devient alors soudainement folie (*Weisheit-Narrheit*), et la logique y perd son latin!

Il se produit ainsi, dans le développement, des bonds, des sauts, des moments de discontinuité brutale. A la suite de Hegel, Marx les tient pour des ruptures qualitatives, et il leur accorde la plus grande importance: elles sont décisives, du point de vue de l'intellection comme du point de vue de la prospective. Au lieu de les nier, ou de s'indigner de leur irruption, Marx adopte la dialectique hégélienne qui prétend se plier à elles pour les mieux saisir, et qui les récupère au profit de la pensée rationnelle. On connaît la théorie fameuse du passage brusque du développement quantitatif lent au saut qualitatif, théorie qui constitue un aspect essentiel de la dialectique.

Elle présente, pour Marx, une importance que l'on ne saurait surestimer. Comment les hommes, en effet, pourraient-ils tirer parti activement de leur connaissance du passé, s'ils n'étaient capables d'intervenir utilement dans ces sauts qualitatifs de l'histoire, de les prévoir, de les préparer, de les orienter, de les moduler?

Or, pour que l'action éclairée connaisse ici une efficacité, il faut que ces ruptures décisives, et par exemple ces révolutions, ne se réduisent pas à des coupures radicales telles qu'elles sont seules reconnues par la logique classique, avec ses oppositions tranchées qui excluent tout tiers et toute médiation possibles: "ou bien...ou bien"!...

Les enseignements du passé ne guident le présent que s'il est lié au passé dans une continuité fondamentale qui comporte certes des ruptures, mais des ruptures relatives. L'histoire se présente alors, pour l'essentiel, comme un processus, c'est-à-dire une continuité d'évolutions progressives et de ruptures brusques. Que l'on songe à ce qu'implique la formule de Marx: "La France est le pays classique des révolutions"!

Bien sûr, Marx savait, et pour cause, que tout le monde n'admet pas une telle représentation du rapport de l'homme au monde et du rapport du genre humain à sa propre histoire. Il comptait un plus grand nombre d'adversaires théoriques irréductibles que de disciples, en son temps.

L'appréciation de la validité et de l'efficacité des leçons dépend de la représentation que l'on se fait de l'histoire, plus ou moins objective, plus ou moins accueillante au phénomène de l'aliénation et à la relativisation du sujet. L'analyse d'une même période historique instruit différemment des sujets différents, car elle dépend des présuppositions théoriques et des préjugés de chacun d'eux.

Le même événement, saisi dans son objectivité, propose des tâches différentes au tyran et à l'opprimé, à l'exploiteur et à l'exploité: tous deux, l'ayant bien compris, s'en inspirent diversement pour leur conduite future.

Est-ce à dire, alors, que chacun choisisse ici l'air qu'il aime entendre? Est-ce l'écoute qui fait la chanson?

Marx ne semble pas le penser. Sans doute, une même connaissance objective se trouve-t-elle utilisée dans des prévisions et des orientations différentes, parfois opposées. Le savoir du médecin lui permet de mieux soigner, mais aussi, éventuellement, de tuer.

Le déroulement de la grande guerre 1914-1918 et de la période qui l'a suivie inspira des activités très différentes à Aristide Briand, à Lénine, à Churchill, à Hitler, et, de même, à la France, à la Russie, à l'Angleterre, à l'Allemagne, et, sur un autre plan, aux impérialistes, au capitalisme, au prolétariat, aux classes moyennes, etc.

Mais cette diversité ne témoigne ni en faveur du subjectivisme ni en faveur du nihilisme, selon Marx.

Certaines gens se montrent, cependant, "imperméables aux leçons de l'histoire."

C'est que si tous, *volens nolens*, tirent des leçons de l'expérience passée et consciemment transmise, tous ne procèdent pas en cela d'une manière également objective et complète.

A un certain niveau de difficulté, l'élève doit être préparé à entendre le maître. Encore faut-il qu'on l'ait envoyé à l'école!

Or, l'histoire réelle ne met pas tous les individus en situation aussi favorable pour saisir la signification de leur propre passé. Chacun se trouve là où le cours de l'histoire l'a fait apparaître: "Je suis là, et je n'y puis rien."

La même condition de réalité objective qui fonde la possibilité des leçons de l'histoire impose aussi des situations individuelles et collectives. Les hommes de la Restauration n'avaient rien appris, ni rien oublié. Il y a des choses que ne comprendront jamais ceux qui n'ont jamais eu faim. Des obstacles sociaux interdisent parfois une intellection satisfaisante du passé.

MAÎTRE ET ÉLÈVE

Compte tenu de ces conditions de possibilité, nous pouvons dire que, pour Marx, l'histoire ne donne de leçons que dans la mesure où elle est capable d'en recevoir. Tout se passe *comme si* le passé, en même temps qu'il l'engendre objectivement, intruisait et guidait le présent dans la conscience humaine. Ainsi, d'un point de vue global, l'histoire accepte d'être son propre élève. En isolant cette manière de voir, et en l'absolutisant, on aboutirait à une conception mécaniste et structuraliste que Marx ne paraît pas avoir jamais envisagée. Au contraire, Marx relativise cette conception en laissant jouer, à l'intérieur de l'histoire, une dialectique subtile, dont seuls quelques moments viennent d'être ici très sommairement rappelés. De plus, sa reconnaissance d'un rôle didactique de la saisie consciente du passé implique l'activité subjective des individus, conçue comme dérivée, mais efficace.

Marx, comme Engels, a aimé suprêmement le drame éphémère, ce que jamais on ne verra deux fois: il a voulu se mettre à son école, et c'est à nous de juger en quelle mesure, poussant à l'extrême la modestie de l'écolier, il a réussi à devenir un maître.

Université de Poitiers

NOTES

[1] *Lettres à Kugelmann*, Paris, 1971, p. 191.

[2] *Ibid.*, p. 190.

[3] *Lettre à Boutroux*, 21 janvier 1876.

[4] *La raison dans l'histoire* (Introduction aux *Leçons sur la philosophie de l'histoire*).

[5] M. Foucault, *L'archéologie du savoir*, Paris, 1969, p. 171.

[6] *Marx-Engels-Werke*, Berlin, 1962, 21: 350-351 (Désormaîs: *MEW*).

[7] *Ibid.*, 22: 197-198.

[8] *Etudes philosophiques*, Paris, 1947, p. 75.

[9] *MEW*, 13: 468-477.

[10] *Anti-Düring*, Trad. française, p. 445.

[11] *MEW*, 26/1: 260.

W E R N E R   B E C K E R

DEMOKRATIE UND DIE DIALEKTISCHE
THEORIE DER GESCHICHTE

ÜBER EIN PROBLEMATISCHES ERBE DEUTSCHER
GESCHICHTSPHILOSOPHIE

SUMMARY. The picture of German philosophy of history is today largely dominated by
Hegel and Marx. But the characteristic feature of the historical theories of Hegel and Marx
does not lie in their being theories of lawlikeness in history, nor are they problematic merely
because philosophical theories of this kind cannot easily be demonstrated with the aid of
empirical methods. It is shown that the most important characteristic of the philosophies of
history of Hegel and Marx should be seen in the fact that they seek to use philosophical
(Hegel) or alternatively scientific (Marx) methods in order to provide a basis for *political
evaluations*. The best known of these political value concents is the concept of alienation.
This concept plays a great role in both Hegel and Marx. It is shown that the paradigm
employed by Hegel and Marx to provide a basis for the philosophy of history and of society,
stands in opposition to the manner in which values and value concepts are legitimated
according to the concept of liberal democracy. This consequently means that Hegel's and
Marx's concepts of the state are in contradiction with liberal democracy's understanding of
the state.

Zwei Pole sind es, zwischen denen sich das Hauptthema der deutschen
Geschichtsphilosophie der Neuzeit bewegt. Sie lassen sich durch die Namen
von Hegel und Marx bezeichnen. Beide Denker spiegeln in exemplarischer
Weise das spezifische Verhältnis, welches die deutsche Philosophie der
letzten 200 Jahre zur Sphäre des Politischen hatte.

Es handelt sich dabei nicht bloß um ein Verhältnis der Philosophen zur
Politik, auch nicht um die verschiedenen Formen, in denen Politik in den
Theorien deutscher Philosophen thematisch geworden ist. Es geht darum,
daß die deutsche Geschichtsphilosophie dem Begriff der Philosophie, wie sie
ihn sieht, selber eine politische Rolle zugewiesen hat. Wie ist dies zu
verstehen? Die Philosophie der Geschichte beinhaltet spätestens seit Herder
ein bestimmtes Wissen über die Entwicklung des Menschengeschlechts, eine
Entwicklung, die für Herder und die Deutsche Klassik, hier vor allem für
Schiller, durch einen Abfall von den Einheitsideen des klassischen

177

Yirmiahu Yovel (ed.), Philosophy of History and Action, 177 –190. All Rights Reserved.
Copyright © 1978 by D. Reidel Publishing Company, Dordrecht, Holland.

Griechentums gekennzeichnet ist. Doch nicht nur Abfall und Herausfallen aus den klassisch-griechischen Harmonieidealen gilt es zu erkennen; entscheidend wird zudem die Vorstellung, wonach die Geschichte wieder auf das Niveau der verlorengegangenen Einheit zu bringen sei. Es ist dies eine geschichtsphilosophische Grundvorstellung, die bei inhaltlich so verschiedenartigen Denkern und Dichtern wie Herder, Schiller, dem Romantiker Novalis und den deutschen Idealisten wie z.B. Fichte leitend gewesen ist. Alle diese Philosophen und Dichter sind unbeschadet ihrer Kritiken aneinander der Überzeugung, daß ihre jeweilige Geschichtsphilosophie das *Ganze* der Entwicklung der Menschheit wiedergibt. Zu diesem Ganzen gehört das Wissen der ursprünglichen Einheit — bei Herder und den Dichtern der Deutschen Klassik die Epoche des Griechentums der Antike, bei Novalis das christliche Mittelalter, bei Fichte die Unschuld des rousseauschen Naturzustandes — ferner die Analyse der Abfallszeit, zu der jeweils die eigene Gegenwart zählt, und das Zukunftsideal wiederherzustellender Einheit und Harmonie.

Zur entscheidenden Frage wird nun: wie kann die Philosophie ihr Wissen vom Besseren an die schlechte, in Entzweiung lebende Gegenwart übermitteln? Soll die gegenwärtige Wirklichkeit sich zur Philosophie hinbewegen, um damit ihre Mangelhaftigkeit loszuwerden, oder soll sich die Philosophie in die Wirklichkeit hineinbegeben, um diese entsprechend dem philosophischen Ideal umzugestalten?

Für beide Seiten der Alternative haben sich prominente Philosophen der Zeit stark gemacht. Von den Vertretern des deutschen Idealismus war es vor allem Hegel, der herausgestellt hat, daß die Wirklichkeit sich der philosophischen Idee anzumessen habe; anders formuliert: daß die Menschen durch philosophisches Wissen die Beschränktheiten der Wirklichkeit zu überwinden haben. In einem berühmt gewordenen pathetischen Satz über die Französische Revolution, in welchem er von der Revolutionierung der 'geistigen Wirklichkeit' mehr erwartet als von der Revolutionierung der historischen Gesellschaft, hat Hegel dies zum Ausdruck gebracht:

Solange die Sonne am Firmamente steht und die Planeten um sie herumkreisen, war das nicht gesehen worden, daß der Mensch sich auf den Kopf, das ist, auf den Gedanken stellt und die Wirklichkeit nach diesem erbaut..., nun aber ist der Mensch dazu gekommen zu erkennen, daß der Gedanke die geistige Wirklichkeit regieren sollte. [1]

Für die andere Seite der Alternative hat sich mit großem Nachdruck Karl Marx ausgesprochen. Vor allem für den jungen Marx ist das Ziel dieses: die Philosophie ist in die zerrüttete Wirklichkeit hineinzutragen; es gilt die Wirklichkeit als das Ensemble aller gesellschaftlichen Verhältnisse zu verändern. Auch hierzu ein berühmtes Zitat, und zwar die letzte der 'Thesen über Feuerbach': "Die Philosophen haben die Welt nur verschieden interpretiert, es kömmt drauf an, sie zu verändern." [2]

Für beide, für Hegel wie für Marx, leidet die Gegenwart unter einem Grundmangel, daran nämlich, daß philosophisches Wissen und die historisch-gesellschaftliche Wirklichkeit einander fremd sind und ohne innere Beziehung zueinander stehen. Für beide zeigt sich darin — in völliger Entsprechung zur Tradition neuerer deutscher Geschichtsphilosophie — der die Gegenwart kennzeichnende zentrale 'Widerspruch von Idee und Wirklichkeit'; ein 'Widerspruch' deshalb, weil die 'Wahrheit' der Geschichte in der *Einheit* der philosophischen Idee mit der historisch-gesellschaftlichen Wirklichkeit liegen soll. Beide sind sich auch darin einig, daß das *philosophische Wissen* als das eine Glied des 'Widerspruchs' sich selber noch im Zustand der 'Entfremdung' befindet. Das Faktum, daß Philosophie und Wirklichkeit getrennt sind; daß Philosophie die Wirklichkeit nicht ergriffen hat, ist für Hegel und den frühen Marx in genau der gleichen Weise das grundlegende Indiz der 'Entfremdung' in der modernen Zeit.

Es ist dies zunächst die systematische Hauptthese Hegels: das philosophische Bewußtsein erklärt sich als das Wissen der absoluten Einheit. Als bloßes Wissen, in Gestalt rein wissensmäßiger Philosophie aber stehen ihm undurchdrungene Wirklichkeiten gegenüber, die Wirklichkeiten der Natur, der Geschichte, der Gesellschaft. Gegenüber all diesen Wirklichkeiten macht das philosophische Bewußtsein die Erfahrung, daß es mit ihnen nicht in Einheit ist: an der Natur, daß es sie durch Erkenntnis nicht völlig zu bewältigen vermag, an Geschichte und Gesellschaft, daß Krieg, Konflikt, Auseinandersetzung, Konkurrenz realer sind als Einheit und Harmonie unter den Menschen. Hegels *Phänomenologie des Geistes* gibt die Geschichte jener Erfahrungen wieder, die das philosophische Bewußtsein macht. Dieses erfährt in Permanenz den 'Widerspruch an ihm selbst': es behauptet, in Einheit mit seinem Gegenstand, der jeweiligen Wirklichkeit, zu sein und muß doch einsehen, daß es ihr in 'Wahrheit' fremd gegenübersteht, daß es ihr faktisch 'entfremdet' ist. Den Terminus 'Entfremdung' hat Hegel denn auch ausdrücklich und aus Überlegung für das philosophische Bewußtsein reserviert, sofern es ein bloßes *Wissen* der Einheit ist. Er nennt deshalb 'Bildung' den 'sich entfremdeten Geist' schlechthin und sieht ihren Mangel, ihren 'entfremdeten' Charakter darin, daß die 'Einheit' nur als das mehr oder weniger zufällige 'gebildete' Wissen einzelner individueller Menschen vorhanden ist. In der *Phänomenologie des Geistes* heißt es: "Wodurch also das Individuum hier Gelten und Wirklichkeit hat, ist seine Bildung. Seine wahre ursprüngliche Natur und Substanz ist der Geist der Entfremdung dés natürlichen Seins." [3]

Warum hat Hegel nun nicht, wie später sein Schüler Marx, die Revolutionierung der realen gesellschaftlichen Verhältnisse gefordert, um die 'Entfremdung' der Philosopie von der Wirklichkeit aufzuheben? Hegel hat das nicht getan, weil er als einziger in der skizzierten Tradition deutscher Geschichtsphilosophie die Vorstellung aufgegeben hatte, die geforderte Einheit sei erst nach völliger Beseitigung der gegensätzlichen Zerrissenheit und Entfremdung herzustellen. Er hat gebrochen mit dem Gedanken, wonach die Einheit, nach der die deutsche Geschichtsphilosophie — von Herder bis Fichte — sich sehnte, erst in der Zukunft — durch philosophische Bildung oder praktisch-gesellschaftliche Revolutionierung — geschaffen werden könne.

Hegel hat — im Gegenteil — das eine seiner beiden Hauptwerke, die *Phänomenologie des Geistes*, mit einer deutlichen Kritik an der Vorstellung eines *zukünftigen* Einheitszustandes abgeschlossen. Nach ihm befreit sich das philosophische Bewußtsein von den Erfahrungen seiner 'Entfremdung' nicht durch die Arbeit für eine Gesellschaft, in der es keine Entfremdung mehr gibt. Nach Hegel gibt es eine Befreiung von der Entfremdung nur dadurch, daß das philosophische Bewußtsein alle aufgetretenen Formen der Entfremdung als Notwendigkeiten *erkennt* und hinnimmt. Man kann deshalb sagen: Befreiung von der Entfremdung heißt für Hegel *Versöhnung* mit der Entfremdung — und damit Aufgabe der utopischen Hoffnung, es könne einmal einen historischen Zustand ohne Entfremdung geben, einen Zustand, in dem der Mensch nicht an die Natur ausgeliefert wäre und der dem Kampf der Menschen untereinander ein Ende setzte.

Da Hegels Position eine Sache der *philosophischen* Einsicht ist, hat die Philosophie bei ihm in der Tat das letzte Wort. Nur darin liegt der von ihm beanspruchte *Primat der Philosophie* vor der gesellschaftlich-historischen Praxis, ein Punkt, für den er bekanntlich von den meisten nachfolgenden Philosophen — Marx war nur der prominenteste — heftige Kritik hat einstecken müssen. Nun kann man zunächst einmal sagen, daß Hegels Ideal nicht zu bewältigen ist — nicht zu bewältigen, weil zum einen kein Mensch in der Lage ist, die *Gesamtheit* aller Entfremdungsformen zu erleben und durch sie hindurchzugehen, und zum anderen nicht zu schaffen, weil die Einsicht in die Notwendigkeit mancher Formen der Entfremdung — dazu gehört nach Hegel auch die Erfahrung der Todesnähe — den meisten Menschen entschieden zuviel abverlangt.

Doch sieht man von solchen realistischen Einwänden des gesunden Menschenverstandes einmal ab, so zeigt sich hier ein überraschender Umstand. Hegel erweist sich ganz offensichtlich als der erste Kritiker des Schemas, welches die deutsche Geschichtsphilosophie seines Zeitalters durchgehend beherrscht. Das Schema ist bekannt: es gab eine Epoche idealer Harmonie, das klassische Griechentum, das christliche Mittelalter oder einen Naturzustand menschlicher Unbefangenheit und ungezwungener Solidarität. Die Geschichte der Zivilisation aber ist die Geschichte der Zerrüttung und Zerstörung der ursprünglichen Harmonie. Diese lebt in der antagonistischen Gegenwart allein in Gestalt abstrakter, von der Wirklichkeit abgelöster, ihr entfremdeter Ideale fort. Philosophie, Literatur und höhere Bildung sind die Stätten ihrer Aufbewahrung. Die Aufgabenstellung an die Gegenwart lautet: Wiedergewinnung der verlorengegangenen Einheit, zukünftige Realisierung der philosophischen Ideale — und damit zugleich *Aufhebung* der Kluft von Philosophie und Wirklichkeit, *Aufhebung* der Entfremdung von Philosophie und Wirklichkeit.

Hegel erweist sich nun deshalb als Kritiker dieses grundlegenden Schemas deutscher Geschichtsphilosophie, weil er die bei seinen Vorgängern und Zeitgenossen (z.B. Schiller, Fichte) übliche Losgelöstheit der Einheit von der realen Wirklichkeit anders sieht. Der Inhalt des 'absoluten Wissens,' in welches seine *Phänomenologie des Geistes* einmündet, fordert nicht zu einer zukünftigen Realisierung der klassischen Ideale auf. Das 'absolute Wissen' verlangt vielmehr die Erkenntnis, daß das Hoffen auf die Zukunft selber die *Täuschung* ist, die es — total und generell — für alle Bewußtseinsstufen — zu durchschauen gelte. Was man sich angewöhnt hat, seit es Hegel-Interpretationen gibt, als Resignation des alternden Philosophen zu deuten, der seinen Frieden mit dem Zeitgeist, vor allem mit dem preußischen Staat der Restauration, gemacht hat, ist in Wahrheit schon immer Hegels objektiv-systematische Überzeugung gewesen.

Die viel gehörte These, in der der 'progressive' Hegel der *Phänomenologie* gegen den 'reaktionären' Hegel der *Rechtsphilosophie* ausgespielt wird, ist eine schiefe These. Es gibt im Hegelschen Werk vom systematischen Konzept her — gar keinen Raum für eine derartige Entgegensetzung. Bei Hegel besteht das Absolute — und dies spätestens seit der *Phänomenologie des Geistes* — in nichts weiter als in der Totalität seiner Entfremdungsformen. Philosophie als 'Wissen des Absoluten,' als 'absolutes Wissen' ist das Wissen von der unumgänglichen Notwendigkeit der Entfremdung, auch derjenigen Entfremdung, die in der Fremdheit der Philosophie und politisch-gesellschaftlicher Wirklichkeit liegt. Nur diesen Sinn hat Hegels Bestehen auf der Selbständigkeit der Philosophie gegenüber Geschichte und Gesellschaft.

Die Linkshegelianer und vor allem Karl Marx haben Hegel stets mehr unterstellt, als dieser hat sagen wollen. Sie haben Hegel vorgeworfen, er habe das Absolute nur im Geist, im reinen Denken belassen, während es seinem eigenen Anspruch nach in der gesellschaftlich-historischen Wirklichkeit realisiert werden müsse. Die Kritik der Linkshegelianer und von Marx ist jedoch der Sache nach mehr als Kritik an Fichte als eine an Hegel aufzufassen, denn Fichte ist es gewesen, der die Hoffnung auf zukünftige Realisierung des Absoluten genährt hat. Allerdings hat Fichtes Philosophie das Zeitbewußtsein in der 1. Hälfte des 19. Jahrunderts nicht annähernd so geprägt wie diejenige von Hegel. Deshalb wurde Hegel zum Exponenten der Kritik und eben nicht Fichte.

Marx hat das klassische Schema der Geschichtsphilosophie wieder aufgegriffen, das Schema von ursprünglicher Einheit, Zerfall und zukünftiger Versöhnung der Gegensätze. Er ist derjenige in der Reihe deutscher Geschichtsphilosophen, welcher das Schema am nachdrücklichsten historisch und gesellschaftlich konkretisiert hat. Der Zerfall ursprünglich-naiver und organischer Einheit menschlicher Vergesellschaftung tritt nach Marx — und zwar in allen Stufen seiner theoretischen Entwicklung — durch das Aufkommen der Tauschwirtschaft ein. Zum hauptsächlichen Indiz für die Zerrüttung menschlicher Verhältnisse in der neuzeitlichen Zivilisationsepoche wird die aus dem Warentausch resultierende Bildung privaten kapitalistischen Eigentums. Im Phänomen des Geldes kommt die ökonomisch bedingte Zerrüttung beispielhaft zum Ausdruck: Geld verdrängt als Darstellungsmittel für den Tauschwert aller Produkte und Gegenstände deren eigene, selbständige

Qualität. In Marxens Aufsatz über die Judenfrage heißt es vom Geld, es sei der "für sich selbst konstituierte Wert aller Dinge," und weiter: "Es hat daher die ganze Welt, die Menschenwelt wie die Natur, ihres eigentümlichen Wertes beraubt. Das Geld ist das dem Menschen entfremdete Wesen seiner Arbeit und seines Daseins, und dieses fremde Wesen beherrscht ihn, und er betet es an." [4]

In allen Phasen seiner Entwicklung ist Marx davon ausgegangen, daß der Grundwiderspruch, welcher die neuere Gesellschaftsperiode charakterisisiert, aufgehoben werden müsse in einer Zukunftgesellschaft, die frei davon ist – die weder das Marktsystem der Tauschwerte kennt noch das privatkapitalistische Eigentum, vor allem nicht das an den Produktionsmitteln.

Zwei Dinge sind klar: Erstens spielt bei Marx das Grundschema der deutschen Geschichtsphilosophie ebenfalls die entscheidende Rolle. Es bildet den Rahmen für die empirischen Einzelanalysen und Theorien, die Marx in seinen Werken – auch den wissenschaftlich-ökonomischen – vorgelegt hat. Zweitens kommt auch bei ihm der *Philosophie* bezw. der philosophischen *Theorie* eine ausschlaggebende Bedeutung zu: die philosophische Theorie ist der Platzhalter der gesellschaftlichen und historischen 'Wahrheit' über die Entwicklung der menschlichen Gattung. Die einzige Frage ist nur, wie man die Theorie in Praxis überführt; wie man gemäß der Theorie die gesellschaftliche Wirklichkeit umgestalten kann. Aber selbst dies ist nicht eigentlich eine Frage für Marx, enthalten materialistische Geschichtsphilosophie und politische Ökonomie doch die 'Wahrheit' sowohl über Vergangenheit, Gegenwart als auch Zukunft der neuzeitlich-kapitalistischen Gesellschaftsentwicklung: aus der wissenschaftlich fundierten Prognose der Zukunftsentwicklung lassen sich nach Marx Handlungsanweisungen zur Beeinflussung der Entwicklung zu dem Zweck ableiten, die sozialistische Gesellschaft zu verwirklichen.

Nun einige Bemerkungen – auch kritischer Art – zum ersten Punkt: Es ist evident, daß die Lehre von Marx in ihren Grundzügen in den großen Zusammenhang der neueren deutschen Geschichtsphilosophie seit Herder gehört. Sie fußt auf dem bekannten Grundschema von ursprünglicher Einheit; Zerfall in Entfremdungsformen und wiederzugewinnender Einheit. Das Schema bildet zugleich die Grundlage der dialektischen Methode, denn diese ist nichts anderes als die Nachkonstruktion des geschichtlichen Verlaufs. Im Rahmen der Dialektik – hauptsächlich auch der materialistischen Dialektik von Marx — spielt der Begriff der Entfremdung eine wichtige Rolle. Er kennzeichnet — neben dem der Verdinglichung — die gesellschaftlich-historischen Phänomene der geschichtlichen Zerrüttungsphase in Vergangenheit und Gegenwart, bei Marx vornehmlich die Phänomene, in denen sich der den Kapitalismus grundsätzlich bestimmende 'Widerspruch von Kapital und Arbeit' spiegelt. Nun stellt der Begriff der Entfremdung — und dies gilt für Marx wie auch bereits für Hegel — nicht bloß eine Kategorie der *Beschreibung* wirklicher Verhältnisse dar. Er beinhaltet als deskriptive Kategorie zugleich eine Wertung, die Wertung nämlich, daß die als 'entfremdet' diagnostizierten Verhältnisse mangelhaft und schlecht sind; so schlecht, daß es darauf ankomme, sie zu überwinden. Kennzeichnend für den dialektischen Entfremdungsbegriff ist aber diès, daß die in ihm liegende Wertung sich nicht als solche zu erkennen gibt.

Es verhält sich vielmehr so, daß dasjenige, was uns als eine gesellschaftspolitische und sozialphilosophische Wertung de facto erscheinen muß, als ein *objektives*, dem beschriebenen gesellschaftlich-historischen Tatbestand innewohnendes Moment auftritt. Gerade darin besteht das Charakteristische aller dialektischen Entfremdungsvorstellungen.

Die Dialektik — ob idealistische Hegelsche oder materialistische Marxscher Version — kommt auf diese Weise in den Besitz eines in seiner theoretischen und praktischen 'Fruchtbarkeit' kaum zu überschätzenden Instrumentariums. Sie erreicht so, daß die Frage der *Gültigkeit* gesellschaftspolitischer Wertsetzungen zur Sache einer wissenschaftlichen Analyse von Tatsachen wird. Das wirkt sich auf die Überzeugungskraft einer Parteinahme für bestimmte politische Wertungen — Wertungen, wie sie in der kritischen Verurteilung des kapitalistischen Marktsystems und dem Votum für den Sozialismus-Kommunismus zum Ausdruck kommen — auf den ersten Blick ohne Zweifel günstig aus. In Hegels Philosophie geht es dabei allerdings nicht um die Bevorzugung einer gesellschaftspolitischen Wertvorstellung wie etwa des Sozialismus. Bei ihm drückt sich — in der *Phänomenologie des Geistes* z.B.— die Nichtbeachtung des Unterschieds von Wert und Faktum in der Behauptung aus, daß jede Entfremdungsform des philosophischen Bewußtseins *in sich* — d.h. als Bewußtseinssachverhalt — des Potentials für seine Überwindung und Aufhebung enthält.

Resümieren wir kurz: in der dialektischen Philosophie ist der Entfremdungsbegriff derjenige Begriff, welcher als Faktenbeschreibung zugleich die Gültigkeit einer bestimmten Wertsetzung beinhaltet.

Ich bin nun der Meinung, daß in dieser kritischen Feststellung mehr liegt als der Nachweis eines 'naturalistischen Fehlschlusses.' Die Vermischung von Werten und Fakten, wie sie beispielhaft im dialektischen Entfremdungsbegriff zum Ausdruck kommt, hat eine weitergehende Bedeutung. Sie macht nämlich klar, warum es die deutsche dialektische Geschichtsphilosophie nicht zu einer konsequenten Demokratietheorie gebracht hat.

Die Theorien über Demokratie, die für die politische Entwicklung Westeuropas und Nordamerikas bestimmend wurden, stammen aus dem Umkreis der Philosophie des englischen Empirismus und des mit ihr verbundenen politischen Liberalismus. Den Philosophen des Liberalismus, von Locke über Hume zu Bentham und J.S. Mill, geht es nicht um Geschichtsphilosophie, nicht um globale Erkenntnis des Verlaufs der Geschichte einschließlich des Wissens der 'richtigen' Ziele der zukünftigen Entwicklung. Ihnen geht es im Kern um die Durchsetzung eines nichtautoritären staatlichen Entscheidungssystems für gesamtgesellschaftliche Wert- und Zielkonflikte, gemeint ist die Demokratie in parlamentarischer Form. Hinter dieser Intention steht eine andere philosophische Erkenntnistheorie als es die ist, die der deutschen Geschichtsphilosophie zugrunde liegt. Während diese Geschichtsphilosophie letztlich immer mit der Vermischung von Fakten- und Wertaussagen operiert, basiert das Demokratieverständnis des englischen Liberalismus auf der von David Hume exemplarisch herausgestellten Unterscheidung von Fakten und Werten. Aus dem prinzipiellen Unterschied von Fakten und Werten folgt nämlich, daß man über divergierende Faktenbehauptungen mit Methoden der Wissenschaft diskutieren und letztlich auch Entscheidungen herbeiführen kann, ein Vorgehen, das bei divergierenden politischen Wertbehauptungen nicht möglich ist: im Umkreis politischer Wert- bzw. Zielkonflikte gibt es keine wissenschaftlichen Entscheidungsmöglichkeiten, mithin keine 'Richtigkeits'-Kriterien. Dieser werttheoretische Skeptizismus bildet meines Erachtens die grundlegende Folie des angelsächsischen Demokratiebegriffes. Er steht im deutlichen Kontrast zum Erkenntnisoptimismus der deutschen Geschichtsphilosophie, einem Optimismus, der am Beispiel 'Entfremdung' aufgezeigt — zu bezahlen ist mit der Mißachtung des fundamentalen Unterschieds von Fakten- und Wertbehauptungen.

Wie sehen die Konsequenzen des werttheoretischen Skeptizismus für den Demokratiebegriff des politischen Liberalismus aus? Die Vertreter des Liberalismus verbindet die gemeinsame Überzeugung, daß Wahlen und Mehrheitsentscheidungen die einzige Entscheidungsbasis für gesamtgesellschaftliche Wertentscheidungen sein müssen. Warum nun Mehrheitsentscheide? Nicht deshalb, weil die Mehrheit die 'Wahrheit' bzw. 'Richtigkeit' von Wertentscheidungen garantiert, sondern weil es mehrheitliche Übernahme der Verantwortung für Wertentscheidungen bedeutet, für Wertentscheidungen, die in der Konsequenz die Gesamtheit der Bürger betreffen. Ich kann hier nur die Punkte herausstellen, die in meinen Augen von prinzipieller Bedeutung für das liberale Demokratieverständnis sind. Deshalb auch nur einige kurze Belege für meine Auffassung.

Erstens geben sich alle Liberalen − von Locke bis J.S. Mill − mit dem Konzept repräsentativer, d.h. indirekter Demokratie zufrieden. Wäre für sie Demokratie − wie etwa für Rousseau − gleichbedeutend mit der Hervorbringung des 'wahren' Willens aller Gesellschaftsmitglieder, wäre in ihrem Plädoyer für die Repräsentation der Einzelwillen in der Tat ein Widerspruch zu sehen.

Es geht ihnen zweitens überhaupt nicht in erster Linie um die Realisierung eines 'wahren' Volkswillens, sondern um die Kontrolle und rechtliche Einschränkung der Macht, die durch die Mehrheit im Namen aller Bürger ausgeübt wird. Ausdruck dieses Grundgedankens ist schon Lockes Konzeption der staatlichen Gewaltenteilung. Aber auch J.S. Mills Verteidigung der Rechte von Minderheiten und des Einzelnen hat diesen Sinn. Mill z.B. verbindet mit seiner Kritik an der Macht von Mehrheiten keineswegs eine Kritik am demokratischen Prinzip selber, wonach die Mehrheit legitimiert ist, die Staatsmacht auszuüben. Und dies deshalb nicht, weil es nur politische *Machtansprüche* auf die Vertretung des Gesamtwohles geben kann, nicht aber objektive Richtigkeitskriterien dafür, was das Gesamtwohl ist und wer es adäquat vertritt. Meines Erachtens löst mein Deutungsvorschlag − werttheoretischer Skeptizismus als erkenntnistheoretische Basis des liberalen Demokratiekonzepts − auch die häufig bemerkte Schwierigkeit, die darin liegt, daß die meisten Vertreter des liberalen Staatsgedankens einerseits ihrer philosophischen Grundeinstellung nach antiontologische, antimetaphysische Empiristen sind und andererseits in ihrer politischen Philosophie − z.B. im Zusammenhang mit individuellen

Freiheitsrechten — sich auf *naturrechtliche* Begründungen beziehen. Der scheinbare 'Widerspruch' löst sich auf, wenn man daran denkt, daß Mehrheiten zwar entscheiden sollen, andererseits aber nie Ausdruck eines 'wahren' Willens aller sein können. Die englischen Liberalen haben aus diesem Tatbestand nicht — wie Rousseau und seine Anhänger, etwa Fichte — auf die Notwendigkeit von *Basisdemokratie* geschlossen. Aus der prinzipiellen Skepsis gegen die Möglichkeit, den Gesamtwillen je adäquat feststellen zu können, haben sie vielmehr stets für die Einrichtung von Freiräumen plädiert die durch Mehrheitsbeschlüsse und Mehrheits- meinungen nicht tangiert werden können. Das Naturrecht wird von den Liberalen immer dann bemüht, wenn es gilt, derartige Eingrenzungen des demokratischen Prinzips selber unter Bedingungen seiner generellen Geltung zu begründen.

Soweit einige kurze Belege für meine Meinung, daß der Demokratiebegriff des Liberalismus als Ausdruck eines werttheoretischen Skeptizismus zu deuten ist, eines Skeptizismus, der die logische Konsequenz aus Humes Beweisführung für die strikte Trennung von Fakten- und Wertbehauptungen darstellt.

Weder bei Hegel noch bei Marx gibt es eine Dimension, die mit der skizzierten Rahmenvorstellung des angelsächsischen Liberalismus zu vergleichen wäre. In beider Philosophien ist die Erkenntnis des bestehenden Schlechten wie die Notwendigkeit seiner Überwindung eine Sache theoretisch-philosophischer Sachverhaltensanalyse. Der dialektische Entfremdungsbegriff wird zum Hebel und zentralen Angelpunkt der Analyse.

Dem liberalen Verständnis zufolge ist sowohl die gesellschaftliche *Bewertung* der jeweils gegenwärtigen Wirklichkeit als auch die Festlegung der Gesellschaft auf wirklichkeitsverändernde Zielvorstellungen eine Sache demokratischer Mehrheitsermittlung und nicht das Resultat wissenschaft- licher Sachverhaltserkenntnis. Als Anhänger des liberalen Demokra- tiegedankens wird man jedoch unbeschadet des Votums für Mehrheitsentscheide ständig das Mißtrauen gegen den Anspruch von Mehrheiten wachhalten, die 'Richtigkeit' politischer Wertentscheidungen zu verbürgen.

An der deutschen geschichtsphilosophischen Tradition kommt als wesentliches politisches Kennzeichen so etwas wie ein '*Diktat der Vernunft*' zum Vorschein. Das mag widersprüchlich klingen, hält man sich an die

WERNER BECKER

plausible Überlegung, daß Vernunft und Zwang ohne Einsicht nicht zueinander passen. Der Ausdruck 'Diktat der Vernunft' ist gleichwohl angebracht, wenn von der Verwendung des Wortes 'Vernunft' im Idealismus ausgegangen wird. 'Vernunft' bezeichnet dort die Fähigkeit zu philosophischer *Erkenntnis* der Wirklichkeit in einem umfassenden, absoluten Sinn: sowohl im theoretisch-wissenschaftlichen als auch im ethischen und politisch-praktischen.

Mir scheint, daß dieser Anspruch nur aufrechtzuerhalten war in einer Zeit, in welcher Philosophie die Rolle übernommen hatte, die im Mittelalter und in der beginnenden Neuzeit die Theologie spielte. Und in der Tat nahm die Philosophie — besonders im Deutschland der ersten Hälfte des 19. Jahrhunderts — eine Funktion wahr, die man als 'Religion für Aufgeklärte' umschreiben kann. Mit ihr verband sich durchaus ein *politischer Machtanspruch* 'höherer Bildung.' Weniger wichtig sind dabei die Inhalte der politischen Wertvorstellungen, die mit dem Machtanspruch jeweils verknüpft sind. Wichtig ist allein, daß Philosophie und mit ihr 'höhere Bildung' den Anspruch erheben konnten, *aus sich* selbst heraus die *Gültigkeit* politischer Maßstäbe zu begründen.

Karl Marx wurde zum konsequenten Vertreter des elitären Machtanspruchs deutscher Bildung. Ihm ging es — hauptsächlich in seiner frühen Phase — um 'Verwirklichung der Philosophie,' um das 'Philosophisch-Werden der Wirklichkeit.' Seine gesamte Kritik am Idealismus läßt sich auf die ständig wiederholte kritische Formel reduzieren, die idealistischen Philosophen, in seinen Augen vor allem Hegel, hätten die ihrer Philosophie innewohnende Forderung nach Umgestaltung der Wirklichkeit nicht konsequent genug erfüllt; bei ihnen sei die Revolution im Geiste — im Begriff, im reinen Denken, in der Logik etc.— steckengeblieben. Er fühlt sich als der eigentliche Verwirklicher der Philosophie.

In Wahrheit aber ist er der Vollstrecker des elitären Machtanspruchs des deutschen Idealismus mit seinem überdimensionierten Vernunft- und Bildungsbegriff. Auch Karl Marx ist der Überzeugung, daß Philosophie allein sowohl die Maßstäbe der Kritik der 'bestehenden Verhältnisse' als auch die politischen Wertvorstellungen, nach denen die Menschen in Zukunft die Einrichtung der Gesellschaft betreiben werden, darlegen kann.

Gewiß, man kann einwenden: wo gab es zu seiner Zeit schon Demokratie? Jedenfalls nicht in dem Land, in dem Marx seine Jugend verbracht hatte und dessen Bildungstradition ihn am stärksten beeinflußt hat: Deutschland. Das erklärt vielleicht, widerlegt jedoch nicht die Feststellung, daß er sich keine Gedanken gemacht hat über die für Demokraten entscheidende Frage, wie man allgemein-politische Wertvorstellungen als gültig in Kraft setzt. Um solche Wertvorstellungen aber handelt es sich bei Marxens Kritik am Bestehenden wie bei seinen Zukunftsprognosen. Er hat das elitäre Diktat des idealistischen Vernunftbegriffs in einer Weise exerziert wie kein anderer Geschichtsphilosoph vor ihm. Der politische Machtanspruch für Philosophie ist bei ihm allerdings mit Raffinement kaschiert. Dadurch nämlich, daß er die Arbeiterklasse, im 19. Jahrhundert die Klasse par excellence der Unterprivilegierten und Entrechteten, zum ausschlaggegebenden Erfüllungsgehilfen der 'Verwirklichung der Philosophie' gemacht hat. Seit dieser Zeit gibt es die unkritisch ins Selbstverständnis der deutschen Arbeiterbewegung eingewanderte — mindestens kurios, wenn nicht gar unheilig anmutende — Allianz zwischen Arbeiterklasse und deutsch-idealistischer Philosophie.

Ich glaube nicht, daß in demokratischen Verhältnissen Philosophie oder irgendeine Wissenschaft eine ähnlich dominierende Rolle spielen könnten. Und das ist nicht zuletzt deswegen gut so, weil Philosophie und Wissenschaft gar nicht die Mittel besitzen, langfristig wirksame politische Wertorientierungen in rationaler Weise abzusichern. Wir haben keine Wissenschaft, vor allen Dingen keine Sozialwissenschaft, die in ihrer Prognosefähigkeit so sicher wäre, daß die Folgen von politischen Entscheidungen sich langfristig mit der nötigen Exaktheit absehen lassen. Und wir haben keine Philosophie, deren Legitimationskraft ausreichte, *aus sich heraus* die Gültigkeit politischer Werte und Wertentscheidungen zu begründen. Das bedeutet kein Plädoyer für Irrationalität und gegen Vernunft in politischen Dingen. Es liegt darin lediglich der Appell zu mehr Bescheidenheit in Anforderungen an die Vernunft, einer Bescheidenheit, für die speziell aus der zum Überschwang neigenden jüngeren deutschen Geistesgeschichte, abgesehen von der rühmlichen Ausnahme Kants, kaum Vorbilder vorzuzeigen sind.

Johann Wolfang Goethe Universität
Frankfurt am Main

NOTEN

[1] *Vorlesungen über die Philosophie der Weltgeschichte*, hrsg. G. Lasson, Leipzig, 1923, 4:926.

[2] Marx & Engels, *Die deutsche Ideologie*, Berlin, 1917, S. 595.

[3] Stuttgart, 1951, 2:377.

[4] *MEGA*, Berlin [Ost], Dietz, 1975, 3:603.

MENACHEM BRINKER

TRANSHISTORICITY AND
THE IMPOSSIBILITY OF *AUFHEBUNG*

REMARKS ON J.-P. SARTRE'S PHILOSOPHY OF HISTORY

Some of those who read Sartre's lecture on Kierkegaard "L'universel singulier"[1] were surprised to find there the notion of *transhistoricité* (transhistoricity). Yet it is this notion and the argument based upon it which offers in my opinion the key to a true understanding of J.-P. Sartre's writings in the late fifties and the sixties, mainly *Questions de méthode* (*QM*) and *Critique de la raison dialectique* (*CRD*).[2]

Sartre wanted the *CRD* to be looked upon as a revised version of Marxism. He stated many times that, due to political circumstances, the development of Marxist thought had been arrested: Marxism had become sterilized and needed a revival. He praised the originality of Marx's insights and the fertility of the dialectical method. Yet if the only reasons for the death of true Marxist research are political, it seems strange that contemporary Marxist thought cannot be revived by going back to its sources but must be revived from without and in the form of ontological foundation.

The truth is, of course, that for J.-P. Sartre original Marxian thought lacked an ontological basis. It succeeded in giving good descriptions of some general historical phenomena but did not supply any satisfying analysis of "the being of a class" and the meaning of "belonging to a class."

This has nothing to do with the historical evolution of Marxism. It has to do with the influence of the Hegelian system and its tendency toward endowing historical collectivities with meta-physical and meta-empirical life. For Sartre, however, the being of a collectivity (the group) is problematic and dependent. Since it is limited on every side by the being of the individuals, it is a secondary ontological structure. It is individual praxis and consciousnesses which give rise to the collectivity in so far as this collectivity is supported by them. In order that the "being of a class" be

Yirmiahu Yovel (ed.), Philosophy of History and Action, 191–198. All Rights Reserved.
Copyright © 1978 by D. Reidel Publishing Company, Dordrecht, Holland.

ontologically founded, it is necessary to recover a generative act where individual human consciousnesses, due to similarity of circumstances and vis-à-vis a natural or a social "other," form a group. Sartre devoted his *Critique* to such an attempt.

What is of interest to us here is not so much his attempt to give Marxism an ontological foundation but his way of doing so. It is clear that the processes described in the *Critique* are, at least from the formal, phenomenological aspect, to be found not only in the case of the working class or the class of the capitalists, but in the case of any other human group. Any group will come into being by individual praxis, that is, by individuals discovering similarities of circumstances positing a common goal, turning their circumstances into a historical situation and trying to transcend it in view of their projected goal. I believe that it is possible to discuss the dynamic involved in such a process outside the sphere of the "being of a class" which is the immediate theme of the *CRD*. The title of Sartre's *Critique* reads *Theorie de l'ensembles pratiques*, and an *ensemble pratique* does not have to be a class. The modern Jewish collectivity can – and does – serve Sartre as another example.

This must help us classify some of the most common criticisms of the *CRD*. The one expressed by Lionel Abel claiming that the *CRD* is a partial apology for Stalinism has no foundation at all. The *CRD* was conceived and composed by Sartre after the publication of his detailed analysis of Stalinism, which covers more than four hundred pages.[3] But even without this auxiliary evidence it is clear that the argument of the *Critique* suggests that most of the history of the Soviet Union after the late twenties forms different stages of the alienation of spontaneity inside the group. This alienation comes with the introduction of hierarchy, institutionalization and bureaucracy into the "groupe en fusion." It breaks the solidarity of the group, turns its members against each other and introduces alienation which is neither more desirable nor justified than capitalist alienation. Since a revolution *may* degenerate but does not *have to* degenerate into this, it does not exhibit any conceptual or historical necessity and must, therefore, be morally and politically condemned.

On the other hand, the criticism made by Raymond Aron in *Histoire et dialectique de la violence*,[4] claiming that violence has a special attraction for Sartre's philosophy of history is, in a sense, true. There is a connection in Sartre's philosophy of history between historical creativity and violence, in the same way as there is a connection in his metaphysical imagination between the creative act of the individual *projêt* and violence towards oneself. Since this has to do with basic attitudes towards history in the sense of the human past, let us elaborate it in more detail.

The central motive of historical change in the *CRD* is *totalization*. A totalization arises whenever an individual or a group conceive their need in terms of a projected satisfaction in the future, its origin in the past and a total evaluation of the means existing in the present, which are able to carry on the transformation in the future. A totalization is the unification of all these separate moments. Need being a lack, that is, a negation, brings about totalization, that is, a structure which aims at a "negation of the negation." By this it also gives the basic scheme of time, which differentiates past from future in terms of the totalization.

It is obvious that within a totalization conceived in this way, the past is recognized as something which is going to be transcended. Some of its moments, of course, will be retained in the future and are retained during the struggle for satisfaction which forms the present. But since the dominant element in the totalization, that is, the unifying element, is the projected goal to be achieved in the future, it is clear that the past is subjected to a rigorous selection with only some of its structures retained. In fact, only those which are regarded as conducive to the goal will remain, and even those will not be taken by the present in the same sense with which they were endowed in the past. Totalization, therefore, creates a rupture between past and future, by which some elements of the past are not permitted to enter the new state of affairs, since they have no bearing on the new *projêt*, or are interfering with its attainment.

A totalization, therefore, is not a synthesis. It is not even a synthesis of the past and the present in terms of their more essential features which are going to be incorporated into the future. It is a unification carried out on the basis of a central negation. Thus it is exactly those features of the situation which are all-important to the unification that are going to be negated in the future rather than contained in it under any form. Need disappears with its satisfaction and the new "present" does not have to understand itself in terms of the satisfied need. It will rather understand itself in terms of new needs, new lacks and new totalizations. Totalization will always be a consciousness of a process or a struggle, and never a contemplation of an achievement. It would be futile to preach to a new generation in history not to use the work of earlier generations as tools towards attaining its goals. In the same way it would be futile to preach to a generation not to consider itself as a tool for the attainment of some goal in the future, since this is exactly what is done in history and no group of people can achieve its self-consciousness without creating a disruption between the generations, while the new one uses the old one and itself in the service of the future.

This inevitable "use" which any emerging group, class, or generation makes of past and present groups or generations turns familiar philosophical forms of moral judgement inapplicable to historical reality. When a group posits a new historical goal (an "end") and comes to understand itself in terms of this projected goal it inevitably creates an instrumentalistic attitude towards the past and the present which are now seen mainly as "means." In his political writings Sartre recognized the difficulties inherent in such a philosophical standpoint for the moral assessment of current political events. He emphasized therefore that moral disapproval or condemnation of political behaviour and decisions is always possible not only on the abstract level where one judges "ends" and "goals" by themselves. We must recognize that "means" participate in shaping "ends"; they create deviations in them and a certain choice of certain means may bring us to a point where we shall have to speak of a complete transformation of the end itself and eventually also of its annihilation.

Unfortunately we cannot discuss here in more detail Sartre's attempts in the fifties at making his own moralistic attitude towards political life compatible with his philosophical image of history. There is a certain tension here as well as some basic contradictions that are far from being resolved in a satisfactory way.

History as a living process does not guarantee an *Aufhebung*. It is at this point that we can ask whether history as a body of knowledge does not guarantee it by its mere preoccupation with the manner things become what they are and as they are. A historian may choose to become interested in an event of the past and turn it into an object of historical knowledge. Can the past be retained in this way?

Let us see what is involved in positing such a question. The moment of choice adds a new and important feature to the attitude of a new generation towards an older one. Historical phenomena which depend on the choice of a later age in order to be known or re-lived have a derived historical life. It is a total dependence in the same sense in which the life, and sometimes even the mere name, of a dead person is said to be dependent upon the memory of the living.

Can an *Aufhebung* be achieved on this level? Can we regard the work done by historians as a retention of past events, personalities and the like in a new form?

The work of an ideal historian is the work of reconstruction. This effort of reconstruction cannot be carried out unless people and events are seen exactly as they were seen at the time, and this cannot be achieved unless the historian has "this faculty which German historians and psychologists call comprehension."[5] Comprehension strives to achieve something which defies generalities and any attempt at complete conceptualization. Its object is the singularity of the personality and its situation. For Sartre singularity is not just the epistemic status of the object of ideographic sciences. It arises as the specific ontological characteristic of the human being, since this being is a centre of totalization, achieved by constant interiorization. Any kind or aspect of a situation which might be adduced in order to explain the behaviour of a certain historical figure, must be looked upon as external until we are sure that we have true understanding of the manner in which this externality was seen by the agent, that is, the manner in which it was interiorized.

In history human beings are constantly thrown into conditions which might be described in general terms and looked upon as universals. Yet, as a ground for explanation of the singular person, universals (such as the persecution of the Jews or the unbearable conditions of the working class) will not work. The historian, no less than the psychoanalyst or the writer of a biography, must look for the process which interiorizes external circumstances and singularizes the universal by its mere interiorization. The universal itself is, of course, an objectivation or common result of the objectivations of other agents, even when not recognized by them as such, due to alienation of one kind or another. Yet history is not done by objectivations (such as books, institutions, etc.) but by people, through their objectivations. A person cannot avoid interiorization any more than he can avoid objectivation, that is, engraving his subjectivity on things and objects (including other people). In this sense every individual consciousness or praxis is already a deviation in relation to the universal it is said to embody. (Any Jew deviates from Jewishness by the mere fact of his consciously existing as a Jew.) But by being this deviation in relation to the universal, the individual may also bring about the deviation of the universal itself.

The attempt to understand historical action or person must therefore — at least at a certain stage — avoid any kind of inference, induction or deduction and turn to be a comprehension, that is, a totalizing grasp of the person based upon a comprehension of the kind of totalization he is. Sartre suggests a special method for achieving this and recommends a certain circularity between the comprehending of an act and the stages which preceded it. This progressive-regressive method aims at making the totalization comprehensible by seeing its point of departure and its goal as illuminating one another. Obviously, it is impossible for us to discuss this special technique here. One point is important, however: we can now see that a true comprehension of historical being is hard to achieve not because the faculty of empathy is rare or occult. On the contrary, empathy is trivial, and all our understandings of others in daily life implies the progressive-regressive method. We understand a goal in terms of a condition that motivated its projection, and we come to understand a condition in terms of a goal. We comprehend an activity under the hypothesis of a projected goal, and we grasp the projected goal as based on a certain interiorization of a condition. Historical comprehension is *technically difficult*. It might be impossible to attach to the historical agent the same signification he attached to the general and particular externalities of his life and time. We might, for example, attribute to him knowledge of certain factors of a situation which he could but did not have. These difficulties are obvious in the special case of literature, where a poet's use of a word might derive from its use in a previous period and differ from its common use in his own time. Individual historicity is diachronic in the same sense that language is. The meaning attached by an adult to a certain state of affairs may need an elucidation in terms of his early childhood. And this is one way of explaining why nothing can be directly deduced from the general objective characteristics of a situation in order to explain personal behaviour.

This is perhaps a crude way of saying that comprehension differs not only from deduction, induction, inference (though all these may form parts of it), but also from evaluation. In evaluation one does not have to assume any affinity between a person or an act under evaluation and the point of view, values or norms which determine the evaluation.

Nevertheless, suppose comprehension in this sense is ideally possible, would it help us to conclude that history may retain its signification in a different and new form?

Here Sartre's lecture on Kierkegaard is all important, for it offers a very definite negative answer to the question.

The argument runs briefly in the following way: suppose Hegel was right and the only signification of Kierkegaard is his being one exemplification of the *unglücklisches Bewusstsein*. Yet, in his way of life, Kierkegaard was trying to show the heterogeneity of his existence and that of the Hegelian notion. This is not just the opposition between Kant's concept of the hundred thalers and their real existence, since Kierkegaard still *has to be* (in the future) the kind of existence which Hegel described (in the past).

Kierkegaard's consciousness lives by rejecting Hegel's description of him. He turns subjectivity into a secret and wants to create a state where overt public behaviour will mislead us the moment we shall try to take it as a *signifié* and move towards his subjectivity taken as a *signifiant*. Attempting to shake our belief in the possibility of objective knowledge, Kierkegaard's effort to detach himself from the Hegelian notion endures as long as he lives. He dies: shall we say that at this precise moment his being is absorbed in the all-embracing system and identifies finally with the notion it formed of him?

Sartre sarcastically formulates a possible Hegelian conclusion:

In ontological terms this would mean that the being of Kierkegaard before-his-birth identifies with his being after-his-death, existence seems just a means to enrich the first being [that is, the being of Kierkegaard before his birth] until it identifies with the second one [that is, the being of Kierkegaard after his death]; a provisional malaise, an indispensable means to arrive from the first one to the second, and in and by itself an inessential agitation of being.[6]

Given the difficulties of achieving a veritable signification and assuming (as we did) that Hegel succeeded in overcoming them (an assumption which Sartre accepts, of course, just for the sake of the argument) there is still something in Kierkegaard's existence which is not included in the signification. It is the failure of his attempt to dissociate himself from Hegel's *unglücklisches Bewusstsein*.

This failure, felt deeply in Kierkegaard's life, becomes something fixed forever, an absolute, with his death. It existed and died with Kierkegaard as a pure negation and cannot be retained in the system in the same way that a *privatio* cannot be contained in Spinoza's substance.

The lesson of Kierkegaard is therefore for Sartre the following: If there ever existed an ideal comprehension which was able to comprehend a singularity completely, that is, to the full extent of its deviations from the universals it is said to embody (or exemplify), there would still remain this feeling of the lack which existence *must* feel toward its signification, which is not retained in the signification itself. This aspect of being is completely annihilated in death and it is therefore because of death that man holds in his historical existence a transhistorical dimension which history cannot recapture.

Transhistoricity was misunderstood by Kierkegaard, who used it to make rational historical knowledge impossible. For Sartre, however, rational knowledge of history is possible so far as we remember that our general concepts (structures, epochs, schools, tendencies, even our general concepts of individual men) are surrounded by singularities which only comprehension can comprehend. Universals make their appearance in history only through men, that is, through singularizing agencies. But even an ideal comprehension is never able to retain the historical past, since in order to do this it must divorce individual existence from its transhistoricity.

An *Aufhebung* is therefore no more possible on the levels of knowledge and comprehension than it is on the levels of praxis and totalization.

Tel-Aviv University

NOTES

[1] The lecture was originally read in a colloquium organized by Unesco to commemorate Kierkegaard's 150th anniversary (21-23 April, 1964). It was published in *Kierkegaard vivant*, Paris, Gallimard, 1966.

[2] *Questions de méthode* was written in 1957, *Critique de la raison dialectique* was written between 1957 and 1960. They were both published in one volume by Gallimard, Paris, 1960.

For more details concerning the development of the ideas in these books and the circumstances of their publication see Michel Contat and Michel Ribalka, *Les écrits de Sartre*, Paris, Gallimard, 1970, pp. 311-322 and 337-340. There is an English translation of QM by H. Barnes, *The Problem of Method*, London, Methuen, 1963.

[3] See especially "Le fantôme de Staline," in *Les temps modernes*, Nos. 129-130-131, Novembre-Décembre 1956-Janvier 1957, pp. 577-697; reprinted in *Situations* 7: 144-307. English translation by M. Fletcher, *The Ghost of Stalin*, New York, George Braziller, 1962.

[4] Paris, Gallimard, 1973.

[5] "Pour saisir le sens d'une conduite humaine, il faut disposer de ce que les psychiatres et les historiens allemands ont nommé 'compréhension.'" *QM*, p. 96 (Eng. trans.: p. 153).

[6] "En termes ontologiques, l'être prénatal de Kierkegaard est homogène à son être post-mortem et l'existence parait un moyen d'enrichir le premier jusqu'à l'égaler au second: malaise provisoire, moyen essentiel pour aller de l'un à l'autre mais, en lui-même, fièvre inessentielle de l'être" (*Kierkegaard vivant*, pp. 31-32).

PART THREE

FAREWELL
TO THE PHILOSOPHY OF HISTORY?

RAYMOND POLIN

FAREWELL TO THE PHILOSOPHY OF HISTORY

I did not choose this topic and title without deep regret. It is, in one respect, my initiation to philosophy, my education as a philosopher that I am renouncing. I have the impression that I am perpetrating a sort of philosophical parricide. When I was a young man, French philosophers were re-discovering Hegel with the help of Alexandre Koyré and Kojève's seminar, which I attended, and with the stimulus of the exciting publication and translation into French of the papers of the young Marx.

We used to believe that philosophy of history was the necessary framework for modern philosophy to be taught, to be written and to be practised.

Each of us, according to his own vocation, used to find his inspiration either in the invention of philosophy of history by Jean Jacques Rousseau, writing his *Discours sur l'Inégalité*, or in the reflexions of Kant on the history of mankind. The philosophy of Hegel himself was generally considered the perfect model for a philosophy of history — *the* philosophy of history itself. But some of us were more impressed by its avatars among the post-Hegelians, and above all by Marx, or by the parallel skizza of Auguste Comte.

Anyway, the present essay will concern itself with that type of philosophy of history as the model of philosophy of history. We shall consequently leave aside the philosophy implicit in the work of any historian and the methodology of history as an epistemological approach, however important or topical these may be.

In many respects, it is a sort of sacrifice I have to consummate in this essay.

I

In order to be clear and direct, I shall try to establish, as rigorously as I can and, I hope, without provoking any discussion, the ideal type of philosophy

Yirmiahu Yovel (ed.), Philosophy of History and Action, 201–218. All Rights Reserved.
Copyright © 1978 by D. Reidel Publishing Company, Dordrecht, Holland.

of history as such. I shall put aside the classical myths of history, the myths concerning the beginnings of history, and the eschatologies, together with the interpretation of the principles of Rousseau, Kant, Hegel or Marx, which could be discussed indefinitely.

The *first postulate* of the ideal type seems to me that not simply the human species, but mankind as a whole, exists as the true point of reference for any meaning, for any means and ends in the world. Mankind may be scattered all over the earth, but it nevertheless constitutes a whole with its universal laws, laws of existence, laws of development. It is remarkable that, even if each phase of this development is governed by peculiar historical laws, the whole of mankind obeys the same universal and unique laws of development, passing through the same stages. Mankind does not initially constitute a general society of mankind, *communis societas humani generis*, but the general society of mankind will mark the achievement of its becoming in the end of history.

The *second postulate* affirms that human nature as such is historical. It does not however question the existence of a human nature, of its essence, which is freedom and reason — freedom, that is to say, reason. But it means that human essence does not fulfill itself in any single personal life, but that all along its history, mankind's essence, its concept, becomes its effective and efficient achievement. Especially for Hegel, that move represents a renewal of the concept of entelechy and a transferring of the Aristotelian theory of potentiality and actuality from the existence of the individual to the existence of the species. Man is given in his essence in the human animal. He frees himself from his animal nature and becomes more and more human, when he prefers his values to the value of life, his work to his existence. History, in its efficient actuality, is, in Kojève's word, an *anthropogenesis* through which the human species, the whole of mankind, passes from generation to generation, from the state of an animal, bearer of the concept of man, of reason, of freedom, to the state of a perfectly human being, perfectly free, reasonable and wise, that is to say omniscient and *befriedigt*, peaceful and satisfied.

Hence a *third postulate*: the becoming of effective and efficient history derives from the conjunction, from the conciliation of freedom, which is essential to human existence, and gives birth to its contingent mani-festations, with necessity, which is essential to the successive stages of mankind's historical development.

Everything human happens as if it were necessary for developing the concept of man into the actual reality of man, to pass through necessary stages of a necessary way. But this necessity is purely abstract, defining the condition *sine qua non*, not the sufficient conditions for the achievement of the perfectly human man.

The living forces which produce facts and deeds, the contingent *res gestae*, which constitute the object of historical studies, depend on freedom. The living forces of freedom manifest themselves in very different forms, according to the achievements of history, from instinct and passion to freedom in itself and for itself, to perfectly absolute and efficient knowledge. Freedom, which is just life in its primitive meaning, and mind, which is its ultimate meaning, are the motor, the efficient means of this history of which there is a philosophy. This freedom is properly the capacity of man to produce himself, to create himself, in a specific progress which, from generation to generation, leaves behind what is obsolete and preserves what is essential.

That freedom is properly the modern mode of freedom invented by Rousseau, freedom as a capacity for perfecting oneself, as a faculty of perfectibility, of *Perfektibilität* as Hegel will later say. But, according to a sort of heredity of invented or acquired characteristics, the making of man not only provokes the education, the *Bildung* of man, it produces the progressive transformation of the species from generation to generation, the actualization of the concept of man in mankind.

The facts and·deeds produced by freedom compose what we traditionally call history, the contingent facts and events of history historians are used to studying. They are neither effectively real nor truly significant. The only acts and facts which are effective and efficient in the realization of the essence of man, are those which happen to coincide with the abstract necessary development of man as such. It is as if the tapestry of mankind's real history were composed of the interweaving of the necessary becoming of mankind with the contingent threads, composed by human freedom. When the threads projected by our freedom do not meet and interweave with those of necessity, they are lost, they become vain and insignificant, a simple waste of the historical contingency. Whenever they knit and knot themselves together, they weave the actual tapestry of history. At this level of efficient reality, reason and freedom are identical in actual history, the only history worthy of the name, and the proper object for the philosophy of history.

Reason and freedom — that is, man himself — in their progressive incarnations, constitute the principles as well as the work of history.

Their conciliation, their dialectical unification, in the omniscient and perfectly free human being as well as in the relations between citizens in the achieved modern State, give history its finality, its meaning, and its end. This *fourth postulate* is certainly the most important for it implies all the others. To say that history has a meaning, an end, implies that everything belonging to the becoming of actual history is comprehensible and justified. Is not that becoming of history in fact the actualization of reason? But philosophy of history is possible as such only when history ends, when the meaning of history can be understood as a whole. Inside of history, in any period in which they live, men are only able to have a unilateral, partial consciousness of the historical becoming. They are effectively blind to the meaning of history, even to the meaning of the period of history in which they participate: they do not really understand what they are doing, what the consequences of their acts are. The subjective meaning they give their acts has nothing to do with their objective meaning; they live by illusions.

The moment of wisdom, of lucidity and absolute knowledge, when the meaning of history is revealed, is the moment when history can be understood as a whole, when man can be perfectly conscious of the world and of himself, and perfectly satisfied.

It is also the moment when a science of history, thus a philosophical science of man and of his actions, can be achieved, can become effective and efficient. If the perfectly wise man, the all-knowing man and the perfect statesman, could be united in one person, this person would be like a temporal god, a mortal god on earth.

II

This fourth postulate implies two major difficulties which may possibly be two insoluble mysteries.

The first is the problem of the "end of history." There cannot be any absolute philosophy, other than a philosophy of what has been achieved. Even adepts of philosophy of history do not agree about the date of the end. Is it 1789? 1806? or 1848? or 1917? Who knows? In fact, it is the pretension of understanding the whole of history which determines the date of the end. For the philosopher who announces the end, his book is the best proof and, of course, the only possible proof of his affirmation.

The uncertainty is even greater about the content of post-historical time. Will there be individual histories, or collective histories, or will the end of history just be a formal end with internal adventures and contingent transformations, the type of man having been perfectly realized once and for all? If this does not mean that man is once and for all perfectly human, completely satisfied, what does it mean? That all men are living in temporal permanent bliss? That all men are omniscient and almighty? or some men only? or one man? Would all the others be human and satisfied, just by identifying with the 'number one' in a homogeneous society?

In principle, one should imagine man to be perfectly happy and satisfied in this world, in this nature. But that would mean that he would not have to act, to struggle, to labour any more. Would not that be, as Kojève imagined, the end of a properly human era, the end of man, his return to an animal way of life in perfect harmony with nature? This animal man, beyond history, would be a natural being, perfectly satisfied, not needing to think any more: in that animal, philosophy, the search for wisdom, would be accomplished, but wisdom itself would disappear with the disappearance of the necessity for thought, of the possibility of error, of the imperfection immanent in freedom.

Otherwise, we should have to assume that history ended in 1806; but are they — these human beings living beyond that date, in that post-history—still men? Animal men perhaps, enjoying life in an affluent society according to the American way of life, or human men living, according to the traditional Japanese way of life, in a permanent and purely formal opposition to nature, expressing the human capacity of negation through their snobbery.

Philosophers, even philosophers of history, are not prophets of the future. Futurologists do not act like philosophers, but like men of action: their hypotheses imagine a possible future as men of action do, they agree to run a risk in appreciating the probability of future events.

The knowledge of philosophers stops with the present time. The philosopher does not know anything about post-historical time, because he lives neither beyond history, nor even at its end. Philosophy is the proof that history has not ended. To affirm that history has to come to an end is an arbitrary postulate, and it even contradicts the essential postulate of history that man is free, that he always exists beyond himself, in constant self-renewal, in a constant surpassing of himself. In such a situation, the philosopher is not capable of absolute knowledge. In spite of its internal logic, the end of history cannot be a necessary postulate for the philosophy of history. And that is obviously the first indomitable objection to the very concept of philosophy of history.

This first uncertainty, this first contradiction, constitutes the first mystery of any philosophy of history. But there is also a second uncertainty, a second mystery inherent in the philosophy of history, I mean the problem of knowing whether or not it implies the existence of a God.

Thirty years ago, my answer would have been categorical. There are philosophies of history, like that of Marx, which are explicitly atheistic, and philosophies of history, like that of Rousseau and Kant, which are explicitly theistic. But what of the most perfect model of any philosophy of history, Hegel's philosophy? Is it or is it not, under its mask, the philosophy of an atheist? Throughout the becoming of history, is not man his own creator, in spite of its blindness? Is not history man's own work? Does he not play the part of God? From Rousseau on, freedom is no longer the power and possibility of realizing one's own essence; it is the power to add to what one is, to surpass, to transcend what one is, to create oneself otherwise than what one is. Is not man what he does? Is not even the meaning of history his own work? After all, Hegel deals with Religion before dealing, in the last chapter of the *Phenomenology of the Mind*, with Absolute Knowledge — Absolute Knowledge, and not Religion, bringing Revelation, the gospel of the Philosophy of History.

But today, I am more dubious about Hegel. I am certainly convinced of man's capacity to transcend himself, to go beyond himself and beyond everything given or imposed upon him, to be the principle of the creation of his values and actions. But I never confused that simply human power, limited by its conditions, its obstacles, its failures, its falls, with a properly divine power of creation. I have never believed that one could be substituted for the other or play the part of the other. In any case, human creation and divine creation can either coexist or not coexist without contradiction. A philosophy of history can affirm the creative gift of human freedom without necessarily excluding the creative power of God.

I must only indicate here that the theistic interpretation of Hegel's philosophy of history is at least as plausible as the atheistic interpretation. Indeed, if one is allowed to admit that a radical absence of order or initial fortuity do not pose metaphysical problems and require a metaphysical answer, the Hegelian concept of freedom, his concept of man, or his theory of concept itself imply a metaphysical question and a metaphysical solution. Freedom is not a simple fact; it implies a meaningful world, a spiritual world. Hegel himself declares that freedom is mind. Freedom requires finality and teleology, with all the metaphysical requisites of teleology. And what could the concept of man be, what would the concept of man and the design for his development mean, what would man's function in this historical becoming mean, without a thought able to conceive of these meanings? Was not Nietzsche right when he wrote that the philosophy of a meaningful history is but theology masked, *eine verkappte Theologie?*

In spite of the fact that we are dealing with a conceptual reconstruction of an ideal model for a philosophy of history, this model, when perfect, seems to imply necessarily the existence of a God as well as the existence of an end. Only on these two conditions does this model become perfect and acquire all its coherence, all its force of interpretation and of persuasion.

I do not consider it a valid objection that I am dealing only with the group of philosophies of history born with Rousseau and which, with Hegel's help, have inspired occidental philosophy until the present. There had not been any proper philosophy of history before Rousseau: there had just been myths of history: Greek or Judeo-Christian myths of the origin and of the end of the world, eschatologies which reappear even in some present philosophies, myths of progress, myths of decadence, myths of the eternal return. These myths were expressed in different forms: histories, tales, legends, symbols, dogmas. They were esoterically interiorized, they reappeared in the form of poetical philosophies. They have never been explicit philosophies of history as such.

Perhaps this is to their advantage. They rise again and again from their ashes, they are resurrected again and again throughout time and civilizations. On the other hand, our philosophies of history tried in our civilization and in our day to supersede the old myths of history and to play their philosophical role. Myths may be capable of permanent resurrection. But philosophies die with their time. Philosophies of history are already *passé*. And we have to bid them farewell.

III

Perhaps it is their mythical inspiration which gave philosophies of history their fascination. Considered as a whole, a great philosophy of history possesses considerable power to create illusion. Reduced to its fundamental axioms, the same philosophy of history does not resist the force of things and it is easy to observe that its axioms do not obey the principle of non-contradiction.

First, we must observe that the greatest philosophies of history were composed some time before 1817, the year in which the French essayist, Ballanche, used the word civilization in the plural for the first time. A little later, around 1840, philologists would demonstrate the irreducible plurality of civilizations. Rousseau himself, as early as 1756 or 1757, ceased to speak of a "general society of mankind" possessing unity, solidarity and a universal natural right. Beyond the human species, which is an animal species, humanity had only been the object of nice feelings and of nice words. It was a kind of fetish, good enough to demonstrate one's good conscience and good intentions at little cost to oneself.

How could one speak of a general history of the non-existing general society of mankind, of its necessary becoming, of the unique formation and education of man? There is no universal history of mankind considered as a whole. Or else three words would be sufficient to write it: "They were born, they lived, they died." But these three words concern not only mankind, but any animal species. There is nothing to prove that an essential history of mankind could exist, that mankind as such is like a single human individual moving from a stage of potential humanity to a final stage of actual humanity, that the same essential history was to be found among the contingent events of individual lives, in every civilization, in every society, in every people, in every nation.

There are many civilizations, societies, peoples, nations, groups and individuals in the human animal species, and they are characterized by their radical plurality and diversity, by their radical differences. The more distant in space or time two civilizations are, the more incomprehensible, incomparable and unassimilable they are to each other. No education can reduce that unbridgeable gap. Bergson's formula: "the human species is a species in which each individual constitutes by himself a unique species" could just as well be applied to civilizations, societies, peoples, nations or groups.

This irreducible plurality does not jeopardize the unity of the human species. It would be impossible to ground a pseudo-theory of the plurality of human races on it.

There is one element which is coextensive with the whole of mankind, I mean man himself, human nature. If it is always possible to recognize man in his works without any doubt, however diverse and original civilizations are, if there always remains a way for comprehension, a capacity for communication among human beings, in spite of this radical irreducibility, it is because there is a human essence. Even among civilizations capable of writing, that essential encounter and, up to the limit, that unbridgeable distance can be observed. A text is always to be understood wherever it comes from. But there always exists — is it not symbolic? — undeciphered writings and even, for lack of mediations, undecipherable writings. This essence of man, made of freedom and consciousness, more or less perfectly united and identified, actualizes itself into infinitely diverse appearances unbridgeably distanced by freedom each from the other.

The pseudo-essential historicity of the manifestations of human existence does not correspond to any experience. Quite to the contrary. There is no progressive succession of species of men in the history of man, like sub-species within a general species, which would correspond to periods of human history and to progressive stages of development, from the concept of man to the actualization of the perfect man. This theory is a gratuitous and arbitrary extrapolation of the fact, which can be confirmed, that each man is, as Hegel says, "a son of his time" and more or less conditioned by the historical circumstances in which he lives. But what is conditioned in that case, is human nature as such — immutable, constant, marked by permanent characteristics — which makes all men similar, which produces the universal similarity existing among all men living in every time, place, and civilization. Nothing for a man of our time better assures the permanent identity of man than Thucydides' description of human nature, *è anthropopinè phusis*, as a duality of passion and intelligence or Plato's doctrine of human nature as the conjunction of mind, will and desire (*noûs, thumos* and *epithumetikon*). Our civilization has not yet ceased to discuss these two images of ourselves, and the analyses grounded upon them are as convincing as they are familiar: they still deal with man, with ourselves.

For the ancients, human freedom consisted in the perfect and unhindered realization of man's essence and function. Under the influence of philosophies of history, the Moderns have interpreted freedom as a faculty of self-production, as transcendence considered as an action, as a creation. This creation is not, however, the negation of nature proper to man. The philosopher who wrote that each man is his own father did not convince anybody, and not even himself. Others have extrapolated the idea of absolute freedom from the idea of creative freedom. They refuse to recognize that there is an essence of man; they identify freedom with a gratuitous and arbitrary existence; they do what they can to associate a certain philosophy of history with all those elements in their doctrine which are not consistent with the theory of an essential and necessary development of human nature. The vanity of the so-called philosophies of the absurd does seem to be fully recognized nowadays: if philosophy is a search for meaning, for intelligibility, is not a philosophy of the absurd, of radical disorder, an absence of philosophy, a non-philosophy? Anyway, modern-day philosophers have to admit the sins of the philosophies currently *à la mode*. Scylla is not far from Charybdis: it is fashionable to celebrate the non-philosophy, the absurd without philosophy and without any philosophical language.

Philosophy of history cannot accommodate itself to these incoherent and insignificant, provocatively insignificant fulgurations. It affirms an essence of man, which could be defined by Kant's formula: "The nature of man consists in the freedom of making one's own nature freely." But the proper task of philosophies of history is to describe the stages of that making, man's formal essence and the historical avatars of its becoming, the succession of man's historical natures. The force of human realities imposes the affirmation of a formal nature of man, and the observation that there exist, in each historically contingent global situation, multiple variations, multiple radically different manifestations of that same human nature, throughout time, groups and individuals.

I know that Rousseau's ingenious intuitions and their suggestive poetry, Kant's decisive indications, Hegel's philosophical genius utilized the impossible scheme of philosophy of history to enlighten and to reveal fundamental trends of human existence. I know that the period of the great philosophies was also the period of great systematic philosophy, that Kant and, above all, Hegel, and the too much forgotten Auguste Comte, were able to compose admirable systems of understanding and of justification. They were certainly perfectly understanding and understandable, if we consider the resistance and impenetrability of human realities. But their magical power, their fascination and their capacity to transform illusions into illuminations, also derives from these illuminations.

Karl Marx' philosophy of history derives its magical powers from another source. From Hegel, he inherits the theory of the historical development of man through a linear succession of stages corresponding to several totalities (in spite of the efforts made later to enlarge and interpret broadly his analysis of an "Asiatic mode of production"). Marx owes the anthropogenesis which culminates in the advent of a perfectly achieved human being to Hegel. But Marx gives this eschatology, which is a renewal of the ancient myths of an end of times, a lay and atheistic meaning. He insists that the definitive human being will be able to live in this temporal world, without alienation, in a homogeneous society, enjoying a freedom which in fact belongs to the tradition of anarchist utopia. Through man's self-production, Marx uses again the Hegelian metaphysic of freedom, defined as man's capacity to make himself, to be the product of his own action. But he turns the Hegelian system upside down, he denies the function of the mind, the part played by the concept of man at the beginning of the anthropogenesis, the immanent and meaningful necessity of that historical development. He emphasizes the privilege of the economic infrastructures in a determining totality. And that means that he reduces man to something like a misfit animal (reappearance of the myth of Plato's *Protagoras*, deprivedlof the gifts of Prometheus and of Zeus). He opposes this infrastructure to superstructures like culture or politics, whose historical function he systematically minimizes (as it is also confirmed by Engels). For him, culture or politics are just appearances or reflections, materials for the mystified consciousness. That is why the Marxist philosophy of history, which he himself scarcely exposes, loses its fecundity of interpretation and locks itself up in simplistic causal explanations. Compared to the Hegelian model, it is decadent and impoverished.

Some people have tried to strengthen Marxist philosophy and to safeguard it from the disrepute that philosophy as such has fallen into nowadays by treating Marxism as a science rather than as a philosophy. For this reason they make the most of the quantitative data offered by economic life and by all the material needs of human societies. But Marx' power of convincing does not derive from this exaggeratedly scientific treatment of human affairs. It comes from his humanistic inspiration, from the moral and

humanitarian inspiration — in which he follows Rousseau rather than
Hegel — with which he studies the different forms of alienation, human
miseries, the mystifications men are suffering from. This moral inspiration,
which appeals to social demands and struggles, joins the eschatological
inspiration which urges Marx to proclaim a communist, homogeneous,
classless society without social struggles, whose members are perfectly
human, free and satisfied.

It is easy to guess why, if Hegel has philosophers for disciples, Marx'
disciples were mostly political men and militants.

IV

I readily admit that it is not greater or lesser perfection which matters in a
philosophy of history. What is most important is that the reality of history,
the historical force of things, does not agree with philosophy of history as
such.

We are not quarrelling with philosophers of history as historians might.
That would be ill founded, false and vain. There is no historical science
without a philosophy of its presuppositions and of its methods. The history
written by each historian implies its own postulates, which determine the
interpretation he gives the historical data. It is not to these postulates, to that
methodology, that we say "farewell." They are just the kind of hypotheses
without which a historian would be unable to observe, to describe, to
explain, to understand historical reality and unable to provide a narrative
capable of being understood, checked and verified.

But the epistemology of historical science is one thing and the philosophy
of history another. The objects of historical science can be such and such
domains and such and such periods of contingent human facts and deeds
upon such and such territory. The philosophy of history considers the
problem of the meaning of human existence and the becoming of mankind,
the problem of its origin, and of its end. These two types of approach belong
to two radically different orders.

The word *history* itself comes from the Greeks. But when Herodotus used
it, this word did not mean either the necessary process progressively
producing mankind as a perfectly achieved human being, generation after
generation, or even the whole set or a single and particular set of human
facts and deeds. History meant only an inquiry, *istorie*. The Romans had no

corresponding word: they just spoke of *res gestae*, of accomplished things. Hegel himself, setting the word *Historie* apart, would speak of *Geschichte*, to designate effective and efficient reality, reasonable reality, *die vernünftige Wirklichkeit*. But *geschehen* means "what happens," and that is a contingent event *par excellence*. Shall we say that a certain set of historical facts is just the product of chance, or the result of causal determinations, or a system ruled by laws? Shall we say that human decision and human behaviour are determined or free? All these acts and facts remain fundamentally contingent anyway.

Even if historians are looking for causal or legal relations, or for meaningful and comprehensible sets of relations, historical science at best only gets at a narrative of contingent history, of a contingent and hypothetical ensemble of facts and events, an ensemble more or less arbitrarily circumscribed, more or less coherent, more or less homogeneous, happening in a certain area, manifesting a certain style, a certain spirit. It could be the history of a certain group, of a certain population, of a certain nation, of a certain civilization. Once again, we have to emphasize the fact that there is no one unique human history, one total history of mankind, with a specific immanent and meaningful teleology: there are just several histories, an irreducible plurality of histories, which can be observed, interpreted and told about people scattered all over the world, throughout time. There are possible major trends in such and such a history, but nothing in historical reality justifies a global teleology immanent in the total history of mankind, with its initial implicit concept of free, conscious, reasonable man, its necessary stages towards its immanent end, implying the progressive revelation of its innate meaning.

And the distance between historical reality and philosophy of history is greatest, when the latter pretends that it can only constitute itself at the end of history, the indefinite and indefinitely renewing process of which we are constantly observing and shall go on observing as long as there are men capable of freedom and reflection. The illusion of philosophy of history is to imagine that an end to the history of freedom and reason is actually accomplished. An end is conceivable for reason, but not for freedom: the goal of freedom cannot be the end of freedom. There is no goal for freedom as such. Freedom is not achieved as long as freedom remains free, remains freedom. What a marvellous vision it would be for man's labour to end, and its happiness to begin. But what human being could be happy without being free? He would not even be human; he would just be an animal. The tale philosophers of history tell and ask credence for is spontaneously transformed into a fairy tale or into the good news of a temporal bliss, into a gospel without divine Revelation.

Even this rudimentary form of philosophy of history, that caricature which is the notion of progress, explodes under the impact of the reality and complexity of historical facts. History is indeed the fact of a species, the human species, which not only has a past, as does every other animal species, but also a future, and which lives for its future. Even if man's nature does not change, man lives by changing, he lives in change. History is the existence of man in time, a dialectic of continuity and change, of tradition and innovation, resulting in a permanent transformation.

But the theory of progress adds to the fact of change the purely subjective appreciation of a certain teleology of that change, an interpretation of its meaning corresponding to a certain supposed end. Even in the very simplified case of progress by accumulation, dealing with science, with techniques, with the production or consummation of equipment or goods, the estimation of the direction of this progress remains an arbitrary and indefinitely debatable decision. Our present fanatics of the return to nature, our scientists of the *leger de main* trick of zero population growth, show us that incertitude and that arbitrariness well enough. *A fortiori*, there is no meaningful orientation inherent in their transformations when they deal with culture, values, the work of human freedom. However, progress and decadence, rise and fall, can have a more coherent and justifiable meaning for the history of a nation which is born, lives and dies, like a biological entity and whose history could be represented by a Gaussian curve.

Even if it were possible, though improbable, to give these different curves an objective and universal validity, it is clear that they belong to different types, that they are incoherent and unsuperposable. The progress of one of the elements of history (science and technique) does not entail the progress of other elements (morality or happiness, for example). The theory of global progress is absurd and confused, whether we speak of the whole history of mankind or even of the smallest area of one culture. It has no basis of any kind in the reality of historical things.

V

The purpose of discovering progress in history orients our reflection towards practical considerations. History is not only an object of knowledge for historians or a theme of meditation for philosophers. It is a job for every man, and especially for men of action.

In a certain place, in a certain historical situation with every one struggling or collaborating with every one, every group against and with every other group, every nation against and with every other nation, everybody tries, through his intentions, projects, discourses, acts, and labour, to play his part in the building of his own history, of the history of the group to which he belongs, the history of his nation and even of his civilization. Everybody tries to influence his own history, the history of his group, the history of his time. And if certain men are incapable of any positive action, they try to insert their passivity into the history of their group, so that its history will be their own history.

The limits and conditions of efficiency of the historical action or passion of each of us in the historical situation in which we live, with our peculiar form of freedom and lucidity, do not matter. What matters is that each man is a historical being, a being who lives within history and makes history, even if nobody can truly tell whether he actually makes history, even his own history.

To say that history is the work of mankind is just a mythical truth. One no longer tries to write the universal history of mankind, not because it is a tremendous task, but because there is no unique and total reality corresponding to that project. There are just histories, a multitude of histories, which sometimes conflict, which were born, each in a certain area, of the composition and convergence of a multitude of human efforts, collaborations and struggles over the same problems and in the same environment. The spirit of a nation, culture, or civilization, with its dominant values, meanings, and peculiar style, appears and lives in the composition formed from the interaction of historical conditions and traditions with the actions and the work of generations of men. With the help of chance, with greater or lesser success and coherence, each of these histories tends towards the expression of common values, common ends, and clearer meanings.

Is it not each man's, each group's human intention and the proper human vocation to build a meaningful world, which he will understand, and in which others will understand him, so that, with the help of chance, everybody will live a meaningful, valuable and justified life? We are very far from the glory and pride of the classical but mythical philosophies of history. Even this vocation is never fully realized. Men are never perfectly free and reasonable; their histories are never perfectly meaningful. Men live from their desire to desire, from their desire for freedom. They are never satisfied and their histories are never fully justified or fully understandable. It is the essence of a free and intelligent being never to be satisfied, to desire to pursue indefinitely his own truly human desire: to understand, to let himself be understood, to actually be understood. To understand and to be understood, is not this the proper end of man, the proper way for him to be justified? Is it not what Hegel called *Anerkennung*, *Versöhnung*, *Befriedigung* — that is, acknowledgement, reconciliation, satisfaction — symbols of man's actual achievement? The more or less coherent period during which a group of men has the chance to achieve this supreme human goal to some extent, is rightly called a *history*. The intention of philosophies of history in fact corresponds to extrapolations of the absolute of that essential experience: the effort towards reciprocal understanding in a free, reasonable community. Aristotle already spoke of *philia* in the *politeia*. Those words, friendship, acknowledgement, reconciliation, satisfaction are the passionate symbols of the ultimate human end: understanding, *theoria*.

This requirement, which makes man a being for understanding, a being whose end is *theoria*, defines man's permanent nature — his individual as well as his generic nature — in any given historical situation. It is the problem of the transition from potentiality to actuality every man faces within the double frame of his political community and his historical situation, not as an element of the so-called progress of a human totality, since the ideas of a general society of mankind, of progress, of human totality are just specious myths, grandiose, moving but vain and void. They have to be denounced, because they serve as pretexts and as guaranties for pseudo-sciences of history, the source of insufferable political dogmatisms. When they dissolve, philosophies of history are corrupted: either they disappear and die, or they are transformed into dreadful superstitions of history. Philosophies of history, farewell.

Of course, once again, we are considering philosophies of history in the strongest sense of the word which, originating in Rousseau and Kant, found their full expression in Hegel and were integrated into the mentality of our time, among our *idées reçues* by his disciples and the disciples of Marx, the greatest of the Hegelians. For them, philosophy was at best a philosophy of history and of man as a historical being. Even if it does not indulge really philosophical creeds, history, of course, remains the possible object of philosophy. Everything which exists or happens on earth, inside the earth or in the skies, is the possible object of a philosophical interpretation. We only dispute history considered as history of human becoming through the whole of a supposed history of mankind: of that history we observe the dissolution.

Histories of men, as we described them, are of course the object of some philosophy, either at the level of historical description and of the task of the historians, whose duties imply not only methodological principles requiring certain philosophical principles, but the practice of a philosophical anthropology; or at the level of historical ensembles lived or observed by philosophers acting as philosophers. I readily admit that the positive indications I gave about the ends, the means, the behaviours of men, each in his situation, his community and his time, trying to compose a historical set, a historical order, which would be meaningful, in which each one could better understand and be better understood, could feel himself acknowledged and justified, where his theory and his practice, as well as his consciousness and his freedom would be unified — all these considerations propose the principles of a philosophy of these histories. But the philosophy of history of which we record the death was of a very different order.

As long as there are men, they will continue to act and to work, to make their histories more or less freely, not only in order to live and to survive among an inadequate nature, but in order to accomplish their vocation as free and self-conscious beings: to understand, to be understood and acknowledged. Temporal bliss, absolute knowledge, which are the passionate symbols of that vocation, serve as symbolic ends for every human existence, naturally frail and fragile in its finitude. These ends are necessary for free and finite men, because they offer human creators and necessarily unsatisfied beings, the necessary illusion of a possible satisfaction, achievement, perfection. We must not forget that man is the being capable of imagining the absolute. The philosophy of history allows people to believe in an absolute which would be realized and progressively understood throughout the time of the whole of mankind.

Each man of action who knows how to be a philosopher, each philosopher who would like to be a man of action, has a peculiarly exacting consciousness of that unity of existence and thought, of freedom and consciousness, of action and lucidity. Philosophies of history having disappeared, the best of their principles, the unity of theory and practice, preserves our faith and our hope as men, as philosophers without any illusions about the ineluctability of our illusions.

Université de Paris-Sorbonne

IS A PHILOSOPHY OF HISTORY POSSIBLE?

Isaiah Berlin, Stuart Hampshire, Max Black, Paul Ricoeur, Yirmiahu Yovel, Raymond Polin, Donald Davidson, Nathan Rotenstreich; Moderator: Charles Taylor.

Charles Taylor: So far we have heard mostly negative statements about the philosophy of history. We have heard, for instance, about assumptions which can no longer form a tenable basis for it. So now, at the end, let us try to answer the positive question: what can the philosophy of history be today? Can there still be such a discipline as a meaningful area of study, as a distinctive and fruitful kind of philosophical inquiry? Or, to put it bluntly, who needs philosophy of history? And what could be the philosophy of history today?

ISAIAH BERLIN

I think I must have been chosen to start this discussion because I have never been an historian and have long ceased to be a working philosopher. And therefore I have, or ought to have, a neutral attitude to this subject.

Let me begin to say something quite modest in order to try to build a bridge between two very different points of view — between the analytical philosophers and the others, far removed from them, which has occurred in the course of these discussions. It seems to me that there exist apparently quite routine, but in fact very rich, topics towards which the philosophy of history could attract the attention of both: for example, the examination of how certain key concepts are used by historians. This would involve them in the philosophy of history in the most direct and central fashion.

Thus they might consider the apparently simple question (though it is not simple at all), how do historians use the word 'because'? 'Because,' as used in historical speech, is not necessarily a causal term; 'because' can apply to motives, and to more mysterious connections between and within historical

219

Yirmiahu Yovel (ed.), Philosophy of History and Action, 219–240. All Rights Reserved.
Copyright © 1978 by D. Reidel Publishing Company, Dordrecht, Holland.

events. Or again, how do historians use terms like 'therefore'? Why do historians use, from time to time in their narratives, phrases like 'thus we see,' or 'small wonder that,' or 'it is not surprising that'? Why was it not surprising? What is it that calls for such small wonder, and why? And so on. These little coupling links are thrown in because they seem to bridge the account of one event with the account of another event, even of one entire culture with another. For they rest on the assumption of specific concepts and categories, in terms of which plausible history can be written.

A famous distinction was made in the late nineteenth century between the methods of the natural sciences and the humane sciences. It was maintained, reasonably enough, that if one claimed that a phenomenon in the natural sciences was what it was because of another phenomenon, or that an object or event was invariably found in the company of another, such assertions could only be established on evidence provided by recognized procedures of observation and experiment. To use a modern example, one may ask "How do we know that this particular medicine can cure disease, penicillin, let us say, cure pneumonia?" There is no particular reason why this should be believed except on the basis of a large number of carefully tested generalizations, which between them form a logical system, a corpus of scientific knowledge. There need be nothing about the events or objects which are connected in this way, no principle or relation which unites them, except that each event or thing belongs (more or less) to a definable class x, members of which do in fact follow, in a clearly describable fashion, the events or things which belong to an equally definable class y. On the other hand, in the humane sciences this does not seem to be so. One tends to write history, and expect to be believed, because one tacitly takes for granted certain sociological and psychological laws, some of which are usually too elaborate to be stated, which we all recognize, and which are not explicitly based on any scientific procedures.

If one is trying to explain some historical event, say the incidents of a revolution, one might say that a certain amount of discontent or indignation occurred in a certain class within a certain province; and one might add that as a result of concessions made by the ruling class to assuage these feelings, rising expectations occurred among members of the discontented classes; and that this in turn led them to demand more and more, which they might not have done if the ruling class had repressed them more effectively; that weakness and concessions by a ruling class strengthens resistance to it far more than it blunts it; and so on. This kind of argument assumes, takes for granted, that certain kinds of situations, conceived in somewhat general terms, are recognized as being the kind of situations which 'understandably' lead to this or that result: 'understandably,' because human beings can be expected to act in certain ways, given characters, goals, feelings, habits which are implicitly taken for granted. To be human is, in part, to be liable to act in this not sharply definable way; communication with others presupposes this. Hence, to show that a given situation is an example of such behaviour is normally regarded as an adequate historical explanation.

It may be rejoined that one of the developments of writing history in our day is a greater reliance upon methods that are more exact: quantitative measurement and statistical information. But this works best in rather specialized types of history. For example, in economic history: the essential facts about the economic history of England in the thirteenth century can probably be learnt by examining such things as how many bales of wool were sold by various groups of merchants, what prices they fetched, where they travelled, what was done with them, and so on; it is not necessary to ask about the moral or religious outlook of the merchants, their private lives, their personal attributes. Psychological information is neither needed nor helpful. Demographic factors arrived at by statistical generalizations are more relevant; these are obtained by methods not very different from those of the natural sciences. One may well discover that more is known about economic history in the fourteenth century than about that in the seventeenth century, because the facts — movement of goods and prices, for instance — are more easily got at. This is one of the paradoxes of economic history.

The same thing is probably true of the history of technology, and the history of certain other subjects which can be to some extent idealized, that is to say, where the subject is artificially delimited, and therefore models or specialized methods for classification of evidence and inference can be established. Mere common sense does not suffice. But in writing general history, particularly political history, this is scarcely ever true. The categories and concepts in terms of which situations and events and processes are described and explained in such accounts are, to a large extent, imprecise; they have a so-called 'open texture.' They are the everyday notions common to mankind at large, related to the permanent interests of men as such. They may be modified at particular periods, in particular countries, by particular circumstances, but all of them are species of basic human attitudes, outlooks, goals, beliefs. Without some degree of understanding — indeed, sharing of — these concepts, it would not be possible to understand either men or history at all.

If this were not so, we should scarcely be able to understand Homer or Herodotus as, at least to some extent, we claim to be able to do, in spite of the fact that they wrote about societies widely different from our own. If you ask, for example, such a question as why some historical figure acted as he did, the explanation of his behaviour is likely to rest upon the use of concepts, categories and beliefs about human nature, which we take for granted in our everyday lives, and upon the assumption that much, if not all, of these similarly entered the outlook of our predecessors from the beginnings of recorded history.

If one relied solely upon inductive investigation, one would get very thin results indeed. If, to take an example from fiction, one asks why Iago hated Othello, and someone replies that Iago was weak and Othello was strong, Othello was noble and Iago was base, and the weak or base are apt to resent or hate the noble or strong, this would naturally be regarded as going some way towards an adequate explanation of Iago's behaviour. If one then goes on to ask how many instances of envy the interlocutor has himself observed, or how much he knows others to have observed, about the relation of the weak to the strong; how much elaborate psychological investigations he has conducted, in how many places, and on how many occasions; what mountain of regularities he has accumulated on which to erect his hypotheses which he can then test experimentally: one will certainly find that chemists or physicists would not regard such evidence as an adequate basis for scientific conclusions. Nevertheless, this is the only kind of way in which one goes about to explain the greater part of the behaviour of human beings; we could scarcely act or live otherwise. No doubt one is often mistaken, and psychologists and sociologists can expose one's errors; no doubt all kinds of untested assumptions are constantly made; but without them one could not proceed at all.

The point I am making is based not on the famous contrast between uniqueness and generality, or between *Wertfreiheit* and evaluation; it is that of the difference between the application of laws or rules based on observed uniformities, and beliefs based on coherence with experience, whether one's own and that of one's society, or that of other men and other cultures. All experience embodies what Collingwood called the 'absolute presuppositions' of an age or a culture. They are not incorrigible, but it is the grasp of these that distinguishes serious historians from bright storytellers and journalists: it is a faculty which historians require to have in common with imaginative writers.

Why do we call some historians great, and others competent or superficial? May I put it to you that we call historians great not only because they possess narrative skill, and certainly not because they possess more knowledge than other historians, or because their observations are more minute, their findings more accurate — all these are necessary and indeed indispensable attainments, but they do not by themselves make a great historian.

One calls only those historians great who are seen to possess insight into a particular period, or a particular society, as a rounded whole, those who present the reader with a picture of human life — the complete experience of a society as a possible form of life, something which could have occurred, and which the evidence available makes sufficiently probable. The danger of the work of the resurrecting imagination is that it may generate coherent fictions. To prove that one is concerned with facts one needs a solid basis of inference from surviving data. Yet even on such evidence the construction may — as Mommsen towards the end of his life began to suspect — prove to be largely imaginary. The indispensable quality of a great historical work is that the reader supposes, after reading it, that he can say to himself not only what the various actors in these societies thought, or did, or aimed at, on the occasions recorded, but also what they would (or at least might) have thought on other imaginable occasions, or how they would have responded to other particular circumstances and, indeed, to the general circumstances, events, ideas and objects, natural and man-made, of their time. To conceive what living in a society unlike one's own must be, it is not necessary to introduce the somewhat mystical notion of transporting oneself into the past, or making a timeless flight (as Collingwood comes near to saying) into Caesar's consciousness, which would enable one to know by direct introspective means what it was that made him invade Britain, what his feelings and ambitions and purposes were.

If one has an imaginative grasp of what kind of society is being spoken about, one can answer certain hypothetical questions, even if the answers are far from certain. Unless, in other words, one is given some sense of the,

as it were, concrete texture of a society, its structure and "zeel," its moral
and intellectual categories and values, one is not likely to regard the
historian who tries to describe it as a gifted historian; one may, indeed,
accuse him of lacking depth. Neither depth nor greatness, incidentally, are
concepts much mentioned by philosophers, although I daresay it would be
a good thing if they did; for they are not mere rhetorical flourishes. 'Deep' is
a metaphorical expression — a metaphor drawn from wells, perhaps. What
does it mean? What is meant by saying (whether or not this is true) that
Pascal is a profounder thinker than Descartes, or that Mommsen or Fustel
de Coulanges are greater historians than industrious compilers or the
authors of patriotic textbooks?

I do not wish to embark on this topic here, but only to insist that mere
reconstruction of the past in an archaeological sense is not enough. Nor will
the categories of the natural sciences alone do the job. This is plainly
connected with the differences between what is usually called knowledge,
and Dilthey's concept of *Verstehen* — understanding. I am inclined to argue
that what we mean by knowledge is identical in both the natural and the
human sciences, whereas there exists a cognitive function — namely,
understanding — which is involved only when we are speaking of agents,
their motives, their purposes, fears, hopes, feelings, ideas, acts: not only
those of individual human beings, but those of groups or classes or
movements or institutions or entire societies. Discussion of the lives and
outlooks and activities of such agents involves categories and concepts
which cannot be applied to the subject matter of the natural sciences
without anthropomorphism; while treatment of topics which lie on the
borderline between the two kinds of science, or in a no man's land between
them (certain kinds of applied economics, or social psychology, for
instance) create problems of their own. To seek to understand the moral
codes, the social purposes, the cultural or spiritual trends and tendencies of
a given society, is to seek to understand what it must have been like to have
lived in a certain milieu. Capacity for this kind of insight requires the
possession of something akin to an artistic gift, which alone can integrate
and give life to the dry bones of research, the accumulation of relevant facts
which, of course, can be obtained only by empirical investigation.

All this is, of course, a row of truisms. Nevertheless, I cannot help
thinking that the most useful task — indeed, the main one — for philosophers
of history is the analysis of the logic of historical explanation. This means

the analysis of the use of such words as 'because,' 'therefore,' 'in due course,' 'it was not surprising that,' and so on, which act as connecting links between various propositions about the past, and bind them into logical structures (so it seems to me) in a fashion different from that in which such logical cement is used in the natural sciences. Under the latter I include all those sciences which go to the making of, but are not themselves, historical thought: archaeology, palaeography, epigraphy, demography, physical geography and anthropology, astronomical, chemical or biological methods of dating, and all the other ancillary disciplines which are needed for the measurement of time spans, and the analysis of the environmental and other material factors affecting human life, without which there can be no accurate knowledge of the human past.

It may be that what I have said is heretical from both points of view, from the point of view of science-directed analytical philosophers, and from that of those here who are inclined in a Hegelian direction. Perhaps this is just as well: I do not feel inclined to retreat, unless compelled to do so by sheer weight of rational argument.

STUART HAMPSHIRE

I agree that in history you are concerned with explanations, and that they are explanations of the action and suffering of human beings, and that such an explanation is not like an explanation in the physical sciences. All these three propositions seem to me to be true.

One proposition, which Isaiah admittedly implied rather than stated, seems to me not to be true: namely, that all explanation of physical change is of a scientific character in the sense that it is a case of subsumption under general laws. This is not the case. Ordinarily, explanations of accidents do not invoke elaborate theories or covering laws. But given that qualification, I would agree.

I would also agree — and I do not think that this has anything to do with any variety of Hegelianism or particular school of philosophy — that explanations of human actions and sufferings have peculiar features. Of these I wish to point out one that has not been mentioned, but which I think also deserves philosophical study. It is a feature important particularly for history, but also in the social sciences, which are distinct from history because they use methods, and aim at conclusions, of greater generality than do historians.

The feature concerned is this: that when we explain human actions by referring to human motives and purposes, and thus by referring to thoughts — certainly at least to beliefs and desires — what we believe to be the explanation of them affects what they actually are. That is, if I believe that my beliefs and desires had certain causes — either certain types of causes, or specific causes in specific cases — this has an effect on what I believe and desire. Consequently throughout the human sciences there is a playback effect of the explanations which are accepted — whether or not they are true explanations.

This is not the case with physical conditions. No matter what I believe about the causes of a lump on my arm, my beliefs (unless it is a hysterical lump) do not affect either the lump or its real cause. But when I change my opinion about what are the causes of my ambitions, desires and beliefs, I indirectly change those desires and beliefs.

It is a familiar fact, which I have brought up here because it does effect a bridge between analytical philosophy and Hegel and Marx, that the acceptance of historical explanations, and indeed of psychological explanations of any kind, has a playback effect upon the actual phenomena under study. But that playback effect is given another name, and is intimately connected with the notion of the unity of theory and praxis.

Finally, I should like to make a negative point, or to raise a question rather than make an assertion. It is noticeable that, in gatherings such as this, we do make references to spiritual realities which we somehow think we can identify as if we had access to some form of collective consciousness. For instance, we placidly refer to the spiritual malaise of our times. Burckhardt and other great historians have certainly operated in this way. Some of us — and I am one — have constituted subjects and delineated periods in terms of spiritual realities which are collective states of minds, or collective conditions, which they identify. Then they impose these patterns upon history and one sees history through them. This habit of thought has very serious consequences if you transfer it onto the present, because then the playback effect comes into existence and you see the facts as forming a certain constellation, and in these spiritual terms.

Now, I am exceedingly sceptical myself about whether we know that there is a spiritual malaise, or how we know, or what this exactly means. This is where the historical service of Karl Marx seems to me of inestimable value.

MAX BLACK

I should like to begin by repeating a point I made earlier, because I believe it demands further attention. Borrowing an idea of Professor Gallie, I was arguing that history, considered as narrative, not as what actually happened, is an "essentially contested concept." That is to say, there is no *definite* thing called history which we can examine, describe and analyse. Indeed, I might say that there are degrees of essential contestedness, and that compared, say, with science, which is also to some degree a contested concept, history, like art, is even more contested.

To put it in plain language, it seems to me a mistake in method to suppose that talking about history in the way that Isaiah Berlin and Stuart Hampshire did, is like talking about horses or the State of Israel — talking about something that is actually "given."

The "given" consists, in the first place, of a number of written narratives, some of which, for somewhat arbitrary reasons, we choose to call history. It is rather parochial, for instance, to insist upon history being exclusively concerned with human beings. A good deal of history is done by scientists — as in the theory of natural selection. A good deal of cosmology and physics deals with time sequences that involve no human beings. It really is parochial to confine our interest in the past to the dramatic episodes occurring in the thin slice of the last 15,000 or 20,000 years.

In talking about history, and in producing history, people are making debatable choices. If a young history student sets out to do some research, it is not as if the nature of the task is predetermined: it is a matter of controversy as to what he ought to undertake. He might choose to write a history of ideas, a very ambiguous sort of subject, or he might even write a history of the philosophy of history, which would be an even more perplexing and frustrating project.

The rules are not laid down, and part of the trouble in this whole dispute, under the rubric of what I take to be the subject under discussion — Do we need a philosopy of history? — is that we do not know what we should be talking about yet, and it is hard to come to any decision.

I shall now try to say one or two positive things. The prior question, suggested by a famous remark of Henry Ford, might be: 'Do we need history?' (For if we do not need any history then we probably do not need **any** philosophy of history.) And to that I think the short answer is **that we** are going to have history, whether we want it or not. If you try the *Gedankenexperiment* of imagining a community, like that of present-day Israel, losing its memory, becoming all at once senile, able to function but having no recollection of the past, you can see, by that dramatic illustration, what an enormous change would be produced in the conditions of life. It is perfectly clear, then, that having histories in the sense of more or less reliable memories of the memorable past, is part of the human condition.

So the choice cannot be between having history or having no history: the choice can only be between having better histories and worse histories. So much for a preliminary banality.

It is less obvious, but true, that we are also going to have philosophy of history, whether we want it or not. Of course, its quality will depend on the choice one makes of the preferred philosophy of history. I agree with Isaiah Berlin's identification of certain special problems that philosophical analysis can help to clarify, but I would like to generalize his suggestion.

There is some kind of theory implicit in the practice of any historian — and I mean any historian, including those that Carl Becker, a Cornell historian, referred to under the title of "Every man his own historian." Yes, every person is, to some degree, his or her own historian, and behind even the crude and fragmented histories that result some kind of theory can be discerned.

It can be put in this form: Why do you choose to remember what you do? And why, if you were writing your own autobiography, would you choose to include these things and leave out those? From the answers an imaginative philosopher could construct a presupposed theory — a fragmentary philosophy of history. The same is true *a fortiori* of a great historian like Gibbon: whether or not they are stated, the presuppositions are there.

So there again one has the choice, certainly in all developed history, between either doing philosophy of history in the sense of having an explicit theory of the writing of history amenable to elaboration, generalization, evaluation, criticism, and clarification — or else writing history blindly.

I think that blind history will usually be bad history. The blindness will be condemned by a later generation of historians, who can scornfully talk about the prejudices of their predecessors, while ignoring the pre-suppositions that control their own research. And the only cure — though it is really only a sort of alleviation — is for historians, when they can drag themselves away from the fascination of their own technical work, to become philosophers. I hesitate to suggest symmetrically that philosophers should also become historians, because, when they do so, they tend to be such bad ones. But at least, given the state of affairs that must prevail, it seems to me essential that some kind of meta-discipline should emerge, which will be of an analytical and critical nature.

The one thing I would deplore is further effort to create a "philosophy of history" in the sense that people used to think of it. That is, a sort of super-history, in which the philosopher sets out to do what the historian does not manage to do, namely, to uncover the sweeping, over-arching laws of historical development. That seems to me neither good history nor good philosophy, but a sort of bastard offspring of the two.

PAUL RICOEUR

I too think that there must be something like a philosophy of history, because certain unavoidable questions arise. The easiest such question is the one which has been elaborated by Sir Isaiah, while all the difficulties start after that.

Sir Isaiah, in short, indicated the need to distinguish between human actions and physical events, and therefore to recognize the conceptual network which is implied by the vocabulary concerning actions. But this can be done, I think, by a philosophy of action. Once that basic distinction has been made, all the other questions arise, the questions which we have already discussed with Prof. Rotenstreich. I shall enumerate four of these questions which I think are unavoidable.

The first, of course, is why only certain actions are historical and not all of them (as somebody has said: many people crossed the Rubicon, but this was not always a historical event). Then, why are these actions historical and not others? According to what criteria are some actions picked out and put into the records as historical?

A second problem arises with what Prof. Rotenstreich called irradiation, impact and effects. For then the opposition between physical events and human action is more or less blurred. Our action becomes event, is joined to the events of physics, to constitute one time, one development. Consequently, we must ask ourselves: how can human action and physical events form one time?

A third problem is: what is the epistemological status of things like institutions, states, nations and so on? Are they merely the product of the inter-action of all the individuals, or do we want some specific kind of mediation, unlike questions concerning concealed Hegelianism? This is not a question against Prof. Rotenstreich, but a question for myself. Can we do without something like an "objective" *Geist*? For if we decide to do without an "objective" *Geist*, we are condemned to a kind of ascetic methodology, with its obvious difficulties. We must then draw all the consequences of methodological individualism, and it is not certain that this type of approach can succeed. If it indeed cannot succeed, what can we do with all the mediations between individuals, which are not individual actions, but are norms, super-personal goals, institutions and so on?

So I think this is a question, and it is a Hegelian question, not necessarily as producing some "absolute" *Geist* somewhere, but as concerning a *Geist* like our own — the *Geist* of men, the *Geist* working within men and at the level of human history.

Finally, I see a fourth question, which is the most dangerous, but maybe also the most unavoidable. The word 'history' is in the singular and not by chance. It is very difficult to speak of histories. Why do we presuppose that there is something like one history?

Here I return to some questions raised by Prof. Polin. Among all the postulates which he discarded, there is at least one which I should like to preserve: the idea that there is only one mankind. For if I drop this postulate, I can slip into fascism and into a kind of dispersion of human reality, whereas I think that I must suppose that there is something like one mankind, and therefore one history. If I do not suppose that, then — at one time or another — I shall treat some part of humanity as non-human.

But — it will be said — this is not a problem of the philosophy of history, but of ethics: since we have a kind of ideal which floats above history, we try to demonstrate at least some convergences within languages, within cultures, we try to make a whole from what we know of all our contemporaries or predecessors, and this we call history. This sphere of which Prof. Rotenstreich spoke is indeed one sphere. You can speak of several spheres, but finally there is only one sphere. So we are obliged to claim that there are some convergences and to try to recognize them.

Frankly, I see this as the danger. It is precisely the unavoidable danger, because if I can invoke only ethics to say that there is only one **mankind,** then I expose history to dispersion and I face this radical gap between empirical histories and the ideal of mankind.

I should say, therefore, that perhaps each of us must consider himself as the end of history. That is to say, as the point from which he has to make an image of the whole, however precarious and dangerous it may be to anticipate a certain unity of mankind in *the* history within which he lives.

YIRMIAHU YOVEL

The concept of a "philosophy of history" is traditionally used in a dual sense, methodological and substantive. I should like to take this opportunity to suggest a third possibility, over and above (or perhaps in between) the two recognized ones.

Sir Isaiah mentioned problems that relate to the philosophy of history when it is taken basically as a *methodology of historiography*. In this sense, the philosophy of history occupies itself with what the historian does: How he goes about his research, what his criteria for selection are, what causal explanations are open to him, etc. Although this is an important aspect of the philosophy of history, I will suggest that it does not represent an autonomous interest, but one which in the last resort should be subordinate to a different interest underlying history — which I shall define in a moment.

On the other side of the usual dichotomy we have the philosophy of history in the substantive sense (the degenerate form of which has just been criticized by Max Black). This involves viewing history as some object or entity in itself which is governed by certain "forces" or manifests a certain pattern of evolution. History in this sense is no longer what the historian does but what he *writes about* — a real process in the world — construed as a nexus of "events," or of "facts," or of "actions," etc., depending on who does the constructing. The philosopher of history in this sense will try to find some structure or even define certain super-laws over and above what the empirical historian has done. This form of the philosophy of history has given rise to many speculations, and its degenerate form — where the philosopher of history takes the place of the practising historian — has become no less obsolete than the old "philosophy of nature" (as a substitute super-physics) has long become.

Another, more important, task of the philosophy of substantive history is to bring to light the historicality of human existence and the manner in which history plays its role in shaping one's individual subjectivity and life. Due recognition of its importance, however, implies a fundamental shift in the interest underlying historical reflection. I believe that this task should be a focus of a "third way" in the philosophy of history, namely, one which approaches historical reflection as an expanded (and a mediated) form of self-consciousness.

A major difference between this third way and the two traditional ones will be its rejection of a feature common to both of them: both approach history as an external cognitive object — as a part of the real world which we simply encounter and wish to study. In this particular respect, there will be no difference in kind between the study of history and the study of nature, even if their respective methodologies are admitted to be different. Moreover, there will be no difference in principle between studying one's own culture and remote cultures. A Frenchman studying Louis XIV or the Aztecs, a black American studying Abolition or eighth-century Japan, may all treat their subject matter as a purely external object, about which they are trying to obtain some objective body of knowledge. Their fundamental interest will be outward-directed, aiming at the object as such, not at their own existence and consciousness as *reflected* to them through this object. Even if they are not satisfied with pure science alone, but wish to draw practical lessons, promote liberal education or look for strategies of social reform, etc. — this will only be a derivative, a kind of technological corollary. Their basic attitude will remain object-directed, treating history as something foreign and external, like natural entities.

By contrast, I suggest we view history as a form of self-understanding and self-interpretation. Then, the focus of interest for historical reflection resides neither in a historical *entity* (or object) in itself, nor in a story as such, but in the kind of historical *consciousness* it makes possible; this historical consciousness is not primarily outward-oriented, is not a consciousness of some natural object, but rather an expanded and mediated form of *self*-consciousness. We grasp our existence, our human condition, indeed the constitutive layers of our subjective ego, only with respect to the historical context with which they are interwoven. Moreover, it is only in this manner that we interpret ourselves, assign specific meaning to our subjectivity, recognize the origin of our wishes, ideas, prejudices and queries, thus realizing ourselves within the constraints which our freedom must both assume and transcend.

What I propose, in other words, is to approach history from the viewpoint of the "interest of reason" (to use a Kantian phrase) involved in it. This interest is to expand my own understanding of myself and to become more enlightened about my existential situation in the world. Equally, it is the interest of forming, in reflection, a richer self-perception and of further interpreting my life, social role and individual subjectivity within the inevitable context in which they take shape.

This does not mean that I now regard *myself* as an object — as a reified cluster of facts, features and behaviours — which has to be understood deterministically, such that history becomes a mere supplement to the natural sciences. Rather, the self-recognition (always, alas, partial) involved in history becomes immediately self-*interpretation*; and by assigning a meaning, a shape, and a goal to anything relating to myself, I do not simply *assert* my features (historical and otherwise) as given, but *participate* in their constitution. The function of meaning-assignment breaks away from the inert, given datum and implies the negative power of freedom; it is never reducible to a set of given "facts," but involves a reflective distance which transcends (and shapes) facts. And, on the other hand, since my subject matter is myself, not an external object, my self-interpretation equally becomes a form of self-*shaping*. My subjective self is not a finished and given thing, upon which I simply superimpose meanings and interpretations from without. There is no "me" existing fully-formed in advance, which I study externally, or come to know as a given object. Rather, my very activity of interpreting myself has a formative function, in the sense that it becomes a mode of my actual *being*. By self-interpretation I also change, I *become*, I produce myself as a concrete subject.

So in this direction of self-understanding, and perhaps also with an educational or formative corollary, I think that philosophy has still something to do with regard to history.

RAYMOND POLIN

I should like to insist upon three points. First, the very notion of the philosophy of history does have two different traditional senses, giving rise to a certain permanent confusion in using this word. I would distinguish between them as follows. On the one hand, there is philosophy of history in the strongest sense, such as the philosophy of Kant, Hegel, or Marx; this is the philosophy of history in general, but which can also simply consist of the negation of that type of history and philosophy of history. And, on the other hand, there is philosophy of history as just a set of considerations regarding the method of the historian, regarding the function, duties and working rules of historians.

The second point is that I think we should not forget that history is not merely a set of deeds or events — or a narrative of certain such sets. It is also the place of action of man. History is what we are doing, whether willingly or unwillingly. We are historical beings. What does that mean? It means that we try to influence the historical situation in which we are living. We may succeed to a greater or to a lesser extent, but still we are trying, we are intending to do something, and what we do is always something historical. I would say that whenever a man crosses the Rubicon he is performing a historical act. Of course, a certain crossing of the Rubicon had a very great importance, a great influence in the building of history — at least, so Machiavelli and Hegel thought. But any human deed is, to a certain extent — even if to a very simple and elementary extent — a historical act.

The importance of this fact is that any set of historical realities, of historical events and acts, acquires a certain significance; at any time some values are becoming prevalent in a certain type of set we call a nation or a civilization. Now, this is why it is very normal that philosophers or historians should have spoken of the collective conscience, or of the *Volksgeist*, as did Hegel. (Incidentally, I do not quite understand why Prof. Hampshire gave Marx this kind of privilege. Marx did, however, speak of a *Totalität*, of a *Zusammenhang*, which represents the same type of collective existence.)

Moreover, it seems to me that in the perspective in which I put myself, this collective existence is not behind us, it is not a hypostasis of a certain type of reality. Rather, it is in front of us. It is what we are doing, what we are aiming at, trying to establish. So Sir Isaiah gave us an excellent definition of the great historian as a man who is precisely able to understand that peculiar style of existence in a certain society, and who gives us the pregnant impression that there is such a society, that civilization is breathing a certain kind of spirit.

After all, why not speak of a "spirit" if we understand very well what we mean by that word?

My last point concerns the problem posed by my old friend, Paul

Ricoeur, about mankind. Now, I said indeed that I do believe in the existence of a human species, but not in the existence of a general society of mankind. Yet I do not think that in saying this I was a fascist. What I mean is that there are societies, civilizations, which are different, but which are to be understood as a plurality of manifestations of the existence of the same man, who has one and only one nature. So that there are not races — in that respect, of course. It is the same man who is trying — in circumstances which differ because he is a historical man — by his actions and his intentions to establish, as a kind of work, a certain type of civilization, which can be determined by a certain set or order of values.

Thus, I would consider it a manifestation of what Hegel once called "*eine schöne Seele*" to believe that there is a mankind, a humanity before us. That could be the goal of our action — such a general society of mankind — but it is not a presupposition. I think it would be merely a moral pre-supposition, but I am rather distrustful of a good heart and beautiful words. I prefer to see lucidly and perhaps cynically the state of affairs among men, who are often neither good nor pleasant to live with.

DONALD DAVIDSON

I would like to mention one way in which I think philosophy, or a philosophical concern, enters into the writing of history.

What I have in mind is not at all a defense of philosophy of history. It seems to me that analytic philosophers often exaggerate the value, to workers in a certain area, of giving an analysis of the concepts those workers use. Such analysis is often interesting, but mainly to philosophers. It is a mistake to suppose that physics or economics or biology cannot get along without the kind of clear understanding of presuppositions and foundational concepts that philosophy is imagined to provide; philosophy needs the other sciences far more than they need philosophy.

There is, however, a different way philosophy can enter into the writing of history. Sir Isaiah spoke eloquently of the gift great historians have for making actions and cultures intelligible. This is to a large extent the kind of skill shown by any interpreter: the ability to create a meaningful pattern by giving emphasis to some things while leaving other things in the background, the ability to arrange the picture of motives, attitudes, intentions and events so that it makes interesting sense to us. The talented historian makes us see what is significant in history much as a critic can lead us to appreciate the beauty or style of a painting or a string quartet.

When actions are to be understood or explained, interpretation takes on a unique flavour, for it falls under the control of the concept of rationality. Take Thucydides' description of how people behaved during the plague in Athens. He is frank about the fact that he is inventing much on the basis of how he thinks people would have acted under the circumstances. His description is brilliant; you feel this even if you are uncertain about the facts. This projection of the unknown from the known is not mere science with a margin for error, it is the art of the plausible. A story is not good history because it convincingly hangs together; but this sort of coherence is a condition of an important form of excellence in history.

In order to think about what makes a set of motives, beliefs and intentions coherent, you must have a concept of what rationality is. The point is not that people never do irrational things, but that you cannot appreciate irrationality except against a background of rationality. Consequently the ability to find an intelligible pattern in historical events requires, among other things of course, a critical insight into the nature and role of reason in human affairs.

A concern with the nature of rationality, validity and intelligibility is a central trait of philosophy. The concern is normative, or even moral, as well as descriptive and analytic. None of this should be claimed as a domain reserved for philosophers, however. So I do not suggest that historians ought to consult philosophers, but only that they must do one sort of philosophy well to do one aspect of history well. Philosophy and history are not two discrete disciplines which ought to talk to each other from time to time; in a central area they simply overlap.

NATHAN ROTENSTREICH

Listening to these thoughts, it appeared to me that the interpretation of the philosophy of history depends to a very large extent on the interpretation of the nature of philosophy, philosophy being a self-referential enterprise. I would like to make a few short comments.

To begin with, I do not think that what Sir Isaiah suggested can be subsumed under the heading of methodology. It points rather to a mode of cognition; this may imply methods, of course, but there is something which he wants to present as being a mode of cognition, and I think it is a totally different emphasis than just methodological considerations.

Second, in Prof. Hampshire's statement there is an implicit presupposition which I would render perhaps by taking advantage of a saying, that in human affairs *Einbildung ist auch eine Bildung*. According to the playback effect, what we imagine affects our perception of what exists; this presupposes that there is a distinction between reality and imagination, otherwise we cannot use these terms. In this sense philosophy of history becomes part of a broader consideration about, let's say, what reality is, what facts are, what there is.

More specifically, I would like to suggest that there are important thematic points which still need to be explored, even today, in philosophy of history. One is, if I may put it like this, the very paradoxical position of history. On the one hand, we assume a kind of affinity, congeniality between the knower and the known. We can give some explanation about Iago and Othello, as Sir Isaiah says, because we know what envy is and the like. But on the other hand there is an epistemic chasm between the subject matter and the knower. Here I would like to recall what Prof. Gershom Sholem told us at the beginning of our conference, that we do not understand texts or periods by experiencing them. But somehow we do understand them as outsiders. It is not even through taking the role of the other. This is some special sort of cognition which needs to be delineated.

The most paradoxical expression, I think, of this ontological identity and epistemic chasm is the question of prediction. We can predict the eclipses of the sun, but we cannot predict, to any large extent, historical events. Why is it so? I think we are closer, in terms of historical events, to earthquakes, which we unfortunately cannot predict, than to eclipses of the sun, though astronomical time has some importance for historical time.

There are further themes for philosophy of history today, which I can merely indicate. For instance, time as it is used in different disciplines; what is the common structure, what are the specific differences? Or again, the relationship between social science and history: though the work of the social scientist tries somehow to overshadow historical considerations, they are not the same.

My last point is that, after having listened earlier to Prof. Polin's *adieu* to the philosophy of history, we have now heard him say *au revoir* to it. For he has shown that philosophy of history is not necessarily identical with the view that history is a converging process; he has shown that convergence is only one of the possible interpretations of the historical process.

CHARLES TAYLOR

When I consider all these answers given to my opening question, I think that one of our expectations has perhaps been partly disappointed. It may be that we were hoping to learn that philosophy of history is not dead, that it is alive and well in Jerusalem, or even that it has been resurrected in Jerusalem. Yet though a lot of very kind things were said about it today, as against yesterday, they were for the most part not really about the philosophy of history. All the points made, with one or two exceptions which I shall mention in a minute, were really made about philosophy of social science, or sciences of man, or *Geisteswissenschaften* in general.

Thus, what Sir Isaiah Berlin stated at the beginning was really a point about human affairs in general, as he explained. The same goes for what Stuart Hampshire said about what he called the playback effect, and for at least some of the issues mentioned by Paul Ricoeur — such as whether we can speak of institutions and states and peoples as some kind of entity or subject — and for most of the other points made.

There were, of course, a few things which did not fit into that category, but these on their own would not be very exciting as philosophy of history. They were certain methodological problems of historiography — such as why people select certain events as significant and not others. Of course, we can call that philosophy of history, and the subject can go on having some kind of existence, but one can hardly imagine much time being alloted to it in a university curriculum.

Yet since there were one or two defenders here, perhaps we might look at the issues they raised. One of them was Yirmiahu Yovel, who actually dared — particularly after Max Black had spoken — to intimate that perhaps there still was something in the inquiry as to whether or not there might be certain patterns or directions in history, something which might be worth exploring, not perhaps with the same ambition or dogmatism as in the past, but nevertheless. And if there were still something of this kind worth exploring, it might deserve the name "philosophy of history" in a rather exciting way.

I think myself that there is something of this kind, and I would like to mention two issues in this connection. First, although we cannot see an inevitable direction in history through necessary stages towards an end that we can now delineate, it may be the case that certain changes in history, such as urbanization or the growth of a technological society, are irreversible, such that when they happen to certain people, other people are, as it were, swept into the stream one way or another. It may be, therefore, that the distinction we make in history between barbarians and civilized is not arbitrary. For even when the barbarians conquered the Roman Empire they eventually recreated certain of its institutions, while when they lost them temporarily they had nostalgia for them, so that they were no longer in the same predicament as people before urbanization. If that were the case, it would give some kind of sense to the notion of a direction in history.

The second issue is whether there are in certain civilizations, the beginnings of which may have been contingent, certain ideas which are fundamental to those civilizations, once they have begun. Whether these ideas are fundamental to people's self-definition and hence impart a certain direction, or limit the possibilities open of development in that civilization, so that it cannot just go in any direction.

We can perhaps take an example. However successful or striking the régime in China might be thought to be by many people in the West, it might be that this is just something one cannot envisage as a possible régime for Western society, for reasons that have to do with very important earlier developments of this civilization. Something like Merleau-Ponty's "Illusion rétrospective" may arise here — that one may then read it into history as something inevitable. But, however contingent at the outset, now that we have come this far there may be a direction to *our* history. Here too we have something more exciting to ponder on than simply the methodology of history, or questions to do with social science.

There is also a point that Yovel mentioned and which gives, I think, a way of distinguishing the philosophy of history from the philosophy of social sciences, since the questions which concern simply the philosophy of social science are those which would arise whether or not it was of any importance whatever to human beings that they had a long past. Yovel was talking about the very identification of oneself, and of what one is, in terms of one's history — something that is, of course, extremely relevant right here in Israel. If this kind of identification is important for what human beings are, then in order to understand them we have to take into account not just social science in some general sense, which could be purely contemporary, but history — the whole development of the past. This would be another way in which to regain philosophy of history of a more exciting kind.

So the question with which we are left is whether there is any life in these or other significant possibilities for philosophy of history. Or are we, from now on, to give this title only to those other rather empty and less exciting issues?

INDEX OF NAMES

Abel, L.   192
Anscombe, G.E.M.   54 59 79 110
Aquinas, T.   66
Arieli, Y.   109
Aristotle   5 36 55 63 64 65 66 216
Arnold, M.   28
Aron, R.   192
Atwell, J.E.   110
Austin, J.L.   72 74 84 110

Barnes, H.   198
Becker, C.   228
Bentham, J.   185
Bergson, H.   208
Berlin, I.   32 219 225 227-229 231
   234-238
Black, M.   59 110 219 227 231 238
Bloch, M.   12
Boutroux, E.   163
Bratman, M.   59
Briand, A.   173
Bryce. J.   27
Burckhardt, J.   226

Carlyle, T.   28 33
Chomsky, N.   10
Collingwood, R.G.   32 71 72 84 97
   98 223
Comte, A.   201 210
Constantine   40
Contat, M.   198
Croce, B.   32

Dagognet, F.   13
Danto, A.C.   78 100 108
Davidson, D.   61-67   85-89   92-95
   99-103 105 106 110 219 235
Descartes, R.   115 130 224
Dewey, J.   34 78

Dilthey, W.   13-15 224
Donagan, A.   84
Donne, J.   53
Dray, W.H.   97 98 101 109

Eisler, R.   126
Emerson, R.W.   28 33
Engels, F.   168 169 170 174 175 190
   211
Eusebius   28

Feinberg, J.   99
Feuerbach, L.   179
Fichte, J.G.   178 180 181 182 187
Foucault, M.   175
Frankfurt, H.   145
Frege. G.   14
Fustel de Coulanges   224

Gadamer, H.G.   10 11 18 19
Galilei, G.   22 36
Gallie, W.B.   227
Geach, P.T.   59
Gibbon, E.   30 228
Glaucon   151
Goldman, A.I.   110
Grice, H.P.   50 51 59

Habermas, J.   10
Hampshire, S.   59 110 219 225 227 234
   237 238
Hare, R.M.   145
Harman, G.   59
Hart, H.L.A.   100 101
Hayek, F.A.v.   108 111
Hegel, G.W.F.   14 15 32 33 35 40 115
   116 120 121 130 136 137 139 140-145

155-159 161 164 166 167 172 177-182
184 187 188 197 201-203 206 207
209-213 216 226 233-235
Heidegger, M. 18
Henderson, A.R. 84
Herder, J. G. v. 40 177 178 180 183
Herodotus 29 212 222
Homer 222
Honoré, A.M. 100 101
Hook, S. 33
Hume, D. 55 185 187
Husserl, E. 7 70 84

Justinian 38

Kant, I. 3-5 8 16 30 66 116-130 189
197 201 202 206 210 216 233
Kaplan, A. 38-40
Kemp-Smith, N. 132
Kenny, A. 85
Kepler, J. 36
Kierkegaard, S. 191 197 198
Kojève, A. 201 202 205
Koyré, A. 201
Knox, T.M. 154
Kugelmann, L. 162 175

Lachelier, J. 159 163
Langer, W. 109
Langford, G. 84
Laplace, P.S. de 162
Lemmon, E.J. 94
Lenin, N. 30 173
Locke, J. 151 185 186

Macauley, T.B. 24 32 36
Machiavelli, N. 107 133 234
MacIntyre, A. 107
Martin, G. 126
Marx, K. 32 35 77 107 148 159 160-162
166-175 177 179 180 182-184 187 188
190 191 201 202 206 211 212 217 226
233 234

Mead, G.H. 29
Merleau-Ponty, M. 239
Mill, J.S. 151 185 186
Mommsen, T. 223, 224
Morawetz, T. 84

Newton, I. 22 36
Nietzsche, F.W. 33 207

Oakeshott, M. 75 76 84
Orwell, G. 29

Parsons, T. 84
Pascal, B. 31 170 224
Petrarch, F. 108
Plato 3 12 13 32 115 123 125 130 209
211
Pocock, J.G.A. 39
Polin, R. 219 230 233 237
Popper, K. 32 108 111
Poznanski, E.I.J. 109

Ranke, L. v. 27
Rawls, J. 72 73 84
Reichenbach, H. 30
Ribalka, M. 198
Ricoeur, P. 21 23 24 38 166 219 229
235 238
Robespierre, M. 130
Rotenstreich, N. 219 229 230 236
Rousseau, J.J. 107 148 149 151 153
186 187 201-203 206-208 210 212 216

Sachs, D. 59
Santayana, G. 36
Sartre, J.P. 145 191 192 194 195-197
Scheler, M. 75 84
Schiller, J.C. 177 178 180
Schutz, A. 8 84
Shaw, G.B. 36
Sholem, G. 237
Skinner, B.F. 107
Socrates 19 143

Spengler, O.   35
Spinoza, B.   197
Stern, W.   83
Strawson, P.F.   4

Taylor, C.   38-40 155 157 158 219 238
Thalberg, I.   59
Thompson, E.P.   151
Thrasymachus   151
Thucydides,   32 209 236
Tocqueville, A. de   27
Toffler, A.   133

Toynbee, A.   35
Trotsky, L.   29

Vico, G.   32 35
Voltaire, F.M.A. de   28

Walsh, W.H.   97 109
Weber, M.   23 79 80 81 84 134
Weil, E.   16
Woodward, L.   108
Wright, G.H. v.   99 104 106 110

Yovel, Y.   219 231 238 239

PHILOSOPHICAL STUDIES SERIES
IN PHILOSOPHY

1. JAY F. ROSENBERG, *Linguistic Representation*. 1974, xii + 159 pp.
2. WILFRID SELLARS, *Essays in Philosophy and Its History*. 1974, xiii + 462 pp.
3. DICKINSON S. MILLER, *Philosophical Analysis and Human Welfare*. Selected Essays and Chapters from Six Decades. Edited with an Introduction by Lloyd D. Easton. 1975, x + 333 pp.
4. KEITH LEHRER (ed.), *Analysis and Metaphysics*. Essays in Honor of R.M. Chisholm. 1975, x + 317 pp.
5. CARL GINET, *Knowledge, Perception, and Memory*. 1975, viii + 212 pp.
6. PETER H. HARE and EDWARD H. MADDEN, *Causing, Perceiving and Believing*. An Examination of the Philosophy of C.J. Ducasse. 1975, vii + 211 pp.
7. HECTOR-NERI CASTAÑEDA, *Thinking and Doing*. The Philosophical Foundations of Institutions. 1975, xviii + 366 pp.
8. JOHN L. POLLOCK, *Subjunctive Reasoning*. 1976, xi + 255 pp.
9. BRUCE AUNE, *Reason and Action*. 1977, xi + 206 pp.
10. GEORGE SCHLESINGER, *Religion and Scientific Method*. 1977, vii + 203 pp.
11. YIRMIAHU YOVEL (ed.), *Philosophy of History and Action*. Papers Presented at the First Jerusalem Philosophical Encounter, December 1974. 1978 (forthcoming).
12. JOSEPH C. PITT (ed.), *The Philosophy of Wilfrid Sellars: Queries and Extensions*. Papers deriving from and related to a workshop on the philosophy of Wilfrid Sellars held at Virginia Polytechnic Institute and State University, 1976. 1978 (forthcoming).
13. ALVIN I. GOLDMAN and JAEGWON KIM (eds.), *Values and Morals*. Essays in Honor of William Frankena, Charles Stevenson, and Richard Brandt. 1978 (forthcoming).
14. MICHAEL J. LOUX, *Substance and Attribute*. A Study in Ontology. 1978 (forthcoming).